D0117289

IMAGES OF
BARBAROSSA

THE GERMAN INVASION OF RUSSIA, 1941

IMAGES OF BARBAROSSA

THE GERMAN INVASION OF RUSSIA, 1941

Christopher Ailsby

BRASSEY'S

First published in the United States of America by
Brassey's, Inc.
22841 Quicksilver Drive
Dulles, Virginia 20166

ISBN 1-57488-319-4

Brassey's books are available at special discounts for bulk purchases for sales promotions, fund raising or educational use.

First Edition
10 9 8 7 6 5 4 3 2 1

Editorial and design:
Brown Partworks Ltd
8 Chapel Place
Rivington Street
London
EC2A 3DQ
UK

Editor: Peter Darman
Picture research: Antony Shaw
Design: Brown Partworks
Production: Matt Weyland

Printed in Singapore

Pages 2–3: A German cavalry column in Belorussia, July 1941.

CONTENTS

Introduction

For Adolf Hitler and his Nazi Party, conflict with the USSR was inevitable, not only because the Soviets occupied lands that Hitler wanted for German "living space", but also because communism was the antithesis of National Socialism.

▲ German dictator Adolf Hitler shakes hands with the Chief of the German Army General Staff (OKH), General Franz Halder, during the campaign in Poland, September 1939. An officer of the traditional Prussian school, he abhorred many aspects of the Nazi regime.

▶ A Nazi Party mass rally in the 1930s. One major theme of Nazi ideology was that some areas of the Soviet Union were ripe for German colonization. Yet another was that the USSR was the centre of the "Jewish-Bolshevik conspiracy", and hence the cause of many of Germany's problems.

The war between National Socialist Germany and the Soviet Union was inevitable. Ever since his days as an extremist in the political wilderness in the early 1920s, Adolf Hitler had been obsessed with what he called the "Jewish-Bolshevik conspiracy", emerging from the USSR. Also, from the earliest days of Nazism, Hitler had looked eastward to find *Lebensraum*, or living space, for the German people. "If we speak of new land in Europe today, we can primarily have in mind only Russia and her vassal border states," he wrote in *Mein Kampf*.

The attack on the Soviet Union stemmed directly from three driving concerns of National Socialism: anti-communism, space and race. War

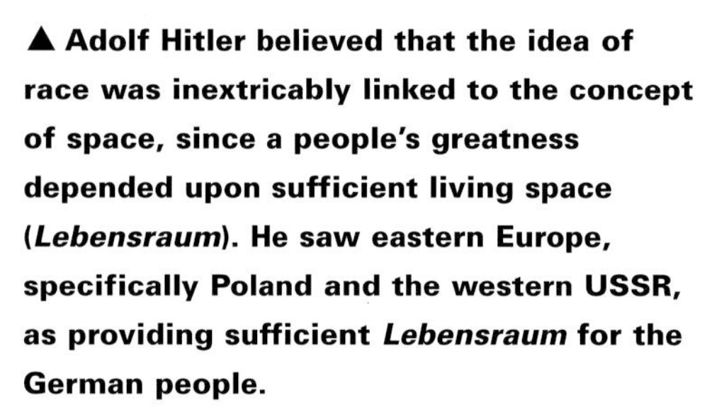

▲ Adolf Hitler believed that the idea of race was inextricably linked to the concept of space, since a people's greatness depended upon sufficient living space (*Lebensraum*). He saw eastern Europe, specifically Poland and the western USSR, as providing sufficient *Lebensraum* for the German people.

▲ It would be wrong to assume that Josef Stalin, the Soviet dictator, did not recognize the threat that Nazi Germany posed. However, he was reluctant to fight Hitler without allies, and British and French inaction over the German annexation of Czechoslovakia in 1938 led him to believe both would sacrifice the USSR if need be.

with the Soviet Union is perhaps less baffling to the neutral observer if viewed not as strategic or military rationality in the normal sense, but as Hitler's own ideologically tainted view of such concepts. The Führer and his Nazi Party had total contempt for the Slavs. Hitler lumped them with the Jews as an "inferior race" and equated Bolshevism with Zionism. The Slavs, he said, were "vermin" and "subhumans" whose only use was to serve the Aryan master race.

Hitler's sense of destiny in the East dictated his overall strategy during the war. To ensure success, he had signed a non-aggression pact on 23 August 1939 with the Soviets, who were given the franchise to absorb eastern Poland and the Baltic states after Germany had conquered western Poland. His strike into Poland on 1 September 1939 was in fact the first step in his "Eastern Crusade".

The guarantee of peace in the East served Hitler's interests by protecting Germany's rear while the Wehrmacht (German armed forces) invaded Scandinavia, the Low Countries and France in 1940. During June 1940, while the Germans were preoccupied in Western Europe, the Soviet dictator Josef Stalin struck. The Soviet

▶ **Panzers parade in Berlin on the occasion of Hitler's birthday in April 1938. The campaigns in Poland in 1939, the Low Countries and France in 1940, and in the Soviet Union in 1941 illustrated the need for aggressive, confident panzer commanders and a good supply of quality tanks to ensure the success of the Blitzkrieg.**

Red Army occupied the three Baltic nations of Estonia, Latvia and Lithuania and the eastern Romanian province of Bessarabia. All of which, under the Nazi-Soviet Non-aggression Pact, Hitler had granted to the Russian sphere of influence. Hitler regarded the pact as a temporary expedient of German strategic planning, a fact he never concealed from his generals. The agreement with the Russians "was meant only to stall for time", Hitler smugly told members of his inner circle – "We will crush the Soviet Union." He advised his commanders in November 1939: "We can oppose Russia only when we are free in the West. Russia is not dangerous for the moment," he assured them. The victory in the West gave him the freedom of action he required to concentrate on the East.

The British problem

Race and ideology, however, were only part of Hitler's philosophy. His other stated reason for the invasion of the USSR related to Britain. Hitler believed that the British were holding out in the hope of Soviet intervention. "Russia," he argued, "is England's continental sword." Once the Russians were defeated, Hitler contended, the British would capitulate.

The prospect of fighting on two fronts, as in World War I, caused Field Marshal Walter von Brauchitsch, army Commander-in-Chief, and General Halder, Chief of the German Army General Staff, to question the advisability of the invasion of the USSR. Their arguments fell on deaf ears. The Führer had decided irrevocably to "settle accounts with Russia as soon as fair weather permitted." Hitler instructed his military leaders to prepare for the invasion of the USSR on 21 July 1940, barely a month after the conquest of France. It was to be launched no later than the following spring.

He cited two immediate reasons for wanting to attack Russia. One was the danger that the Russians would initiate a war against Germany. Stalin *had* acted aggressively and in violation of the Nazi-Soviet Pact: he had seized a strip of western Lithuania reserved for Germany under the treaty, and marched into the Romanian province of Northern Bukovina. Finland, a friend of the Reich and its chief source of nickel, had also been attacked by the Soviets.

▲ SS chief Heinrich Himmler (second from right). In instructions attached to Hitler's Directive No 21 he was given "special tasks ... resulting from the necessity finally to settle the conflict between two opposing political systems." These included executing Communist Party officials, commissars, Jews and other "extremist elements".

Planning for the Russian offensive was inherently difficult because of the scope of the venture, and was further complicated by the German military's overlapping command structure. In 1938, Hitler dismissed his leading generals and promoted himself to the post of commander-in-chief of the Wehrmacht. He then created his own military staff, the Organization of the Supreme Command of the German Armed Forces (OKW), but this immediately became embroiled in conflict with the High Command of the German Army (OKH).

The two staffs developed plans, which shared many common features, for the invasion of Russia during the latter part of 1940. Both proposed the use of the Blitzkrieg doctrine that had been a stunning success against Poland and France. This doctrine was characterized by ruthless action at great pace directed against an enemy's command and communications system; the enemy front was breached by an overwhelming concentration of force, especially armour, to make possible the encirclement and annihilation of enemy armies. Rapid armoured strikes would encircle the Soviet armies deployed in western Russia. Red Army units would then be prevented from retreating farther east to relative safety. The Germans envisioned conquering only the western quarter of the Soviet Union: the Wehrmacht would stop roughly 1920km (1200 miles) beyond the 1939 border, along a line running south from Archangel on the White Sea to Astrakhan on the Caspian Sea. Beyond this line lay a vast expanse of Asia that the Germans regarded as "unproductive wasteland".

OKW and OKH were divided concerning the strategic conduct of the campaign. Hitler personalized these differences in a dispute between the chief of the army High Command, General Franz Halder, and himself. Hitler preferred a three-pronged attack along the lines submitted by his OKW staff. A northern army group would strike through the Baltic states towards Leningrad, a southern group would push through the Ukraine to Kiev and beyond, and a central group would slice through Belorussia, the Soviet republic that lay astride the route to Moscow.

For a combination of reasons, the Führer was drawn by what he perceived to be opportunities on the two flanks. The northern attack would secure the vital ports on the Baltic Sea and eliminate an important economic centre, the city of Leningrad. In addition, the latter was the philosophical cradle of the Bolshevism which Hitler detested. The southern thrust could lead to the occupation of the Soviet breadbasket of the Ukraine, while beyond lay the coal-rich Donets Basin. Naturally, successful flank attacks would also provide protection for the advance on the Soviet capital. The capture of Moscow itself, Hitler told his generals, "was not so very important." After all, he pointed out, it was at Moscow that Napoleon's campaign had foundered in 1812. "Only completely ossified brains, absorbed in the ideas of past centuries," said Hitler, "could see any worthwhile objective in taking the capital." Moscow thus became of secondary importance to Hitler, while General Halder made it the centrepiece of his strategy.

A product of the Prussian General Staff, the 56-year-old Halder was professional in manner

▼ Hitler had never made a secret of the role the conquered Slav population would have in the Third Reich: "Our guiding principle must be that these people have but one justification for existence – to be of use to us economically ... anyone who talks about cherishing the local inhabitant ... goes straight off into a concentration camp."

◀ **Field Marshal Walter von Brauchitsch (centre) was Commander-in-Chief of the German Army from 4 February 1938 until 19 December 1941. Though brave and able, he lacked the moral fibre to stand up to Hitler. And his wife was described as being "200 percent National Socialist"!**

and appearance and guarded the army's prerogatives with an icy logic and fox-like cunning, even if it meant a confrontation with the Führer himself (Hitler once referred to him as a "chronic know it all"). General Halder commissioned at least three invasion feasibility studies. From these he concluded that Moscow must remain the primary objective of Germany's invasion of the Soviet Union.

Both Field Marshal Walter von Brauchitsch and Halder contended that the capture of Moscow would deprive the Soviets not only of a communications hub but also a major armaments centre and their seat of government. It was their conclusion that the very threat of the capital's loss would compel the Red Army to deploy its units for the defence of the city. This would give the invaders an opportunity to surround and destroy them.

▶ **V.I. Molotov, Soviet Commissar for Foreign Affairs (right), seen here with Stalin, and his Nazi opposite number, Joachim von Ribbentrop, finalized the Nazi-Soviet Non-aggression Pact on 24 August 1939. A temporary expedient, it attempted to settle spheres of influence in Eastern Europe between Germany and the USSR.**

The final plan for the German invasion of the Soviet Union was contained in Hitler's top secret Führer Directive No 21, issued on 18 December 1940. It set out the overall objectives of the campaign, which would be launched in May the following year. This Directive included the following words:

"The bulk of the Russian Army stationed in western Russia will be destroyed by daring operations led by deeply penetrating armoured spearheads. Russian forces still capable of giving battle will be prevented from withdrawing into the depths of Russia. The enemy will then be energetically pursued and a line will be reached from which the Russian air force can no longer attack German territory. The final objective of the operation is to erect a barrier against Asiatic Russia on the general line Volga-Archangel. The last surviving industrial areas of Russia in the Urals can then, if necessary, be eliminated by the Luftwaffe."

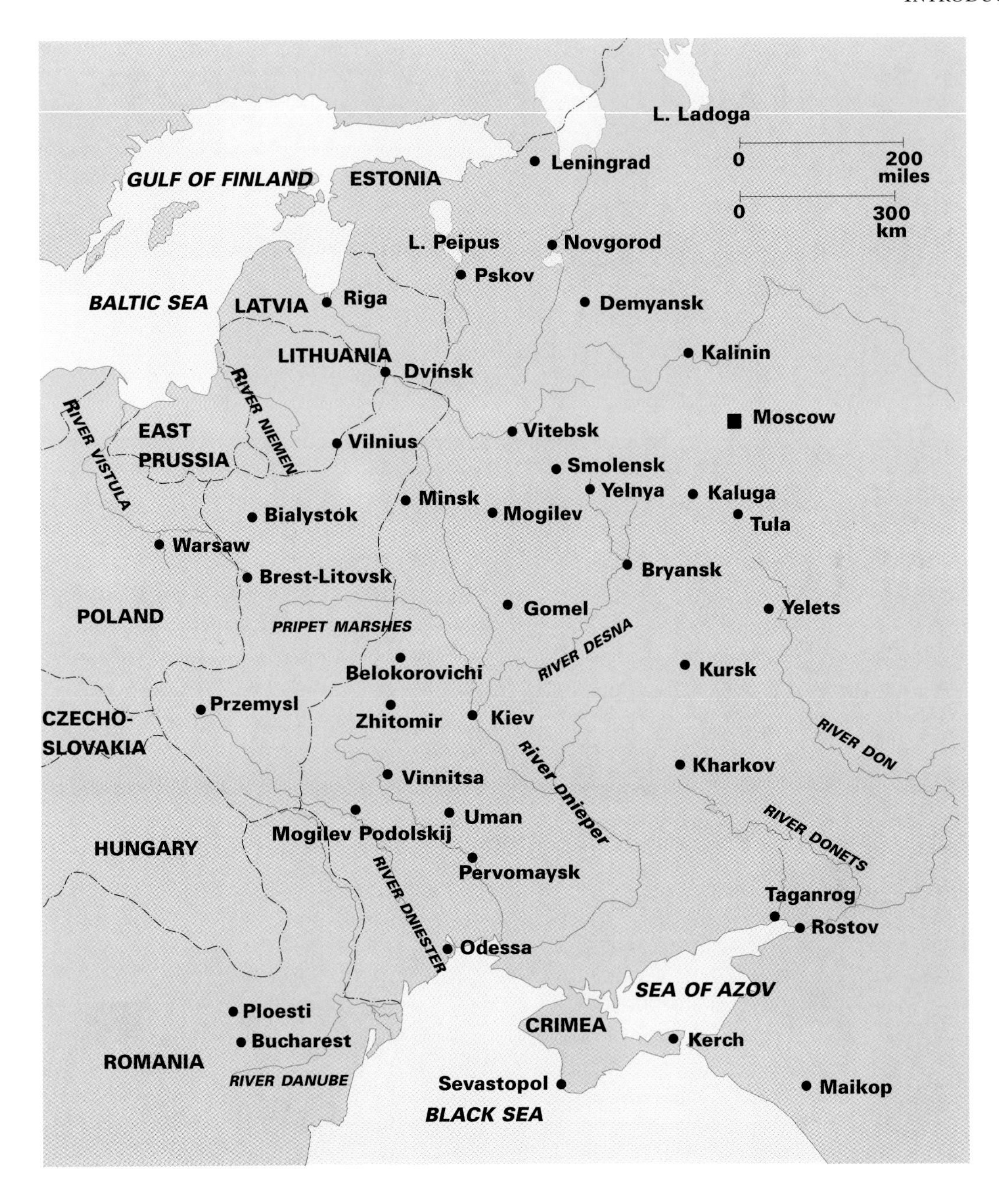

A codename with historical significance was chosen for this grand venture to replace its former nondescript working titles, "Otto" and "Fritz". The Nazi supreme commander now proposed to launch his military crusade to concquer the East under cover of the codename "Barbarossa". This the Führer took from the nickname of one of the heroes of German history: Emperor Frederic "Barbarossa", also known as Red Beard. "Barbarossa" had successfully waged war on the Slavs, and at the close of the 12th century had marched with his knights against the infidel in the Holy Land, where he died a "Holy Death".

On the eve of war

German planning for a campaign in the Soviet Union envisaged a war lasting no longer than 10 weeks, but Hitler had not reckoned on a campaign in the Balkans, brought on by the ineptitude of his Axis ally, Mussolini.

The German plan for an attack against the Soviet Union involved three army groups, which would advance towards Leningrad, Moscow and Kiev respectively. According to Hitler's Directive, Moscow would be a secondary objective. Thus when the central army group reached the area about two-thirds of the way between the border and Moscow, just east of Smolensk, it would divert its armour both northwards and southwards to help clear the Baltic region and help secure the Ukraine respectively. In the words of the Directive: "Only *after* [author's italics] the fulfilment of this first essential task, which must include the occupation of Leningrad and Kronstadt, will the attack be continued with the intention of occupying Moscow." That settled the matter in Hitler's mind, but not in that of General Franz Halder, head of the High Command of the Army (OKH), who envisaged the campaign being conducted differently.

▼ Italian artillery pound Greek positions in early November 1940, during Mussolini's attempt to emulate the success of Nazi arms. The invasion of Greece was a fiasco: the Greeks stopped the Italian Army and then drove the attackers back across the border into Albania. The Italians were badly led, poorly equipped and had low morale.

Halder was in favour of a main thrust towards Moscow, not only because of its economic, political and military importance, but because he believed that it would be around Moscow where the Red Army would make its final stand. Since the most vital aspect of the Barbarossa campaign was to destroy the Red Army, Halder believed the main German effort should be concentrated against the Soviet capital. The Führer disagreed.

In addition to differences of opinion between Halder, Hitler and their OKH and OKW (High Command of the Armed Forces) staffs, other potential problems with the Barbarossa enterprise were revealed by detailed map exercises and other exhaustive war games conducted by the Deputy Chief of OKH, Major-General Friedrich Paulus.

The question of space

Paulus' studies showed that even an army of more than three million men would be spread desperately thin soon after the invasion. As the invaders advanced, the German front would have to expand funnel-like from its start point to a width of well over 3200km (2000 miles). The army would therefore have to adapt its Blitzkrieg tactics in a country so vast. It would have to cover enormous distances, something it was not accustomed to, having only operated within the comparatively limited confines of Western and Central Europe. The armoured spearheads would quickly outrun the infantry divisions, leaving large, vulnerable gaps in between. And as the spearheads penetrated ever deeper into the Soviet heartland, resupply would become critical.

The Soviet Union had few substantial highways, and hard, metalled roads were not a common feature of its transport network: only three percent of the roads in the European part of the country were paved. The packed dirt roads would be transformed into deep quagmires once the rains started – which would slow the advance fatally. In addition, both the German and Central European trains were incompatible with the mostly single-line, broad-gauged tracks that the few east-west Soviet railway lines were constructed of.

▲ Mussolini (left) with Hitler. The German Führer had attempted to prevent the Italian invasion of Greece suspecting, correctly, that it would drag Germany into the Balkans. Italian failure in the region resulted in Hitler having to delay his long-cherished dream of invading the Soviet Union while he secured his southern flank.

German planning presupposed a decisive superiority over the Red Army in the quality of fighting men, equipment, leadership and tactics. German intelligence also believed that the enemy possessed huge quantaties of war material, but assumed the great bulk of Soviet hardware to be outmoded and useless for modern

▶ Soviet infantry training on the standard Red Army machine gun in World War II, the Maxim water-cooled model. Like many Red Army infantry weapons, it dated back to Tsarist times. And, like much Soviet hardware that would take part in Barbarossa, it was cumbersome and archaic compared to the German MG 34.

warfare. Most of the aircraft, for example, lacked radios and pilots had to resort to wing wagging in order to send signals.

On paper the Red Army appeared to be a formidable adversary. It fielded 230 divisions totalling 12 million men, supported by 24,000 tanks and 8000 aircraft. Against this force the Wehrmacht would deploy 3.3 million soldiers – about 87 percent of its 3.8 million total – accompanied by 3330 tanks and 2770 aircraft. Moreover, the Russians made full use of natural obstacles like the Rivers Pruth, San, Bug and Dnieper and deployed their lines of defences opposing Army Group South (see page 28).

However, the Germans knew that the Soviets lacked experienced leaders. The Soviet armed forces had been decimated by Stalin's political purges, which were named after the most prominent officer executed: Marshal Mikhail Tukhachevsky. Between 1937 and 1941, Stalin carried out the systematic destruction of the Soviet High Command, the primary motive being to secure his position as absolute ruler of the USSR by removing anyone he suspected might pose a challenge to his authority. In June 1937 Tukhachevsky was executed, thus beginning a cull of the entire Red Army officer corps: three out of five marshals of the Soviet Union, 11 deputy commissars of defence, 13 out of 15 army commanders, all the military district commanders of May 1937, and the leading members

◀ Essentially the Red Army was a vast peasant force drawn from a society that was backward compared to the states of western Europe. The rank and file of the Red Army in June 1941 were conscripts with little military training. Against the well-trained German Army it would suffer a series of catastrophic defeats.

▲ The image of the Red Army that Stalin liked to portray to the world – a modern, fully mechanized force. These T-38 light amphibious tanks and T-26 light tanks parading in Red Square in 1938 look impressive. However, tank crew training was poor, mechanics were scarce, and many models were obsolete in 1941.

of the naval and air force commands were shot or disappeared without trace. The same fate was suffered by the political apparatus, which was supposed to advise the professional soldiers. During this period some 35,000 officers of the armed forces were either dismissed, imprisoned or executed. These purges were to cause incalculable damage to the ability of the Red Army to resist the German invasion in June 1941.

The purges led Hitler and his planners to underestimate their enemy's military potential. German intelligence services had, for example, failed to get an overall picture of the Soviet system. They saw only emasculated armed forces, failing to notice the new industrial cities springing up in the Ural Mountains, and farther east in Soviet Asia. They had also been unable to produce accurate projections regarding future Soviet weapons production, let alone adequate topographic maps of the areas the German Army would be operating in.

The Soviet invasion of Finland in November 1939 only served to reinforce German beliefs that the Red Army would be incapable of withstanding the Blitzkrieg, when more than one million ineptly led Soviet troops attacked the numerically inferior Finnish Army. The Finnish commander, Marshal Gustaf Mannerheim, likened the Soviet performance to that of a badly conducted orchestra whose players could not keep in time.

▲ **Corps commander Georgi Zhukov (centre) at the Battle of Khalkhin-Gol in August 1939. At this battle the Red Army under Zhukov smashed the Japanese, which ensured that Tokyo would not trouble the Soviet Union in the future, and freed up units for Stalin's Moscow counteroffensive in 1941. It also signalled the rise of Zhukov.**

The Germans overlooked the fact that Soviet forces had been rushed into an ill-prepared offensive against the Finns, that they had been given almost no time to prepare, and lacked intelligence concerning the enemy and terrain they would be fighting in. But then, in early 1941, euphoria arising from recent victories had caused the Germans to overlook the flaws in their own military machine, while at the same time overestimating their strengths. What were the strengths and weaknesses of the German Army on the eve of Operation Barbarossa?

In 1941 the German Army was still dependant on infantry that travelled on foot. Even the motorized infantry divisions were short of trucks, despite thousands of commercial vehicles captured in France or commandeered in Germany having been pressed into service. The movement of the army's supplies and artillery relied heavily on horses. Since crushing France in June 1940, the much-vaunted panzer divisions had suffered a reduction in their offensive capacity. Hitler had doubled the number of panzer divisions from 10 to 20 by reducing the number of panzer regiments in each division – from two to one – and thus halving the number of tanks that were assigned to each division. This reduced the number of tanks per division to about 160, compared to around 324 in a typical 1939 panzer division. Notwithstanding the reduction in tank numbers, however, by 1941 panzer divisions were a fairly potent mix of Panzer III, Panzer IV and lighter Czech tanks. Most of the smaller, lightly armed Panzer Is and IIs, which had fought in Poland and France in 1939–40, were limited to reconnaissance duties or had been cannibalized for their chassis.

The next generation of tanks was still in the prototype stage or on the drawing boards of German engineers. Indeed, at this period Germany's panzer situation was a paradox. The Wehrmacht lacked tanks and trucks because Germany's industry was not geared up for total war. The failure to fully mobilize the economy made the Blitzkrieg, which promised quick victory through intense, short campaigns, all the more vital. And yet the Blitzkrieg depended on mobility for its success, which in turn required the increased production and improvement of trucks, tanks and other military vehicles that were fast and easily manoeuvrable.

What of the Soviets? Aside from the fact that they had 17 million males of prime military age, they were actually ahead of the Germans in tank development. For example, a Russian military commission which visited German tank factories during the spring of 1941 refused to believe that Germany's heaviest tank was the Panzer IV. They knew that at home their assembly lines were starting to produce heavier and faster Soviet tanks, notably the T-34.

▲ Marshal Semen Timoshenko commanded the Western Front at the start of Barbarossa, and had the unenviable task of stopping Army Group Centre. An iron disciplinarian, he replaced Marshal Budenny as leader of the Southwestern Front. Despite his failings at the front, his insistence on strict discipline endeared him to Stalin.

▲ An altogether more able commander was Konstantin Rokossovsky. Arrested during Stalin's purges of the Red Army, he was released and took command of a mechanized corps during Barbarossa. He commanded an army in late 1941, was a front commander at Stalingrad, and finished the war as a marshal.

▲ **Finnish troops examine Russian dead during the Winter War of 1939–40. Though the Red Army outnumbered the Finns, its attacks were clumsy and ill coordinated, suffering heavy casualties for little gain as a result. The Finns, by comparison, were trained for winter warfare and fought from well-prepared positions.**

Hitler and many of his generals were convinced of their military invincibility and of the Soviets' inferiority. Hitler boasted to one of his generals: "We have only to kick in the door, and the whole rotten structure will come crashing down." They were so confident of victory that they made no serious attempt to enlist the aid of Japan, their Axis partner, for the coming attack on the USSR, even though an attack from the Far East would have diverted Soviet formations that otherwise could have been deployed against the Germans. In fact, Hitler did not even inform the Japanese of his aggressive intention.

After Napoleon's failed invasion of Russia, Carl von Clausewitz, the 19th-century German military theorist, concluded that Russia could only be conquered from within. However, the Germans chose to disregard the potential support of the millions of oppressed Soviet subjects who longed to throw off their communist yoke, especially in the Ukraine and the Baltic states. Hitler's racism precluded him from trying to win over people to the anti-communism cause with the promise of local independence.

Instead, he intended to wage a ruthless campaign and spoke of a war of extermination. "The war against Russia will be such that it cannot be fought in a gentlemanly fashion," he told a gathering of his senior commanders in early 1941. "This struggle is one of ideologies and racial differences and will have to be conducted with unprecedented merciless and unrelenting harshness." Accordingly, German soldiers would not be bound by the rules of warfare laid down in the Hague Convention, or by the guidelines on the treatment of prisoners as dictated by the Geneva Convention. What followed was a series of decrees to exterminate "ideological and racial enemies" and for eradicating Russians. These measures were to be carried out by the Einsatzgruppen (SS special action squads), which would follow the conquering armies into the Soviet Union.

One decree protected members of the Wehrmacht from the legal consequences of crimes against the Soviet population, while another order empowered the army to summarily execute civilians who took up arms against the German invaders. And a so-called Commissar Decree required the liquidation of the communist political commissars who shared control with military commanders in every unit of the Red Army. Many army officers were dismayed by the prospect of carrying out these gruesome orders, but their objections went no further than the army Commander-in-Chief, von Brauchitsch, who chose not to provoke Hitler.

Balkan diversion

Through the late winter of 1940 and into the spring of 1941, the Germans amassed their forces in East Prussia, Poland and Romania. Some 17,000 trains rolled eastwards bearing men and equipment.

In April, part of the build-up was temporarily diverted south for the brief campaign against Yugoslavia and Greece. Hitler did not want a conflict in the Balkans and had restrained his Axis partner, the Italian dictator Benito Mussolini, from initiating plans for an Italian invasion of Yugoslavia and Greece on several occasions during the spring and summer of 1940. Mussolini reluctantly accepted Hitler's wishes, as he was dependent on Germany for raw materials needed for armaments. In March 1940, though, an official German communiqué which proudly announced Germany's military achievements after only six months of war elicited Mussolini's grudging admiration and deep envy. He had nothing to compare with Hitler's territorial gains, and felt that his prestige as Europe's first fascist dictator demanded that he take action. At the beginning of June 1940, Mussolini's frustration was further heightened when the German armies drove British forces off the continent and brought France to her knees. It now seemed certain that Germany would win the war. Mussolini had an understanding with Hitler that in the "New Europe" Italy would be rewarded with pickings from the French Empire. To reinforce this right and give Italy these spoils by force of arms, on 10 June 1940 Mussolini announced his declaration of war on Britain and France. Yet, he was caught in what Italian Foreign Minister Galeazzo Ciano ironically called "an outbreak of peace" (though not before French forces had given the Italians a mauling).

▼ A knocked-out Soviet T-26 Commander's Tank during the Winter War. The poor performance of the Red Army, which had lost an estimated 48,000 dead and 158,000 wounded against the Finns, reinforced the view in Berlin that the Soviet Union would succumb to the Blitzkrieg when Barbarossa was launched.

▲ German panzers during the invasion of Poland in September 1939. The lightning Nazi victory in Poland alarmed the Soviet Union, whose analysts had anticipated a campaign lasting several months. The invasion was effectively over in four weeks, demonstrating to the world the speed and power of the Blitzkrieg doctrine.

But Mussolini was not to be deprived of his share of the limelight. On the morning of 28 October 1940, Italian forces based in Albania crossed the frontier into Greece to initiate one of the most surprising campaigns of World War II. Benito Mussolini proclaimed the birth of a "New Roman Empire" that was intended to recreate the ancient glories of Rome. A month later, the Greeks had expelled the Italians from their homeland, and went on to occupy a quarter of Albania by the middle of January 1941. The rot had set in by early December when the Greeks captured Progradec, bringing dismay to Italy. The Italian commander, General Soddu, was now openly talking of settling the situation by political intervention. Foreign Minister Ciano was told by Mussolini: "There is nothing else to do. This is grotesque and absurd, but it is a fact. We have to ask for a truce through Hitler." But Ciano persuaded Mussolini not to do so. Instead General Cavallero was sent to the Albanian Front to report on the situation.

▶ The Wehrmacht in France, May 1940. The conquest of France and the Low Countries at the hands of the panzer divisions further frightened the Red Army's High Command. In response, the Soviet Council of Ministers ordered the creation of eight new mechanized corps, each one consisting of 1031 tanks.

221

▲ General Ernst Busch commanded the Sixteenth Army during Operation Barbarossa. Part of von Leeb's Army Group North, it comprised II, X and XXVIII Corps. During Barbarossa he told von Manstein that he wanted to lead his army southeast towards Kalinin and then Moscow. He was not allowed to do so by von Leeb.

Mussolini's "Greek disaster" had engendered a fundamental change in the relationship between the two fascist dictators. Diplomatic relations with Greece had not been broken off by Hitler – a severe slight to his Axis partner – though he had refrained from openly criticizing *Il Duce* for invading Greece. However, Hitler now made no attempt to conceal his displeasure at the "Italian adventure", which had jeopardised the Axis position in southeast Europe. For the first time, Hitler advised the Italians how to run their war. Most impartial observers held the view, one also shared by Hitler, that the Italian forces would be unable to defeat the Greeks unaided. General Metaxas, the Greek dictator, died suddenly on 29 January 1941, and with his demise Hitler hoped that German diplomacy would be able to bring Greece into alignment with Nazi policy (the political situation in Greece made the country potentially suitable to to join the Axis – Metaxas had copied Nazi methods). But the King of Greece made it clear that the death of Metaxas did not affect the determination of the Greek people to continue the struggle against Italy.

In November 1940, as part of his ambition to control the Balkans, Hitler formulated plans for a more effective invasion of Greece, code-named "Operation Marita". It required the deployment of 16 divisions in bases in southern Romania, from where they would attack south

▶ **German panzers in the Greek port of Thessaloniki on 9 April 1941. As usual, superior German hardware and tactics ensured a speedy victory – it took the German Army only 20 days to reach Athens. British aid had proved ineffectual, and her army left behind 104 tanks, 400 guns, 1800 machine guns and 8000 vehicles.**

into Greece. The initial plan was for the seizure of Greek territory north of the Aegean Sea, but with the landing of British troops in Greece in early March 1941 (a month earlier Britain had promised 100,000 troops to fight alongside the Greeks), the plan was refined and the decision was taken to occupy the whole peninsula and the island of Crete. The objective now was to drive British and Commonwealth troops out and force the Greeks to surrender.

What of Yugoslavia? The Tripartite Pact formed between Rome, Berlin and Tokyo was the cornerstone of the Axis. Hungary, Romania and Slovakia had joined the Pact in 1940. Bulgaria had joined in 1941, and on 25 March Yugoslavia followed the Bulgarian example and became a signatory, albeit under intense German diplomatic pressure. The route to the Greek border had been secured. However, the Yugoslavs overthrew the government that had joined the Pact. At 02:20 hours on the morning of 27 March, General Bora Mirkovic struck. After which, the Yugoslav military revolted, the government fell and the young Peter II was proclaimed king, forming a new anti-German government in Belgrade. In Britain there was jubilation in the War Cabinet, and across the Atlantic there was quiet optimism. It was the reaction in Berlin that was critical, though. The Germans

◀ **Waffen-SS troops in Belgrade. Hitler was so incensed by Belgrade's "treachery" that he ordered the destruction of Yugoslavia militarily and as a national entity. The Wehrmacht carried out its orders clinically. The Luftwaffe, for example, having destroyed the Yugoslav Air Force, bombed Belgrade and killed 17,000 people.**

▶ **German machine-gun teams on exercise. In 1941 the German Army was undoubtedly the finest fighting formation in the world. Flushed with nearly two years of victories, its morale, training and equipment were excellent. In addition, and crucial to mobile operations, its junior commanders and NCOs were of a consistently high quality.**

had decided in late November that they would assist the Italians to overcome the Greeks once spring had thawed the Balkan roads. By the first week of April the snow was melting, and Operation Marita was set to begin. But a hostile Yugoslavia now menaced both operations Marita and Barbarossa.

Hitler received news of the Belgrade coup early on 27 March and at first refused to believe it. "I thought it was a joke," he said later. His anger was immense, as he saw the coup in Belgrade as a personal affront. Hitler ordered that Operation Marita be expanded to include an invasion of Yugoslavia, codenamed "Punishment", stating: "Politically it is especially important that the blow against Yugoslavia is carried out with pitiless harshness and that the military destruction is done with lightning rapidity." No ultimatum would be presented to Belgrade – war would come with the first bombs that fell on the capital. Operation Marita would be launched simultaneously with the invasion of Yugoslavia, while Barbarossa was to be postponed for "up to four weeks".

The Balkan diversion affected the launch of the Russian offensive, however. Originally targeted for the latter half of May, Barbarossa had to be postponed for roughly five weeks. The delay was attributed largely to shortages of military vehicles in the newly formed panzer and motorized infantry divisions, and to heavy

◀ **Field Marshal Fedor von Bock, commander of Army Group Centre, was once described as having "Frederican Prussianism ... deeply ingrained in his character" and as "a violent nationalist, a stern disciplinarian and intent only upon strengthening the army and advancing his own military career." He was killed in an air raid in 1945.**

spring flooding in Eastern Europe that rendered the border rivers largely impassable.

By late December 1940, the Russian military attaché in Berlin had received an anonymous letter containing the details of the Barbarossa directive issued one week earlier. Over the following months, the Soviets received dozens of warnings of the impending dangers. The Germans' eastward movements had not escaped the notice of the Soviet dictator Josef Stalin. Although a German ruse suggesting preparations for an invasion of Britain was staged by sending a score of second-line divisions westwards, Stalin was not deceived. However, aware that mobilization by Tsar Nicholas II had triggered the German declaration of war in 1914, Stalin was determined not to give Hitler a similar pretext.

Tension along the border

Throughout the spring of 1941, frequent border violations by German armed reconnaissance patrols and by specially equipped high-altitude spy aircraft kept the Russians on the alert. Stalin appeared to ignore these indications of an imminent invasion. He breathed not a word of public protest, forbade discussions of them in the government-controlled press, and gave no evidence that he was mobilizing his armed forces. The Soviet leader apparently believed that Hitler, unless he was provoked, would not attack without first issuing an ultimatum. Meanwhile, Stalin prudently negotiated a neutrality treaty with the Japanese. In an attempt to appease the German Führer, Stalin even continued shipments of grain and other commodities to Germany under the terms of a trade agreement.

There is no doubt that Stalin knew the Germans would attack the USSR eventually. Aside from the ideological rivalry and hostility between National Socialism and Marxist Communism, both states had ambitions in Eastern Europe that made them competitors. The Soviets wished to establish a number of buffer states in the region as a safeguard against invasion from the west, the traditional route by which Russia was attacked. For their part, the Nazis regarded the same area as essential to fulfil the territorial ambitions of the Thousand Year Reich. But Stalin was desperately trying to buy time for his armed forces, hence such expediencies as the Non-aggression Treaty.

▲ Field Marshal Gerd von Rundstedt (centre left) commanded Army Group South. Described as the "Black Knight of the German Army", he had an uneasy relationship with Hitler. Nevertheless, the latter knew that von Rundstedt was highly respected by the officer corps and thus treated him with some respect.

To correct the deficiencies exposed during the Finnish War, the Red Army was undergoing a modernization programme. At the same time, the recently appointed Chief of the High Command, General Georgi Zhukov, was rushing to implement his plan for an in-depth defence of the motherland. Zhukov's scheme was a variation on a Soviet offensive strategy developed by the Red Army during the 1930s. Rather than deploy the bulk of the Soviet defences near the border region, it called for three successive lines of defence reaching more than 240km (150 miles) into the rear. Zhukov hoped that these zones of resistance would absorb the energy of the German armoured thrusts, enabling the last echelon, the strategic reserve, to mount a decisive counterattack. It was a good plan, but turning theory into reality takes time, and by mid-1941 the Red Army was still poorly deployed and inadequately trained and equipped to meet the impending invasion.

▲ The Germans were fully prepared for the river barriers they would have to cross during Barbarossa. The River Bug stood in the path of the Second Panzer Group, while to the north the Niemen would have to be crossed by the Third Panzer Group. Upon these two formations rested German hopes of victory in the East.

The invasion force

The German invasion force that had taken up positions along the frontier by late spring 1941 outnumbered the estimated one million troops in the Soviet first line of defence by more than three to one. The German force consisted of 150 divisions, 17 of which were panzer and a further 13 motorized infantry. The attacker's main objectives were to encircle the Red Army with deep armoured thrusts and then destroy it in the area between the frontier and a north-south line formed by the Rivers Dvina and Dnieper, about 480km (300 miles) to the east.

As planned, the invaders were divided into three groups for the June invasion. Army Group North was the smallest force, with only three panzer, three motorized and about 20 infantry divisions, and was commanded by Field Marshal Ritter von Leeb. It had SS-Gruppenführer Theodor Eicke's powerful and totally ruthless SS *Totenkopf* Division assigned to it as part of General Erich Hoepner's Fourth Panzer Group. Another Waffen-SS unit, the *SS-Polizei* Division, was part of Army Group North's reserves. The weakest of the army groups, its divisions were poised to move northeast from East Prussia into Lithuania, clear the Baltic states and capture the city of Leningrad.

Finland would provide support by attacking from the north with 21 divisions two-and-a-half weeks after the Germans moved. To bolster this far-north effort, SS-Kampfgruppe (Battle Group) *Nord* and SS Infantry Regiment 9 were deployed as part of the Norway Mountain

Corps under the command of Colonel-General Nikolaus von Falkenhorst, and committed to the far northern sector of the front in Finland.

Army Group Centre, under the command of Field Marshal Fedor von Bock, formed the largest German force. It comprised nine panzer, six motorized, 30 infantry divisions, three security divisions, a cavalry division, the *Grossdeutschland* Regiment and a reserve division (the SS *Das Reich* Division was allocated to General Heinz Guderian's Second Panzer Group). This made a total of 50 divisions, and OKH deployed a further six divisions behind the group's front. Army Group Centre would attack north of the Pripet Marshes, a vast swampland that stretched along the front for 240km (150 miles). The group's two parallel columns would knife eastwards into Belorussia towards Smolensk and Moscow. However, after Smolensk had been taken by Army Group Centre, the force would cooperate with Army Group North to destroy "enemy formations in the Baltic area". Only after this had been achieved would Moscow become an objective.

Army Group South

Army Group South was commanded by Field Marshal Gerd von Rundstedt, and was made up of 41 divisions, which comprised five panzer, four motorized, 28 infantry, one mountain and three security divisions, plus a division as an immediate reserve. This group included the SS *Leibstandarte* and *Wiking* Divisions, which were with General Edwald von Kleist's First Panzer Group. In addition, OKH deployed a further six divisions behind the army group as a reserve, one of which was a mountain division. In the southern sector of the front there were also 14 Romanian Divisions, the Hungarian Brigade and two Italian divisions.

Security divisions were intended to secure the rear of the armies that would be fighting on the Eastern Front. Mostly made up of poor-quality troops, such as older-aged men who had

▲ It is often forgotten that the spring of 1941 was exceptionally wet in the East. Rivers remained at flood levels until well into May, rendering much of the surrounding ground impassable for large-scale military movements. By the time Barbarossa started, levels were much lower.

▼ Bridging and engineering skills were crucial if the Barbarossa campaign was to succeed, the more so since many Russian bridges had been poorly constructed. Fortunately for the Germans, the speed and tactical surprise of the panzer divisions resulted in many bridges being captured intact. These were then strengthened.

▶ **Field Marshal Gunther von Kluge, commander of the Fourth Army, Army Group Centre. During Barbarossa he was Guderian's superior, but the two bickered over the latter's desire to push his panzers ever farther east. Von Kluge was promoted to command Army Group Centre in December 1941.**

fought in World War I, they were equipped with second-rate weaponry. Each division comprised only two infantry regiments (standard infantry divisions had three), the first to carry out active operations and the second – of even lower-grade personnel – to undertake guard duties in the division's static areas. Considering the mission they were tasked with carrying out, the security divisions were woefully deficient in both manpower and equipment.

Campaign objectives

Army Group South was given the initial task of cutting off all the Soviet armies west of the River Dnieper. Hitler was determined that the Russians must not be allowed to retreat into their interior with their forces intact, from where they could launch a counterattack against an overextended Wehrmacht. This was echoed in the army's deployment directive of 31 January 1941: "The first intention of the OKH within the task allocated is, by means of swift and deep thrusts by strong mobile formations north and south of the Pripet Marshes, to tear open the front of the mass of the Russian Army – which is anticipated – will be in western Russia. The enemy groups separated by these penetrations will then be destroyed."

The First Panzer Group had the objective of breaking through the Russian lines south of Kowel and cutting off Red Army units to the southwest, trapping them until the infantry could move up and eliminate them – an advance of over 480km (300 miles) had to be undertaken across difficult terrain.

Once the Soviet armies in its path had been surrounded and annihilated, the army group would advance to capture Kiev, Kharkov and the Crimea, before pushing on to the River Volga, the city of Stalingrad and the all-important Caucasian oil fields. Army Group South was divided into two widely separated wings. The strong northern wing was to advance eastwards along the southern edge of the Pripet Marshes into the Ukraine. Its targets were the River Dnieper and the city of Kiev. A smaller southern wing, made up of six German divisions and about 200,000 Romanian troops, would cross the border from Romania on 1 July.

The role of the Luftwaffe in the campaign was first to gain aerial superiority and then to support ground operations. The German Navy had a more limited role: operating in the Baltic, its aim was to prevent enemy forces from breaking out of that sea. Once Leningrad had been taken and the Soviet fleet had been destroyed, it would safeguard supplies through the Baltic.

The panzer divisions

For the German Army, the successes of Barbarossa would depend largely on the panzer divisions, which were its hitting power. Composed of one panzer regiment, two motorized infantry regiments and support elements that included artillery, antiaircraft, antitank, engineer and reconnaissance units, each panzer division was a well-balanced formation that totalled around 17,000 men.

Much more than the number or types of tanks that they fielded, the real strength of the panzer divisions were their personnel. After nearly two years of spectacular victories, the panzer crews were élite troops who were well trained, knew their job and the capabilities of their vehicles, were led by excellent commanders, and possessed a high *esprit de corp*. On the eve of Barbarossa the panzer crews were in a high state of morale, and had great confidence in their equipment, their leaders and their cause.

Although the Red Army could deploy as many as 20,000 tanks – some 1000 of which were the excellent T-34 and the heavy KV-1 – the majority of these vehicles were inferior in quality to German tanks, being light cruiser tanks of the BT series. In June 1941, some 60 percent of the older designs of Soviet tanks were out of action for mechanical reasons, which gives a telling insight into the reliability of many Soviet tanks and the ineptitude of their crews. In addition, though new T-34s were rolling off the production lines, their crews were far from being battle ready.

▲ A final briefing before Hitler's Crusade against Bolshevism. Most German soldiers who took part in the Barbarossa campaign knew little about the Soviet Union. They knew that it was a large country, but only when they were marching across the seemingly endless steppes did they fully appreciate the size of their task.

If the Germans had one main deficiency at the beginning of Barbarossa it was in antitank weapons. The famous 88mm antiaircraft gun has attained legendary status since the end of World War II, but it was the 37mm-calibre gun that was the main antitank weapon in the army. It would prove deficient against the well-sloped armour of the T-34.

Another potential problem was the question of spares. The panzer divisions did not have the maintenance capacity to conduct a long campaign. Spare parts and trained mechanics were always in short supply (during previous campaigns tanks had been shipped back to Germany for repairs), and the fighting in the Balkans had depleted the supplies of spares and tank treads. However, everyone in the Wehrmacht believed that the campaign in Russia would be no different to those in Poland, France and the Balkans: a quick victory seemed certain.

Kicking in the door

On 22 June 1941, during the early hours of the morning, German artillery opened up along the entire length of the Soviet border. Some 25 minutes later, the first German Stuka dive-bomber attacks went in – Barbarossa had begun.

Last-minute preparations had to be honed and polished by the German military machine; it was time to organize hundreds of units along a front that twisted and turned for 2160km (1350 miles) between the Baltic and the Black Sea. This great arc running from the Arctic Ocean in the north to the Black Sea in the south was a front crammed with vehicles, artillery pieces and troops. Hitler confided to an aide before the launch of Barbarossa: "At the beginning of each campaign, one pushes a door into a dark, unseen room. One can never know what is hiding inside."

By the end of May 1941, Germany proceeded to close ranks with her proposed co-belligerents in the forthcoming campaign. Chief of the Finnish General Staff, General Heinrichs, visited

▼ A German flame-thrower team deals with a Red Army position during the initial phase of Barbarossa. The weapon is a bulky Flammenwerfer 35, which weighed 35.8kg (78.75lb). It had enough fuel and nitrogen to project 10 one-second jets of flame to a range of 25–30m (83–100ft). Because of its weight, it was operated by a two-man team.

▶ **German field artillery shell Soviet positions on the first day Barbarossa. The Red Army had built up giant supply depots, filled with weapons, ammunition and fuel, close to the frontier, which were within range of German artillery – they were destroyed with clinical precision.**

Jodl, chief of Wehrmacht operations, and Halder, his opposite number in the German Army. They had discussed the German attack plans and Finland's role in the venture. On 7 April, the German "Norway Army" received its full operational directives for Operations Reindeer (if necessary, seizing the vital nickel deposits of northern Finland) and Silver Fox (to prepare bases for a possible attack on Murmansk and its railway). Marshal Gustaf Mannerheim would command purely Finnish forces, while German officers would control German-Finnish forces. On 3–5 June, in preparation for these operations on the very rim of the world, the Chief of Staff to the "Norway Army", Colonel Buschenhagen, discussed German deployment in northern Finland and the subordination of the Finnish III Corps to German command.

Hitler met Marshal Ion Antonescu of Romania a week later, in Munich, on 12 June. Here, more of the secrets of Barbarossa were given to the Romanian leader. While in Romania itself, German officers worked on the final details of the German-Romanian plan of attack.

Special conferences were held during the first week in June chaired by General Halder, each one split into 15-minute periods. The Operation Barbarossa timetable had already been approved by the Führer on 5 June. General Halder visited the Fourth Army, Army Group Centre area, on 9 June to discuss the surprise attack across the River Bug. On 10 June 1941, the German General Staff set out the following dates for units along the Soviet Union border: 22 June

▶ **After the artillery bombardment and dive-bomber attacks, the tanks and infantry went in. Here, an infantryman is knocking out a Red Army bunker with a Stielgranate (stick grenade). It was customary for troops to carry stick grenades with the throwing handles jammed into their belts.**

▲ **Ju 87 Stuka dive-bombers on their way to attack Soviet targets during the opening phase of Barbarossa. The Luftwaffe deployed nearly 300 of these aircraft along the front, distributed between Luftflotten I, II and IV. To maintain secrecy, Luftwaffe aircraft were only moved to their forward bases at the beginning of June 1941.**

▶ **For the attack on the Soviet Union, the Luftwaffe used a new type of fragmentation bomb: the SD2. Some 76.2mm (3in) in diameter and 89mm (3.5in) in length, after being released in rapid succession the bombs' casings opened up to form a pair of "wings". The bombs would then drift to the ground, exploding on impact.**

was d-Day; at 13:00 hours on 21 June either the codeword "Dortmund", denoting the start of the attack, or the codeword "Altona", signifying its postponement, would be transmitted; on 22 June, at 03:30 hours, the Luftwaffe would cross the Soviet frontier and the German Army would commence operations. In the event of bad weather preventing air operations, land forces were to open the offensive by themselves. That weather conditions should not delay the attack had been emphasized by Hitler himself. The same day, the various panzer group staffs were ordered to their forward headquarters.

Hitler called a final conference on 14 June. Army group, army and panzer group commanders and their staffs, plus their Luftwaffe and Kriegsmarine counterparts, assembled in the Reich Chancellery in Berlin. To try to maintain secrecy around this large gathering of senior officers, several entrances to the Reich Chancellery were used.

Inside, the subjects of this final conference concerned timing and the whole scope of Operation Barbarossa. Before noon, the officers reported their individual assignments to the Führer. All the assembled senior officers then attended lunch, after which Hitler pronounced his reasons for war. He stressed that Britain would now, finally, be forced to throw in the

towel. He also emphasized, as he had previously on 30 March, that this was the "decisive round" between two conflicting ideologies. Moreover, he stressed to his officers the need for them to bend their wills to the necessary brutalities that the coming conflict would demand; this was to be a war without mercy.

Meanwhile, General Halder discussed with General von Falkenhorst of the Norway Army the details of Operation Silver Fox. He also went over the details with Army Group South command regarding how the Romanian forces would remain under Antonescu's "independent" command until D-Day. Thereafter, the German

▲ Against "soft" targets, such as rows of parked aircraft, the SD2 proved to be very effective. Due to weak Soviet antiaircraft defences, German aircraft were able to make low-level runs and plant their fragmentation bombs accurately among the lines of enemy aircraft.

▶ "During the first days of the war enemy bomber formations launched massive attacks on 66 frontier airfields ... The result of these raids and the violent air-to-air battles was a loss to us, as at noon on 22nd June, of some 1200 aircraft." (*History of the Great Patriotic War of the Soviet Union*)

▲ German infantry on the attack during the first day of Barbarossa. The flimsy Soviet forward defences were destroyed by the initial artillery barrage, allowing the mass of German armour and infantry to advance. The soldier on the right is carrying a 7.92mm MG 34 medium machine gun.

Eleventh Army, functioning as Antonescu's "work staff", would assume operational control of the Romanian Army, and the German military mission would serve as a liaison staff between Antonescu and the Eleventh Army. Hungary, on the other hand, while a member of the Axis, had not yet committed itself to Barbarossa, although she was concerned at Soviet troop concentrations on her borders.

Three days later, on 17 June, the Führer approved 22 June as D-Day and 03:00 hours as Y Hour. On the same day, Guderian examined for himself the lie of the River Bug. The whole

◀ A German motorized assault boat crossing the River Niemen at speed in June 1941. Army Group Centre had to open its operations with crossings of both the Niemen (in the north) and the Bug (in the south), but lack of opposition resulted in the Germans quickly establishing a footing on the east banks of both rivers.

of the Soviet defences and terrain were scrutinized in detail. However, the first barrier was the River Bug itself, which his panzer group, like Army Group Centre as a whole, had to cross. The tanks of Guderian's Second Panzer Group, Army Group Centre, sported a white letter "G" as their tactical signs, while the tanks of Kleist's First Panzer Group, Army Group South, were identified by a white letter "K".

Men and machines were carefully hidden in the great forests of Augustovo. The panzer formations, held back to the last, began to move into their jump-off positions, and on 19 June heavy bridging equipment and artillery were unloaded at Biala Podlaska. The attack line on the southern Bug and the deep-echeloned Soviet fortifications behind it were surveyed by reconnaissance elements of the northern wing of von Rundstedt's Army Group South. Out of the June morning mist, Army Group North planned to move with the minimum of artillery preparation against Soviet earthworks, so ground and air commanders could select special targets in the operational zone – including bridges, signal centres and radio stations – for the special attention of the Luftwaffe.

"The world will hold its breath"

After 19 June German U-boats proceeded to their war stations, while in the Baltic German warships began laying mines. On 21 June at 13:00 hours, all army group headquarters were alerted that Barbarossa would begin as scheduled. A courier plane stood by to take the letter Hitler had written to Mussolini on that Saturday afternoon from his new underground headquarters: Wolf's Lair at Rastenburg in East Prussia. In it he announced to Mussolini that "the hardest decision of my life" had been taken, and he went on to list the main points of Barbarossa. Other courier planes had already flown out the Führer's eve-of-battle message to his troops, and as companies, gun crews and special parties fell in, it was read to them. In this missive Hitler addressed them, for the first time, as "soldiers of the Eastern Front", in an order of the day that defined their mission. They were about to take on their biggest task to date. "The world will hold its breath," Hitler declared, without exaggeration. Never before had a nation assembled such an enormous force to launch a military operation. More than three million men were deployed on the Soviet Union's western border, supported by 3330 tanks, 600,000 other vehicles, more than 7000 artillery pieces, 2770 aircraft and 750,000 horses.

The mighty German Army was at the peak of its efficiency and confidence was high: in less than two years it had triumphed in whirlwind campaigns against Poland, Norway, Denmark, the Netherlands, Belgium, Luxembourg, France, Yugoslavia and Greece. On the other hand, the magnitude of its latest task was sobering indeed. The Soviet Union sprawled over one-sixth of the

▼ With the Red Air Force largely destroyed on the ground on the first day of the invasion, the Luftwaffe reverted to its usual task of supporting ground forces. Bombers and dive-bombers targeted enemy communications, though this particular bridge over the River Styr was destroyed by the Soviets in an attempt to stop the Nazi advance.

▲ **Soviet 3in divisional field guns captured by the Germans during the first few days of Barbarossa. These weapons dated back to the days of the Tsar, but had been improved in 1930 by extending the barrel for longer range. The result was the 76mm Model 03/30 divisional gun. Most were lost in the summer of 1941.**

earth's land mass, and was occupied by a population of an estimated 200 million people, more than twice that of Germany. The USSR also experienced severe extremes of temperature and terrain. Nevertheless, Hitler and most of the army High Command anticipated a short campaign. They believed Operation Barbarossa would last no longer than 10 weeks. So certain were the planners of swift summer success that they had ordered winter clothing for only one-third of the invasion force.

The situation report for 21 June indicated no major change in Soviet dispositions or activity. The Brandenburgers and other special regiments, in many cases dressed in Russian uniforms, silently infiltrated across the frontline. Many were Russian speakers, and they proceeded to sabotage power stations and signal centres, and seize vital bridges ahead of the invasion troops. They were extremely effective. The command of the Soviet Fourth Army, for example, after finishing interrogating a German deserter who provided details of the forthcoming invasion, began to circulate this intelligence. It never reached its destination – the telephone lines had already been severed.

Their bomb-racks fully loaded, German aircraft flew into the night sky and across the Soviet frontier. Below them, the infantry watched the tail lights of the Stuka dive-bombers and German fighters fade as they flew east to their targets (Luftwaffe planners intended to have their bombers hitting Soviet airfields and other targets by dawn on the 22nd).

The Army of the East maintained radio silence, but shortly after midnight on 22 June higher formation headquarters transmitted their readiness-state call-signs. The short summer night was on the wane, artillery in the assault divisions and supporting units was zeroed in on

◀ **In towns and cities German aircraft bombed railway lines and stations, refineries, roads and barracks with great precision. Junkers Ju 88 ground-attack aircraft, Heinkel He 111 bombers and Dornier Do 17 bombers flew far behind Soviet lines seeking out targets, especially railways, bridges and supply depots.**

▲ **Soviet railway stock and field artillery lie destroyed following a heavy Luftwaffe attack. The record of German Air Force success was high during the initial stages of Barbarossa. Luftflotte II, for example, destroyed 356 trains, 14 bridges and numerous troop concentrations between 22 June and 9 September.**

▼ **Urban centres were on the receiving end of several waves of Luftwaffe bombers. The result was widespread destruction of civilian property and loss of lives. Terror against civilian populations was an integral part of the Blitzkrieg, but was especially so in Hitler's ideological war in the East.**

all its targets, and the lead tanks were ready to roll. As the German invasion force waited to be unleashed, just after midnight the Berlin-Moscow express passed over the rail bridge and on to Brest-Litovsk as per usual.

Although it was the shortest night of the year, the wait until dawn on Sunday 22 June 1941 seemed endless to the German troops massed on the frontier of the Soviet Union. They waited expectantly in fields and forests. The rank and file, buoyed by their succession of previous victories, had good cause to share their leader's high spirits. As the minutes ticked away

▲ Military historian Basil Liddell Hart explains how the poor condition of Soviet roads helped save Russia: "If the Soviet regime had given her [Russia] a road system comparable to that of Western countries, she would probably have been overrun in quick time. The German mechanized forces were balked by the badness of her roads."

before the beginning of the largest and bloodiest campaign in modern military history, groups of sleepless men toasted the success of this new adventure with special rations of brandy and vintage Champagne they had brought with them from France. The soldiers did not dwell on the fact that 129 years earlier, nearly to the day, Napoleon's doomed legions had crossed the River Niemen en route to Moscow. Soon, with the first hint of light in the eastern sky, the flash and thunder of their heavy artillery and the drone of aircraft engines would announce the opening of Operation Barbarossa.

On the morning of 22 June 1941, at 03:15 hours, what was to become the greatest continuous land battle history has ever witnessed erupted. The sudden flashes of thousands of artillery pieces seared the pale dawn, heralding the onset of Operation Barbarossa. The battles in the Soviet Union would herald spectacular victories for the German Army, but would also witness unimaginable brutality, with both sides giving and receiving no quarter. The Third Reich's military and ideological élite, the Waffen-SS, waged a quasi-religious struggle of the *Herrenvolk*, or master race, against the *Untermenschen*, or subhumans, to bring about the subjugation of those the Nazis despised most – the Jews, Slavs and Bolsheviks – as well as providing *Lebensraum* (living space) for the German people.

From the Carpathian Mountains to the Baltic Sea, the whole of the German frontline moved forward across the demarcation line following a short artillery bombardment. Above the ground units, hundreds of bombers and fighters streaked over the frontier and flew far into Russia, to strike at Soviet airfields and troop concentrations located as far as 320km (200 miles) east of the border. Then the panzers, their sides draped with the all-important jerry cans of extra fuel and sacks of rations, began to roll forward. Accompanying Army Group South during the early hours of the campaign, a war correspondent graphically described the scene: "The exhausts of the panzers belch out blue tongues of smoke. The air fills with a pungent bluish vapour that mingles with the damp green of the grass and with the golden reflection of corn. Beneath the screaming arch of Stukas, the mobile columns of tanks resemble thin lines drawn with a pencil on the vast green slate of the Moldavian plain."

Soon after the beginning of the attack, Army Group Centre reported good progress. In the centre its units faced the River Bug, which since

▲ German cavalry in a burning Russian village. It is a misconception that the German Army was fully motorized in World War II. In fact, it relied on horses for over 80 percent of its motive power. At the beginning of Operation Barbarossa, for example, the German Army entered the Soviet Union with 750,000 horses.

▼ An infantry squad moves through a burning Russian village. Though it was the panzers that set the pace of Barbarossa, it was upon the infantry that the main burden of battle fell. It was the infantry who had to clear innumerable villages, as well as reduce the Soviet pockets created by the panzer divisions.

1939 had marked the frontier between Germany and the Soviet Union. The Russian frontier units, desperately trying to obtain orders from the High Command and trying to assemble under heavy enemy attack, fought without cohesion, their artillery fire was weak and there seemed to be no plans either for organized defence or retreat. This led to most of the bridges over the River Bug falling into German hands intact.

The Soviets' lack of preparation for invasion was quite astonishing, especially as the lengthy and extensive German planning can hardly have escaped the notice of the Soviet leaders. Wherever Russian forces put up local resistance, tactical surprise was achieved and they were outflanked. One can only speculate as to Stalin's thoughts. Did he think that the vast movements of troops and vehicles in Poland and East Prussia was a mere political demonstration? Did he rec-

▲ **One advantage for the invading armies in delaying Barbarossa until late June was that the summer heat had reduced water levels of rivers and streams. As a result, rivers could be forded easily and streams, such as here, became only minor obstacles. As a precaution, many German tanks had been fitted with wading equipment.**

ognize the German peril too late? Whatever the reason, his frontier units were systematically carved up and annihilated by the Germans as a consequence. It was only in the fortress of Brest-Litovsk and in the field-works to the north of the city that the Soviet soldiers put up a tough resistance, but after four days the fortress was captured by a German division left behind for the purpose.

The main crossing of the River Bug on the south wing of Army Group Centre was blocked until 26 June, however, and this had an adverse effect on the deployment of the units of the Second Panzer Group, leading to much congestion in the area. The timetable for this important river crossing was upset, and the traffic police were at first unable to deal with the jams. Motorized units had to be diverted south towards assault bridges hastily thrown across the Bug. But here, too, there were further delays caused by the poor and marshy approach roads. Nevertheless General Heinz Guderian, Second Panzer Group's commander, urged on his tanks tirelessly and some of his advanced units reached the two important roads near Kobrin and Pruzhany during the evening of 23 June. Meanwhile, to the north of Brest-Litovsk, the Fourth Army penetrated enemy territory to a depth of nearly 16km (10 miles). Simultaneously, farther to the north, the Third Panzer Group captured the Niemen bridges at Alitus intact, while to the south, Grodno fell on 23 June. Luftflotte II carried out surprise raids on the Russian airfields and inflicted severe losses on the aircraft sitting on the ground. All along the front the Luftwaffe established air superiority over the Red Air Force, which was of vital importance to the Germans at the outset of the offensive.

These initial successes opened the way for the thrusts of the motorized units on the two

▼ **German infantry cross the River Styr in inflatable boats as a bridge burns in the background during the first week of July. At the beginning of Barbarossa the Russians started fires to slow the Germans. These could be very effective. In July 1941, a fire in a pine forest on the River Luga nearly wiped out a German brigade's command post.**

▶ **It was the task of the infantry and assault pioneers to cross rivers and knock out Soviet fortifications. Some squads would cross silently using their paddles, while others would swim across; motorized boats were used for speed. In this way the Germans crossed the Memel, Bug, Prush, Narev, Pripet and Dniester.**

wings of Army Group Centre, which were planned to bring about a wide encirclement of enemy forces in the general direction of Minsk. The Russian forces overrun in the Bialystok region were to be dealt with by shorter pincers thrown out by the Fourth and Ninth Armies. On 23 June, air reconnaissance reported many enemy columns retreating eastwards from the Bialystok area. A number of questions went through the mind of von Bock, Army Group Centre's commander: had the disorganization caused by the initial surprise been so quickly overcome by the Soviets; had the Soviet High Command taken the reins back into its hands and made up its mind to withdraw its forces eastwards to avoid the danger of encirclement and to regain freedom of movement? Von Bock thought so, and reports of the growing resistance of Soviet units convinced him that the latter were apparently intended to cover the general retreat which he suspected. He was afraid that strong enemy contingents might escape into the marshlands around the Berezina before the ring around them could be closed near Minsk. On the evening of the 23 June, therefore, he decided that the Third Panzer Group, which had advanced the farthest, should forthwith occupy the crossings over the Dvina at Polotsk and Vitebsk in order to prevent in good time the enemy from building up a new front on the Dvina itself.

The northern arm of the pincer movement near Minsk could safely be left to the Ninth Army. However, in an exchange of views with OKH the latter saw no advantage in such a deep and isolated thrust by the Third Panzer Group; rather, it was viewed as an unnecessary risk. OKH insisted on the junction of the two panzer groups near Minsk in accordance with the original Barbarossa plan. Further developments

▶ **An infantry squad crosses a river at the start of Barbarossa. The German Army's immediate tactical aim was to trap the Soviet armies in front of the Dnieper and Dvina river lines to prevent their retreat into the interior. The main weight of the attack was to the north of the Pripet Marshes; to the south the aim was Kiev.**

showed that this decision was the right one. On 24 June the spearheads of the two panzer groups reached Slonim in the south and Wilno in the north. Always edging farther to the east, the Fourth and Ninth Armies swung gradually to the north and south respectively, pushing into a trap Soviet forces that had been outflanked by German tanks. The Soviets fought in separate, uncoordinated groups, apparently without unified leadership – obstinate resistance combined with fragmented withdrawal. Some Red Army units disappeared into the vast forests in the region, only to turn up again in the rear areas of the advancing German Army. The result was a series of local engagements carried out by day and night, with severe losses to both sides.

Time and again, portions of the Russian forces succeeded in breaking out eastwards at points where the gaps in the net drawn around them were widest. There was no question of surrender. Nevertheless, the general German view was that such tactics would be unable to prevent the planned encirclement and elimination of the majority of the Soviet forces. But, the creation of a vast pocket extending from Bialystok to Minsk had become a difficult problem.

The original scheme was therefore quickly altered to conform with the current course of events. The old plan had depended on the speed of the armour. The panzers had indeed disrupted the Soviet forces along their lines of attack, and had cut their rearward communications. But they were unable in their unceasing forward thrust to create a solid ring around the encircled pockets. The panzer groups expected the

▲ A German officer and his men take a break to record their participation in Barbarossa for posterity. The first days of the offensive saw major German gains. Army Group North captured Kaunas and Vilna on 24 June, while the next day the First Panzer Group took Lutsk and Dubno in what was formerly Poland.

◀ Their morale high, a German infantry unit marches east into the Soviet Union. Infantry units sometimes marched up to 70km (44 miles) a day in an effort to keep in touch with the panzers. But the tanks travelled at speeds of up to 80km/h (50mph), and OKH was worried that they were outrunning their infantry support.

infantry corps to do this, but for all their efforts the latter could not keep up. Vehicles could move faster than marching infantry. In addition, the reduction of Soviet pockets was requiring more time than had been initially anticipated, especially as the panzers had moved on. The result was that the gaps between the infantry and the tank columns became progressively wider, and at Minsk the enclosing ring was very thin on the east side. The enemy soon discovered the weak spots, and strong forces tried to break out through Volkovysk and Slonim. At Volkovysk they succeeded. As a result, the Second Panzer Group, advancing partly on Minsk and partly on the Dnieper, found its overstretched left flank lines of communications to the rear threatened. Differences arose between the impetuous Guderian and the more cautious von Kluge, commander of the Fourth Army, because the infantry was held up by the unexpectedly bad roads and enemy resistance on the edges of the pocket. Von Bock, looking beyond Minsk to the Dnieper and the Dvina, took the side of Guderian.

The Waffen-SS in Russia

With the exception of the *SS-Polizei* Division, within the first few days of the campaign all the Waffen-SS formations under army command were in action (the *SS-Polizei* Division first went into action in early August). Russian troops bypassed during the main advance were dealt with by two brigades of Reichsführer-SS Heinrich Himmler's Kommandostab RFSS (headquarters of the Reichsführer-SS while in the field) – SS Infantry Brigade 1 and the SS Cavalry Brigade – which were deployed immediately behind the front. On 27 June, the *Leibstandarte* Division, some 10,796 strong, was committed to battle, leaving its assembly area and joining the First Panzer Group's reserves. It finally went into combat on 1 July, when it crossed the River Vistula at a point southwest of the town of Zamosc.

The First Panzer Group's pincer movement had extended deep into Soviet territory by this time, and General von Mackensen's III Panzer Corps had been cut off near Rovno. The first major task of the Waffen-SS on the Eastern Front was therefore to re-establish contact with General von Mackensen's corps. The motorized *Leibstandarte* Division roared into action. The German forward elements soon engaged Soviet tanks. While pushing through a densely wooded area, one SS column was joined by two Russian tanks that mistook it for a retreating Soviet unit. The column came to a brief halt just outside

▼ Accompanying the three army groups were Waffen-SS units. Though numerically insignificant when compared to the numbers of army personnel involved, Reichsführer-SS Himmler's legions brought an ideological fanaticism to the campaign that gave them a significance out of all proportion to their numbers.

▲ "Tactical surprise of the enemy has apparently been achieved along the entire line. All bridges across the Bug River, as on the entire river frontier, were undefended ... That the enemy was taken by surprise is evident from the fact that troops were caught in their quarters." (General Halder, Chief of OKH)

Klevan as night began to fall. The Soviet tank crews realized the awful truth and broke away, speeding off into the night under cover of darkness. Klevan was quickly taken and the advance relentlessly moved on. A spot was reached a few kilometres to the east of the town by the forward elements of the *Leibstandarte*'s reconnaissance battalion, where they discovered an empty, blood-soaked ambulance beside an abandoned German howitzer. A few hundred metres away, the corpses of several German soldiers were found, their bodies mutilated and barbed wire bound their hands. The war of atrocity and counter-atrocity had begun.

Even if such instances had not happened, the Waffen-SS would still have committed atrocities in the East, for it was in the vanguard of Hitler's crusade against "Asiatic Bolshevism". In particular, it was emphasized again and again to the soldiers of the Waffen-SS that the people of the Soviet Union were subhuman and their ideology was the antithesis of National Socialism. By thus dehumanizing the foe, the soldiers of the Waffen-SS, and the German armed forces as a whole to a lesser extent, were freed from feelings of guilt or remorse for atrocities. Therefore, as the war in the East developed, the side effects of this ideological view became apparent: the murder of civilians, the shooting of prisoners and the wholesale destruction of property. Small wonder that the enemy responded in kind.

In Moscow, meanwhile, Stalin at first believed that the attack was merely a "provocation", but after it became clear that a full-scale German invasion was under way, he issued Directive No 2, on the prompting of Chief of Staff Georgi Zhukov, stating that all "troops in full strength and with all means at their disposal will attack the enemy and destroy him in those

▼ Despite their victories on the frontier, the Germans were noticing differences in the nature of the fighting compared to that which they had experienced in the West. On 23 June, Halder had complained about the "absence of any large take of prisoners". Soviet troops were showing a willingness to fight and die rather than surrender.

places where he has violated the Soviet frontier." Point two ordered air attacks against enemy aircraft and troop concentrations, which the Germans had been doing to Stalin's own forces since the opening of the offensive! The order was issued at 07:15 hours on 22 June, but events over the next few days illustrated how hollow this directive was.

Disaster for the Red Army

Only 16 hours after their invasion, the Germans had dislocated two Soviet Fronts – the Northwestern and the Western – by smashing the Eleventh Army located at their junction and mauling the left flank of the Eighth Army and the right flank of the Third Army. Other horror stories soon revealed themselves: the Fourth Army had been paralyzed, and the Tenth Army, located in the centre of the Western Front, was under threat of having its flank turned. Initial Soviet dispositions had aided the Germans enormously; in Army Group Centre's sector, for example, three Soviet mechanized corps had been deployed in exposed positions in a salient and had been duly encircled and annihilated.

On the ground Soviet commanders struggled to organize their forces. The obstacles to any sort of success were massive. The aircraft that might have provided some cover had been shot to pieces on the ground by the Luftwaffe; artillery could not be moved due to transport deficiencies; fuel shortages affected both tanks and trucks; and poor organization resulted in many units suffering shortfalls in ammunition.

The Soviet General Staff issued its first operational digest at 20:00 hours on 22 June from Moscow. Its wording was somewhat fanciful: "During the second half of the day, with the arrival of forward elements of the field forces of the Red Army, the attacks of German troops along most of the length of our frontiers were beaten off and losses inflicted on the enemy." As the days passed, however, the extent of Red Army losses became apparent: average divisional

▲ Soviet prisoners taken in the first days of Barbarossa, during which the Germans were introduced to a favourite trick of Soviet soldiers: feigning surrender. Units and individuals would often approach German soldiers waving white flags and with hands in the air, only to then open fire at close range on Wehrmacht personnel.

strength, which had stood at 10,000–12,000 in early June, was down to under 6000 by July. Vast stocks of fuel, ammunition and stores had been captured or destroyed, weapon shortages had been massively increased by battlefield losses, while ammunition, both ordinary and specialized, was in critically short supply. In addition, thousands of tanks and aircraft had been lost, either through enemy action or abandonment.

In fact, the tactics of Red Army commanders, stung by orders from Moscow to attack, aided the Germans in the first phase of Barbarossa. In the south, for example, front commander Colonel-General M.P. Kirponos threw in his corps as and when they arrived at the front. Soviet tank crews, having been harassed and exhausted by constant Luftwaffe attacks, were no match for the experienced tank crews of General von Kleist's First Panzer Group. Many Russian tanks drove straight into

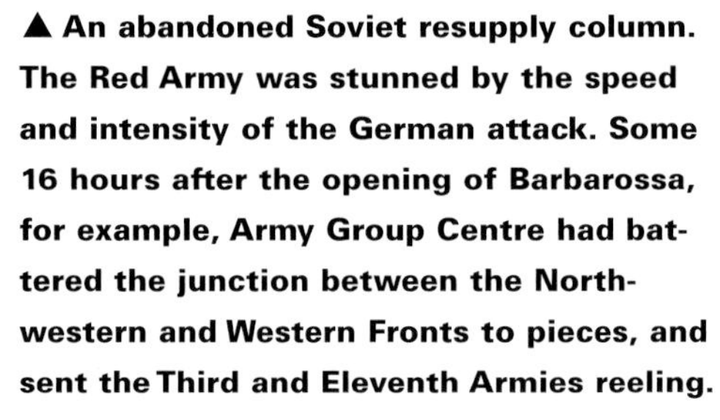

▲ An abandoned Soviet resupply column. The Red Army was stunned by the speed and intensity of the German attack. Some 16 hours after the opening of Barbarossa, for example, Army Group Centre had battered the junction between the Northwestern and Western Fronts to pieces, and sent the Third and Eleventh Armies reeling.

ambushes, or broke down before they got to grips with the enemy. However, despite wasting his men's lives and their vehicles, Kirponos did inflict losses on the enemy, as Halder noted: "The enemy leadership in front of Army Group South is remarkably energetic, his endless flank and frontal attacks are causing us heavy losses."

For the Germans, despite the baffling resistance of individual enemy units that had no hope of survival and chose to fight rather than surrender, Barbarossa was yielding massive gains. In the north, for example, General Erich von Manstein's LVI Panzer Corps advanced a staggering 296km (185 miles) in four days, while Guderian's panzer group had covered 432km

◀ Destroyed Soviet war material. Red Army tactics were desperate during the early stages of the war: on 25 June the 100th Rifle Division deployed northwest of Minsk to halt Army Group Centre's panzers. But it had no artillery and was brushed aside. Two days later German forces trapped three Soviet armies in a pocket at Minsk.

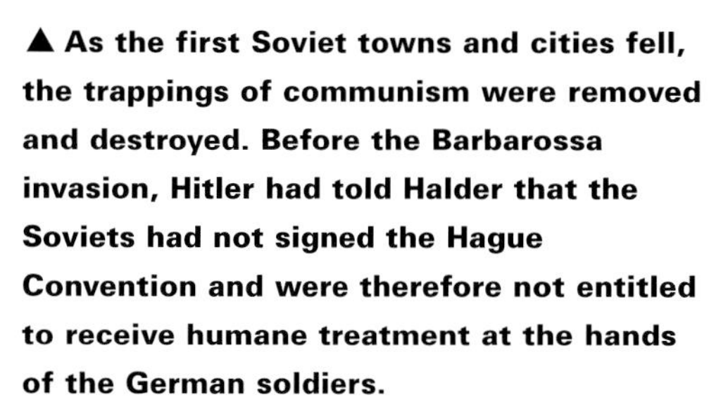

▲ As the first Soviet towns and cities fell, the trappings of communism were removed and destroyed. Before the Barbarossa invasion, Hitler had told Halder that the Soviets had not signed the Hague Convention and were therefore not entitled to receive humane treatment at the hands of the German soldiers.

▲ Another communist symbol is removed. Many Soviets welcomed the Germans as liberators, but soon came to appreciate the true nature of Nazi rule. Hitler viewed the Russians as fit only to serves as slaves, to be ruthlessly subjugated once under "Aryan" domination. "At present," he stated, "they can't read, and they ought to stay like that."

(270 miles) from Brest-Litovsk to Bobruysk in only seven days. By mid-July, therefore, the overall situation on the Eastern Front was most favourable for the Third Reich: the three army groups had gained positions that would allow the army to bring about a victorious end to the campaign. In the south, German spearheads had reached the approaches to Kiev; in the north the Fourth Panzer Group had secured bridgeheads over the River Luga and thus gained the "gateway to Leningrad"; and in the middle Army Group Centre was only 310km (194 miles) from Moscow. For the moment, Hitler's great gamble seemed to have worked.

However, the German armies that so confidently crossed the Russian frontier found themselves in an alien land of stupefying magnitude. The vast forests of the north were as impenetrable as jungle. Swamps larger than entire German provinces blocked the advance. In the south, the undulating plains of the Ukraine swept unbroken from horizon to horizon. Boundless Russia seemed able to swallow the German armies whole. Likewise, there was no end to the defenders' resilience. Despite the loss of half a million men either killed or wounded in the first two weeks of the campaign, the Soviets kept coming from an apparently bottomless reserve.

The great military theorist Antoine Jomini had remarked on the eve of Napoleon's invasion of Russia in 1812: "Russia is a country which is easy to get into, but very difficult to get out of." Operation Barbarossa seemed to illustrate his wisdom, as German and Axis armies drove ever deeper into Russian territory. The Germans had kicked in the door, but the superstructure had not crashed to the ground.

▲ German Army field artillery, StuG III assault gun and Panzerjäger antitank guns in Russia, late June 1941. By the start of July the first phase of Barbarossa was over: Army Group North had broken out of the Dvina bridgehead, and Army Group Centre was advancing to Smolensk.

▶ A German casualty during the frontier battles. The German Army had made allowances for losses, and had anticipated 275,000 casualties for the period June–August 1941. It had this number of replacements available in its field replacement battalions and the Field Replacement Army to replenish anticipated losses.

◀ German infantry moves through a Russian town. At the beginning of July 1941, the German Army had lost a total of 11,822 killed, 39,109 wounded and 3960 missing (a mixture of captured and killed) on the Eastern Front. By the same date the Red Army had lost 200,000 killed alone.

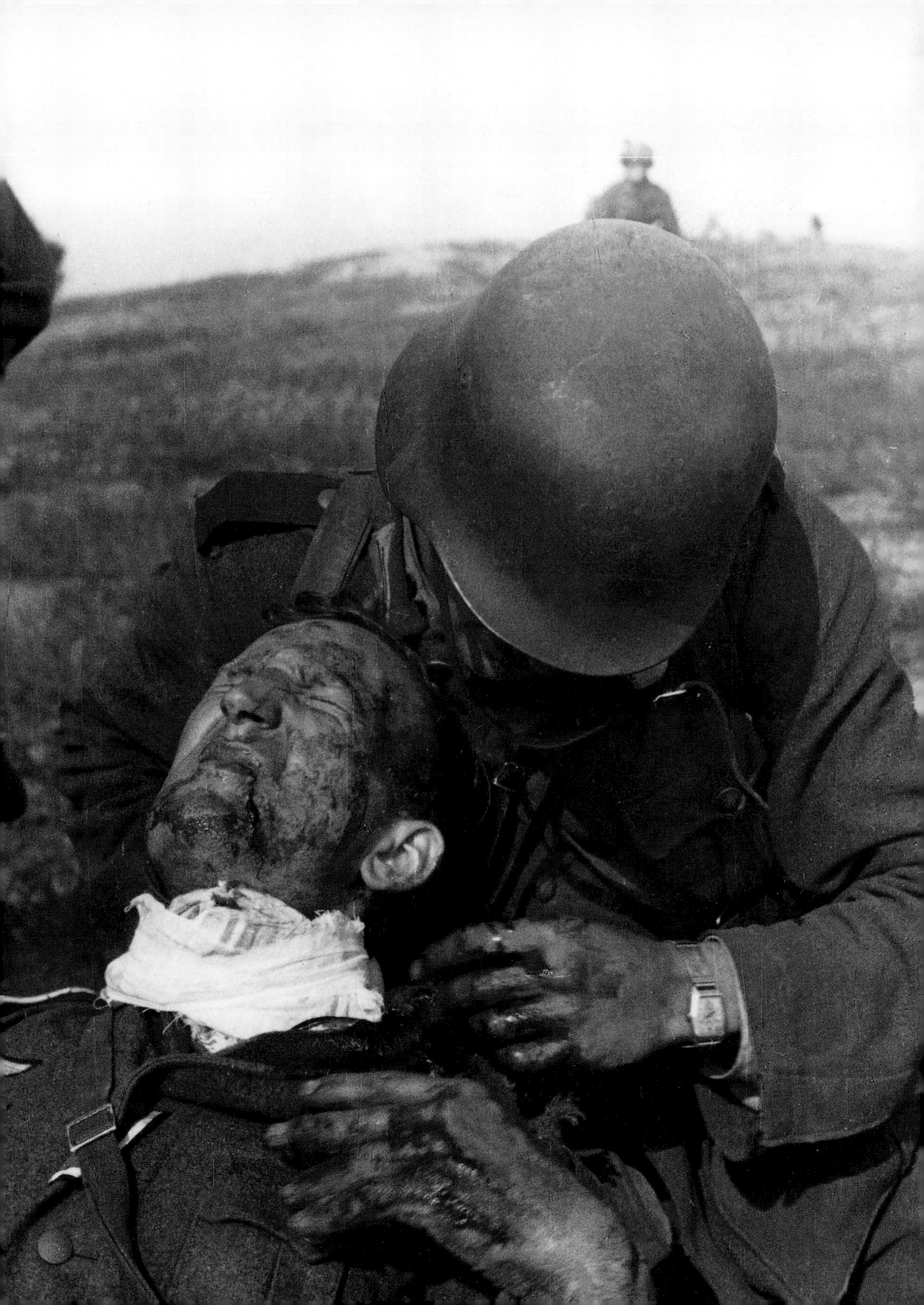

Guderian's panzers

The two panzer groups of Army Group Centre held the key to winning the war against the Soviet Union, and in Heinz Guderian the panzers had a master of armoured warfare – but would he be given the freedom to exploit his success?

The Russians had fought and lost the "battle of the frontiers". Now von Bock's Army Group Centre could begin the long drive to Smolensk, plunging into White Russia. The Germans were confident that they could encircle both Minsk and Smolensk. The decisive element in these objectives would be the performance of the Second and Third Panzer Groups, commanded by Colonel-General Heinz Guderian and General Hermann Hoth respectively. And it would be Guderian, a headstrong but inspiring leader, who would demonstrate exactly what well-led armoured units could achieve.

The original plan for Army Group Centre was to conduct two closely linked encirclement operations. The first, to be conducted by the Fourth and Ninth Armies, was to annihilate

▼ Infantry of Army Group Centre take a ride on a Panzer III during Barbarossa. It was upon Army Group Centre that the greatest expectation fell. It possessed two panzer groups – a total of nine panzer divisions – and was stronger than the Soviet forces that opposed it. And in Guderian and Hoth it had expert leaders.

▲ **General Heinz Guderian, "the Father of the panzer divisions". In the interwar years he had specialized in the military uses of mechanical transport, and by 1938 was Hitler's general of panzer troops. The commander of the Second Panzer Group during Barbarossa, he won a series of victories that took him to the gates of Moscow.**

▲ **Guderian's panzers head east. With the Luftwaffe ruling the skies – its supporting contingent, Luftflotte II, had destroyed most of the enemy aircraft on the ground – the tanks roamed at will. The Second Panzer Group advanced from Brest-Litovsk to Bobruysk in the first seven days of the campaign – some 432km (270 miles).**

enemy formations around Bialystok. The second, also involving the Fourth and Ninth Armies but spearheaded by the two panzer groups, was to encircle enemy divisions 160km (100 miles) farther east around Minsk, thereby trapping any Soviet units trying to escape into the interior. In this way Army Group Centre hoped to destroy 36 Soviet divisions, including 10 armoured formations.

The plan relied on the speed of the panzers, which had disrupted the Russians along their lines of attack and rearward communications during the first few days of the attack. But in their unceasing forward thrust, the Germans were unable to establish a solid ring encompassing the pockets. The Germans needed more time than had been anticipated to deal with Soviet forces driven off the main lines of attack. The result, as the tanks moved on, was gaps between the infantry and panzer columns which

▲ **Field Marshal Fedor von Bock (second from right), head of Army Group Centre, confers with three of his subordinates in the early phase of Barbarossa, including General Hermann Hoth (right), commander of the Third Panzer Group.**

became progressively wider. The weak spots were soon probed by the Soviets, and whenever strong forces tried to break out through Slonim and Volkovysk, they generally succeeded.

Advancing partly on Minsk and partly on the Dnieper, the Second Panzer Group found its overstretched left flank threatened and its lines of communication in danger. Differences now arose between the more cautious von Kluge, commander of the Fourth Army, and the impetuous Guderian, because the unexpectedly bad roads, and intense fighting on the edges of

◀ **At the start of the campaign Soviet infantry had few weapons that could pierce the armour of the Panzer IIIs and IVs. Their antitank rifles were useless, and the 47mm antitank gun had still to be issued in large numbers. The panzers therefore pushed on at speed – at times achieving a rate of advance of 80km (50 miles) a day.**

▲ A composite force of Panzer IIIs, half-tracks and antitank guns on the advance. The Third Panzer Group's panzers sliced through the boundary between the Soviet Northwestern and Western Fronts. On 26 June, Lieutenant-General D.G. Pavlov, the latter's commander, reported to Stalin that "there is no way to oppose them".

the pocket, had held up the infantry. Looking beyond Minsk to the Dnieper and the Dvina, von Bock sided with Guderian. To Hitler, though, the Minsk Pocket seemed too large, and thus von Bock's two panzer groups were confined to the Minsk area.

However, in order to join the expected infantry corps of the Fourth Army in buttressing the pocket being formed farther to the east around Volkovysk, the Second Panzer Group, though unwillingly, was compelled to leave part of its force at Slonim. At this juncture (25 June) the encircling forces of the Ninth Army on the north side of the pocket were stronger than those of the Fourth Army on the southeastern side. As the Soviets probed the pocket, they discovered the weak spots and attempted to break through them, and for a time several corps of the Fourth Army were in a serious predicament. On 25 June, therefore, OKH insisted on strengthening the pressure exercised by the Ninth Army on the north and the Fourth Army on the south side of the pocket. In bitter fighting, first around Bialystok then Volkovysk, this resulted in several fragmentary pockets being created instead of one large one.

Russian resilience at this stage of the campaign was becoming an irritant to the Germans. The Soviets did not fight like their Western counterparts. They made use of the trackless forests to infiltrate through German lines, and being largely self-sufficient, they would live off the land (that their supplies had long since been cut off by the Germans seemed irrelevant). But most alarmingly, when their ammunition was exhausted the Soviet soldiers were not afraid to resort to hand-to-hand combat.

At Minsk, large numbers of Red Army troops had slipped northeastwards through the thin net to Novogrudok, before the door was

▼ German armour on the advance (the tank on the left is a Panzer IV). Panzer divisions simply chewed up the initial Soviet counterattacks, which lacked cover, coordination and logistical support. An attack by VI Cavalry Corps (around 13,000 men) towards Grodno, for example, resulted in 50 percent casualties, mainly due to air attack.

closed on the eastern side of the Volkovysk Pocket on 28 June. But they found themselves entangled and encircled again on 29 June. On the same day near Minsk, the spearhead of the Second Panzer Group joined up with units of the Third Panzer Group, which after a bitter struggle had arrived the day before. In the closing days of June, it fell mainly to the Third Panzer Group to repel attacks by fresh Soviet tank units thrown in from the east, which were desperately trying to help the forces trapped in the German pocket.

The preliminary objective of the two panzer groups had been attained by 28 June, though behind them the Fourth and Ninth Armies were still fighting hard to clear up the pocket. The fighting around Bialystok and Volkovysk was more or less over by 30 June. This victory released a number of German infantry corps to advance and relieve the panzer groups in the great encirclement near Minsk. The Soviet Third, Tenth and Thirteenth Armies were destroyed in the two pockets, eliminating some 417,000 men from the Soviet order of battle. The Germans also captured 3332 tanks, 1809 guns and 250 aircraft. The lagging infantry once again sorely tested the patience of German panzer commanders anxious to forge ahead. Part of the tank forces had to be left at the front of the pocket in a crescent on either side of Minsk, for example, for an entire week. Despite forced marches, on the rough and dusty roads the infantry could not maintain the desired speed.

The Battle of Minsk was a disaster for the Red Army. The Western Front had ceased to exist as an organized military formation. (The prewar Soviet mobilization plan had allocated army divisions to a number of military districts of the western Soviet Union; when war broke

▼ A German casualty is loaded onto a Fieseler Fi 156 Storch during the reduction of the Bialystok and Minsk Pockets. This huge encirclement operation, which involved the two panzer groups and the Fourth and Ninth Armies, netted 324,000 prisoners, 3332 tanks and 1809 artillery pieces. The Soviet Third, Tenth and Thirteenth Armies were smashed.

▲ An ecstatic welcome for the German Army from the citizens of Lemberg (Lvov), which fell to Army Group Centre on 30 June 1941. On the same day, Luftwaffe fighter pilots of squadron JG 51 (flying Messerschmitt Bf 109s) shot down 100 Soviet bombers attacking German ground troops east of Minsk.

out these districts were transformed into five army group headquarters called fronts – roughly equivalent to German army groups.) Such a calamity did nothing to sweeten Stalin's temper, and the Soviet leader began to exact harsh punishments. The front's commander, Lieutenant-General D.G. Pavlov, was arrested and shot. Marshal Timoshenko was given the unenviable task of assuming command of what was left of the Western Front.

At a lower level, the defeat at Minsk had seen a change in the conduct of ordinary Red Army soldiers. Fatigued by the earlier fighting and suffering from poor morale, to which a shortage of ammunition and other supplies may have contributed, Soviet units were now more inclined to surrender: over 300,000 prisoners were taken at Minsk. Nevertheless, a large number of Soviet troops did reach the comparative safety of the large forests in the area, where they organized themselves into partisan groups. When partisan warfare became increasingly rife in the later stages of the campaign, it was to produce very disturbing effects. Army Group Centre had to employ some of its reserve frontline divisions in an attempt to mop up the areas behind the frontline, as there were not enough German security divisions available to undertake the task. However, even the frontline divisions were only partially successful in anti-partisan missions.

Soviet breakout attempts from encirclement were not sophisticated and well-planned operations – quite the opposite. German units were continually baffled by suicidal mass frontal charges, often repeated at the same spot, without artillery support against entrenched machine-gun positions. The motivation for such assaults seem to have been a fear on the part of local Soviet commanders and commissars of criticism

▲ A German 37mm antitank gun scores a hit on the dusty steppe. The 37mm Pak 35/36 had a muzzle velocity of 762m/s (2500ft/s), and at a range of 500m (1640ft) could easily penetrate 48mm (1.9in) of vertical armour or 36mm (1.4in) of 30-degree sloped armour. In Russia this weapon proved ineffective against the T-34.

and punishment meted out by the command, compounded by the commissars' fears of being shot out of hand if captured (in which they were justified). In addition, most Red Army soldiers believed, no doubt encouraged by commissar warnings, that they would also be executed if captured by the enemy. And though German frontline units generally did not execute their prisoners, those who were commissars, communists or Jews were shot out of hand. It is a tragedy that, after suffering horrendous losses (at this period of the war it is estimated that for every German soldier killed in battle, approximately 29 Red Army soldiers were being killed), Soviet troops who reached their own lines were subjected to interrogation, and sometimes arrest and execution, at the hands of the NKVD (Peoples' Commisariat of Internal Affairs).

After the defeats at Bialystok and Minsk the centre of the Soviets' front was left wide open. At first, Russian troops were seen retreating eastwards across the Dnieper as a result of the battle, but OKH had realized some days before that the Soviets had decided against any general retreat into the depths of the country. From 29 June onwards, air reconnaissance reports confirmed large-scale troop movements *westwards* from the Smolensk area by road and rail. To the Germans it appeared that a new defence line along the Dnieper, Dvina and on the "land bridge" between the two rivers was being set up. This was proof that Soviet Commander-in-Chief Marshal Timoshenko had retaken "the reins of command" firmly into his own hands.

The forces at his disposal looked formidable on paper – seven armies – but he had only 200 tanks and 389 aircraft to rebuild his front. His front directive ordered a "durable" defence of the Polotsk "fortified district", the Western Dvina, Senno, Orsha and the Dnieper itself, to

▼ A Soviet position under devastating Luftwaffe attack. Over half the operational strength of the Luftwaffe was concentrated in Russia during Operation Barbarossa. As in previous Blitzkrieg campaigns, the rapid German advance demanded much of the fighter and fighter-bomber squadrons, which provided air cover and support.

◀ A knocked-out Soviet T-26 light tank. At the beginning of Barbarossa the Red Army fielded 24,000 tanks, which outnumbered the panzers by seven to one. However, Soviet tank crews were poorly trained and led. The T-26 was the most common Soviet tank in 1941, comparable in performance to the German Panzer I, II and 38(t).

prevent any German breakthrough to the north and east. This new directive was given *Stavka*'s approval (*Stavka Glavnogo Komandovanita* – Main Command Headquarters – was chaired by Timoshenko and included Stalin, Molotov and most senior Soviet commanders).

The movement of Soviet forces was seen in Army Group Centre's headquarters as being proof of an attempt to buy time for the build-up of the Dnieper defences. If so, it showed that von Bock's fears of 23 June were far from illusory. It explained why he and his tank commanders were so keen on pushing forward without delay to the Dnieper and Dvina, and why, because of their long-term aims, they had been so reluctant to take any part in the engagements connected with the encirclements. In tactical warfare time is of the essence: every day lost helped the Red Army to bring up reserves and construct a new defence line on the Rivers Dnieper and Dvina. More valuable time would be lost breaking through a fresh front, and would cause unnecessary German losses before the first great objective of the campaign – the Orsha, Smolensk, Vitebsk "land bridge" – could be reached: the essential base area for the final attack on Moscow. In addition, if the momentum of the offensive could be maintained Soviet manpower reserves would be irrelevant, since Army Group Centre was moving so fast, and was so superior when it came to operational-level manoeuvre, that the Russians were running out of space to trade for time to allow them to organize reserve formations.

From the beginning, German field commanders had fixed their sights on the Dnieper and Dvina, and had kept large parts of the two

▶ Another knocked-out T-26. This tank was designed primarily for infantry support. The state of the Red Army's armoured force may be judged by the fact that in June 1941 over 65 percent of the light tank force required major repairs. Many Soviet light tank units broke down before they reached the front.

◀ **Guderian (centre left) and Hoth (right), the architects of Army Group Centre's staggering advances. Guderian in particular always wanted to race farther east, which brought him into conflict with Hitler. He wrote in his diary: "[Hitler] wanted to halt the panzer groups and turn them against the Russians in and about Bialystok."**

panzer groups moving eastwards without letting them take part in the fighting around the pockets. These decisions had now proved correct. At the beginning of July, Army Group Centre was at the starting point for the next advance to the east. On its right wing, encountering only slight resistance, one corps of the Second Panzer Group had crossed the Berezina and reached the Dnieper near Rogachev. On the northern wing, another corps had reached the Berezina near Borisov. A bridgehead on the road to Smolensk was then established after a hard struggle. On the encirclement front at Minsk, other corps units were still waiting for the infantry to relieve them. Elements of the Fourth Army not tied to the Minsk Pocket were pushing towards the Berezina, but with up to 200km (125 miles) to travel they could hardly be expected to be there in much less than a week (advancing in forced marches along roads deep in dust was exhausting in the extreme for both man and beast).

On the edge of the Pripet Marshes, at the far end of Army Group Centre's southern wing, sending out reconnaissance patrols among the swamps, the 1st Cavalry Division, part of XXIV Corps, was holding the long flank. It was known that comparatively strong enemy bands were

▶ **A Panzer IV on the advance. The heaviest German tank in service in June 1941, the Germans only possessed 450 of them at the start of Barbarossa. Armed with a short-barrelled 75mm gun and served by a five-man crew, the main gun was in reality a low-velocity howitzer designed for anti-personnel fire support.**

▲ A Panzer III, the mainstay of the German panzer force that undertook Barbarossa. Some, as here, were armed with a 37mm gun; others mounted the more powerful 50mm model. The three army groups began the campaign with a total of 1440 Panzer III tanks. Their average road range was 175km (109 miles) at a speed of 40km/hr (25mph).

operating skilfully on the south side of the River Pripet, and were causing a considerable nuisance to Army Group South's Sixth Army.

Meanwhile, the Third Panzer Group was thrusting towards the Dvina near and above Polotsk, while Army Group North's southern wing had already crossed the river near Daugvapils (Dvinsk). The Ninth Army with the bulk of its infantry was following in the tracks of the Third Panzer Group (its route to the Dvina was much shorter than that of the Fourth Army's to the Dnieper).

During this period it was discovered that the number of Soviet aircraft had been greatly underestimated by German intelligence, but this did not hamper the Luftwaffe's domination of the Russian skies or hold up the advance. A combination of better aircraft and more highly trained crews resulted in heavy Soviet losses: on 29 June alone, for example, the Luftwaffe shot down 200 Soviet aircraft. There had also been no great supply problems reported. Advanced dumps had been established at Slutsk and Molodechno and in the Minsk area, and as far as Baranowice the conversion of the railways to European gauge had been completed.

The German Army Commander-in-Chief, Field Marshal Walter von Brauchitsch, and von Bock had held a discussion on the strategy to be followed in the next phase of operations as far back as 26 June. Both agreed that no time was to be wasted in engaging the enemy around Smolensk at the expense of the thrust towards Moscow. Von Brauchitsch advocated a measure that would allow better use of the fast-moving armoured units. This was the merging of the two panzer groups, under the command of Field

Marshal Gunther von Kluge. Bock had serious misgivings, based mainly on the self-willed personalities of Guderian and von Kluge, but his objection was dismissed as of no great significance by Brauchitsch, who ordered the new arrangement to come into force on 3 July. The former High Command of the Fourth Army was therefore renamed Armour Army High Command IV to occupy a place in the hierarchy of command between Army Group Centre Command and the Second and Third Panzer Group Commands. The Fourth Army units were taken over by the new High Command of the Second Army, with General Maximilian Freiherr von Weichs at its head.

New objectives

Army Group Centre received a new instruction on 1 July, which was relayed to the various subcommands. The new Fourth Panzer Army was to be in a position on 3 July to break through into the direction of Moscow. The Second Panzer Group, with this objective in view, was to force a crossing of the Dnieper in the Rogachev-Orsha sector. Then, its spearhead, following the lines of the Minsk–Moscow highway, was to capture the heights of Yelnya on the River Desna.

The Third Panzer Group was to bypass the marshes of the upper Berezina and, following the line of the Dvina between Polotsk and Vitebsk, break into the region north of Smolensk. The Second and Ninth Armies were to follow the fast-moving units with all possible speed and send forward mobile detachments to support them. The capture of the Orsha–Vitebsk "land bridge" was of vital importance to both armies. Cooperation with the Luftwaffe was to remain as before. Both the Second Army and Second Panzer Group were to be supported by II Fliegerkorps and the Ninth Army and Third Panzer Group by VIII Fliegerkorps.

This time, though, the element of surprise had failed: the Fourth Panzer Army's attack was held up on the first day, 3 July, when it met tough resistance on the river courses. On the outer wings, bridgeheads were eventually formed near Rogachev on the Dnieper and Polotsk on the Dvina. The Soviets put up a stubborn defence between the two on the Berezina and showed intense activity near Borisov. Luftwaffe air reconnaissance reported further troop movements from the rear, leading to the conclusion that the Red Army was trying to halt the Germans at the river barriers. The approach to Moscow via Smolensk was, it seemed, certain to grind to a halt. Von Bock was faced with an urgent dilemma on the first evening. Should the Fourth Panzer Army's attack be continued alone or should it await the arrival of the Second and Ninth Armies? The first divisions could be expected in a week at the earliest. The advanced detachments with artillery might provide some minor reinforcements at an earlier date, but that

▼ A Soviet fort near Brest-Litovsk under artillery bombardment. The advance of Army Group Centre was not held up by fortresses. Brest-Litovsk, for example, held out for a week and commanded an important crossing over the Bug. However, von Bock left a division to keep it contained while his units built alternative crossings farther south.

◀ Soviet infantry lying in wait for the Germans. In fact, this photograph gives a false image of Soviet infantry tactics. During Barbarossa many Red Army infantry attacks were of the human-wave variety, being largely uncoordinated and often across open ground. The inevitable result was large-scale slaughter.

would not compensate for the loss of time while the bulk of the forces arrived.

Von Bock, with von Kluge's agreement, acted at once and ordered the scattered units of the Second Panzer Group to concentrate on either side of Mogilev, then to deliver a strong attack at both Mogilev and Borisov. The Third Panzer Group caused him less concern because its advance had been shorter and it could call on nearer reinforcements from the divisions of the Ninth Army. Although heavy rainfalls, which softened the dirt roads, had hindered and delayed the regrouping, the Third Panzer Group, fighting hard east of Polotsk, was able to roll up Soviet defences on the Dvina defences and occupy Vitebsk on 9 July. This was a key success, and the staff of both the army and the army group, seizing the opportunity, decided to transfer the spearhead of the operation to the north wing by moving units from the Second Panzer Group to the Third Panzer Group. This idea was abandoned, however, due to bad weather conditions and poor roads. On 10–11 July, the Second Panzer Group succeeded in crossing the Dnieper on both sides of Mogilev at Stary Brykhov and at Shklov, rendering the transfer unnecessary.

Air power – the key factor

Luftwaffe air superiority was proving of immense importance to the German Army, and was having a detrimental effect on Red Army operations. An assault against XXXIX Panzer Corps' flanks from north of Orsha was launched by Timoshenko on 6 July. The Soviet V and VII Mechanized Corps, fielding 300 and 400 tanks respectively, though with no air cover, few anti-aircraft guns, and inadequate supplies of fuel and ammunition, advanced on Senno and ran into the 17th and 18th Panzer Divisions. As the tank battle raged, Luftwaffe dive-bombers attacked the Soviet vehicles – the result was the destruction of both Soviet corps.

On 13 July, a double German breakthrough on the wings set in motion the operation for the encirclement of Smolensk. The Orsha–Smolensk road served the armoured spearheads well. Advancing from the northwest, one division of the Third Panzer Group reached the Smolensk–Moscow high road and blocked it at Yartsevo on

▲ "Minsk was enveloped in a pincer movement; the first pocket was closed and a large number of prisoners were taken. Our infantry, whose inhuman hardships made us feel sorry for them, followed up on foot and took care of the surrounded Russians." (Hans von Luck, 7th Panzer Division, Third Panzer Group)

5 July. The following day, a division from the Third Panzer Group made a surprise attack on Smolensk and captured the city. This meant that enemy forces, estimated at about 300,000, were cut off between Orsha and Smolensk. The Germans had once again formed a massive pocket, which they set about annihilating.

As usual, Soviet efforts to prevent this happening had been desperate, heroic – and futile. Remnants of the Thirteenth Army, having just escaped from the Minsk Pocket, attempted to halt Guderian's Second Panzer Group around Mogilev on 10 July. Having no armour, they

▼ The panzers may have been the spearhead of the Blitzkrieg, but to keep moving they required trucks to bring up spares and other essential supplies. Amazingly, there had been no Reich plan for national production of wheeled military vehicles, thus the army's requirements were met by requisitioning and confiscation.

◀ The army was able to pad out its transport requirements with captured and requisitioned trucks, coaches and even private cars, aside from its own standard lorries. However, it soon discovered that vehicles built to travel upon the well-maintained roads of Western Europe suffered intolerable wear and tear on Russia's roads.

were penned up in Mogilev for two weeks before being destroyed. The men of the Soviet Nineteenth Army went into action as they dismounted from railway carriages on 11–13 July in an attempt to retake the Vitebsk salient. By the evening of 13 July, though, the whole army was in tatters.

By 17 July, the Second Panzer Group, having left its XXXXVII Corps on the south edge of Smolensk Pocket, sent XXXXVI Corps to the River Desna on either side of Yelnya, and XXIV Corps to the River Sozh on either side of Krichev. Meanwhile, the Third Panzer Group's XXXIX and LVII Corps constituted the northern section of the trap, fighting their way forward to the Yartsevo/Nevel line. Displaying a recklessness greater than in their thrust for Minsk, the panzer units rushed to deal with the Soviet forces threatening the Germans' flanks. Strong Soviet forces, numbering some six or seven divisions, had been left behind near Mogilev, while northeast of Vitebsk were another three or four. In addition, there were several enemy formations deployed on both sides of Nevel, perhaps some 10 divisions in all.

It was imperative that the lead German units awaited the arrival of the infantry corps of the Second and Ninth Armies, both to deal with enemy units on the flanks and to annihilate the huge pocket at Smolensk. However, as with previous pockets, it was not possible to seal off the Smolensk Pocket entirely, due to a small gap left in the tangled valley of the Dnieper. Guderian was responsible for this sector, and he tried to close the gap with artillery fire and air raids. But the enemy could still infiltrate eastwards through it. When urged by the army group to effect a definitive junction with the Third Panzer Group, he replied that with all the tasks he had in hand he simply did not have enough

▶ "There was no water, only sweat that burned in the eyes and made the shirt flap wetly against the skin. The companies, battalions and regiments had regrouped after the breakthrough and now they were on the march again ... But it was hot, so mercilessly hot. There was no water but there was blood and that ran in streams." (German officer)

▶ The Blitzkrieg demanded that mobile infantry keep up and fight with the panzers. The need for an armoured personnel carrier was met in the SdKfz 251, seen here, which had good cross-country performance but was complicated to maintain. Each 1941 panzer division had two motorized rifle regiments transported in such vehicles.

tanks to comply. In fact, Guderian was less interested in closing the gap than in continuing his thrust eastwards and creating a springboard for the advance on Moscow. But, on 20 July, when he established a bridgehead across the Desna near Yelnya and proposed to follow this up with further thrusts to the east, von Bock intervened to remind him of his prior duty to close the Smolensk gap. This was not done until 27 July, and it was not until 5 August that the enemy in the Smolensk Pocket was finally liquidated. In the fighting since 10 July, 310,000 prisoners, 3205 tanks and 3120 guns had been taken. The Soviet Sixteenth Army, plus parts of the Nineteenth and Twentieth Armies, had been annihilated. These large numbers and the timescale of their resistance are explained by the fact that the gap so tardily closed was used for bringing in supplies, rather than as an avenue of escape.

In a vast curve some 800km (500 miles) in length stretched the loose front of the fast-moving units of the German Fourth Panzer Army, which were fanning out with the support of the infantry divisions of the Second and Ninth Armies. The first main objective of Army Group Centre had been obtained in the break out from the Orsha–Smolesk–Vitebsk "land bridge". Soviet forces had been crushed and scattered on a wide front, and their attempts to form a fresh defence line along the Rivers Dnieper and Dvina had been extensively defeated. From mid-July

◀ German troops pass an abandoned Soviet KV-2 heavy assault tank. Armed with a 152mm howitzer and protected by 100mm (4in) of armour, it was designed to destroy heavily reinforced bunkers. However, it was too slow, presented too big a target and was unreliable. As a result, most of the 334 built were lost in 1941.

onwards, the German staffs were aware of the new battle order of the Soviet "fronts", or army groups, and that Marshal Timoshenko had assumed the leadership of the Western Front opposite Army Group Centre.

It was becoming clear that the new Soviet Commander-in-Chief was displaying a fresh spirit of strong will and initiative. If there was anything to be salvaged from the loss of six Soviet armies, it was that their sacrifice had at least given the Soviet High Command time to conjure up fresh, if partly improvised, forces from their immense reservoir of manpower and to place them in the frontline. These were now coming into action chiefly on the flanks of the advancing Army Group Centre, and at the points of junction with its neighbouring army groups to the north and to the south. To the south, coming from the Gomel area, the Soviet Twenty-First Army, comprising eight divisions, attacked on 15 July across the Dnieper near Rogachev. Simultaneously from the Pripet Marshes there emerged a cavalry force moving north from Mozyr in the direction of Bobruysk on the Berezina. Both movements were aimed at the southern flank of the German Second Army.

Too many commitments

The Soviet forces were brought to a standstill after several days of fighting, but three German corps continued to be engaged in the area. Army Group Centre's southern wing became pinned down on the Dnieper, and this hold-up, together with the developments on Army Group South's northern wing, were to later play an important role in deciding the strategy of the German High Command. Another corps of the German Second Army had been given the task, as mentioned above, of eradicating the Red Army concentration at Mogilev, estimated to be six divisions. This was successfully accomplished by 27 July.

Meanwhile, von Weichs had only two army corps left to send forward to strengthen the front of the Second Panzer Group. To the north, where the infantry divisions of the Ninth Army had arrived earlier than expected at the Dvina, and where close contact with the right wing of Army Group North could be maintained, the situation was less critical than it was farther to the south. The Ninth Army had to defeat strong enemy forces in order to capture the fortress of Polotsk, which fell on 16 July, but it was then able to detach three corps in good time to help in the fighting around the Smolensk Pocket. The enemy groups at Nevel were eliminated by 24 July. South of Velikie Luki the right flank of the Third Panzer Group had been held up by the obstinate resistance of the Soviet Twenty-Second Army.

▲ Russians taken in the Smolensk Pocket. Once again the two panzer groups had scored a great victory: 310,000 prisoners, 3205 tanks and 3120 artillery pieces taken or destroyed. In accordance with Hitler's Commissar Order, Communist Party officials were shot on the spot, as were wounded or sick prisoners, classed as "useless eaters".

As the Soviet armies and ad hoc forces of Timoshenko's front carried on fighting, the German front from Yelnya to Yartsevo and Belyy was put under strong pressure. At this time the

◀ **Panzer IV medium support tanks move forward to reduce Soviet units in the Smolensk Pocket in mid-July 1941. By this stage of Operation Barbarossa the German Army had lost 102,488 men killed, wounded or missing. Though a large number, it represented only three percent of the total manpower committed on 22 June.**

Desna bridgehead at Yelnya became a focal point, causing great sacrifices of men and material. The Waffen-SS *Das Reich* Division was deployed in this sector. One of the division's soldiers, Heidi Ruehl, later recalled the nature of the fighting: "The gunners, working like fury, finally beat off the first Russian tank attacks, but these were renewed in greater strength and then our motorcycle battalion came under heavy pressure ... because of the severe losses which it had sustained, the motorcycle battalion had to be taken out of the line and was replaced by an East Prussian engineer battalion. With the help of that formation we stemmed the Russian advance, albeit temporarily, for soon ammunition for the guns began to run out and we were only allowed to fire against certain, specified targets."

Army Group Centre found itself in the second half of July on the defensive at many points. Moreover, panzer commanders had to take into account a serious reduction in fighting strength: 40–50 percent in armoured units, 20 percent of vehicles due to wear and tear, and up to 50 percent of tanks. Signs of exhaustion were also appearing among the troops, who had now been fighting without a break since the beginning of the offensive in June. Unexpected crises also occurred in the supply system, usually because of the state of the railways, which engineers were frantically trying to convert to European gauge.

A pause for breath was essential. A rest period of 14 days was thought necessary to allow the infantry divisions to arrive at the front, after which the armoured units could be withdrawn for repair and be prepared for new operations. Rations and other supplies could be replenished at the same time. Of course a rest period was equally valuable to the Red Army, giving it time to reconstruct a solid frontline.

The state of the Red Army

Although substantially weakened in trained personnel, and although most of the cadres now appearing at the frontline bore the stamp of improvisation, the Red Army was not yet beaten. Nor was there any doubts about the efforts of the Soviets to mobilize all their manpower potential to carry on the struggle.

The desperate Soviet attacks against the front of Army Group Centre, and the energy and haste visible in all Soviet movements, made it quite clear that the Soviet leadership was determined to stop any further German advances east of Smolensk. They had obviously realized the danger that threatened their capital city and motherland from this direction. For their part, German leaders rightly suspected that the strongest Soviet forces were concentrated in this area. It was here that they made up their minds to seek a rapid conclusion to the whole campaign in the East.

At this stage of Barbarossa, German strategic planning began to show signs of strain, and to examine why it is necessary to go back in time to early July. At that period the Soviet Supreme

▲ It is ironic that thousands of Soviet prisoners initially welcomed the Germans as liberators. However, Nazi racial policies discounted using prisoners as soldiers against their former masters. Instead, hundreds of thousands were used as slave labourers or simply starved to death.

Command's appreciation of German intentions assumed that Moscow was the enemy's main target. They had therefore decided to concentrate their main forces opposite Army Group Centre, on the grounds that this would not only provide frontal protection for Moscow itself, but would also limit German opportunities for strong offensives in the north or south in two ways. First, it would limit the forces available to them by forcing Army Group Centre to retain strong forces in the middle of the front; second, any German attempt at deep penetration in the north or south would find a large Soviet force hanging over its inner flank. It was decided that a strong defence should be combined with counterattacks aimed at exposed German flanks and at the junctions between them.

The task of the Red Army

If the Soviet troops could carry it through, this was not an unreasonable plan – the more so since enemy troops advancing into Russia from the west were in effect moving out of the neck of a funnel. The farther east they went, the longer the front became and the wider the gaps between their elements. Furthermore, since the essence of German strategy was to achieve deep encirclements by throwing forward mobile

▲ **A German 150mm standard medium field howitzer is unlimbered on the edge of the Smolensk Pocket. German artillery in the early war years was organized by regiments not divisions, since as its role was infantry support OKH simply allocated artillery units as they were needed.**

▼ **German troops at the River Desna in late July 1941. By this stage of the campaign the Red Army was mounting substantial attacks against Army Group Centre. On 30 July, for example, the Soviets mounted 13 attacks on the Second Panzer Group's Yelnya bridgehead over the Desna.**

forces, large gaps were inevitable between the panzer and motorized infantry divisions rushing on ahead at speeds of up to 80km/h (50mph), and the infantry armies following on foot at a rate of 5.6km/h (3.5mph). The German advance therefore tended to disperse their forces into a series of spearheads and shafts, and *Stavka*'s task was to sever the one from the other. The Soviet High Command had clearly grasped the nature of the problem. The question was whether, after their severe mauling during the battle of the frontiers, the Red Army's soldiers could do the job required of them.

A task too large?

The attack by the Soviet Fifth and Sixth Armies on 10 July had been an attempt to sever the First Panzer Group spearhead from the Sixth Army shaft. The Soviet Fifth Army had operated out of the gap between German Army Groups Centre and South, against the north flank of von Kleist's panzers, while the Soviet Sixth Army was meant to strike against his southern flank. The operation had failed, but it had caused the Germans some anxious moments, and its failure had not removed the threat presented by the Soviet Fifth Army, which had merely retreated back to its start line. If this showed anything, it showed that there was still plenty of life left in the Red Army. Similar incidents had occurred elsewhere on the Eastern Front. In places resistance had collapsed with spectacular suddenness, but in many places the Red Army's surrounded formations showed a willingness to fight their way out with fierce vigour, both receiving and inflicting heavy losses.

Many of the senior generals in the German Army – the Commander-in-Chief, Field Marshal von Brauchitsch, the Chief of the General Staff of the Army, General Halder, and von Rundstedt, commander of Army Group South – had opposed the invasion of the Soviet Union. They believed that for any invasion to succeed, the main forces of the Red Army had

▶ **A German soldier surveys the scene during the Smolensk battles. No less than six Soviet armies were involved in the Smolensk and Yelnya battles as Marshal Timoshenko slashed at the German flanks. The price was heavy in terms of blood: some rifle divisions, wartime strength 18,000 men, were down to 2000 effectives.**

to be annihilated before they could retreat east across the River Dnieper.

This decision brought large problems in its wake. It demanded quick encirclements of large forces, which meant large encirclements, which in turn meant that large holes were left in the ring, through which many Red Army units could punch their way out. To achieve encirclements of the requisite size without leaving such holes, the panzer forces had to be held back until the infantry could be brought up. The alternative was to settle for more modest encirclements, which would mean leaving large parts of the Red Army free to mount counterattacks.

The fact was that the job was too big for Germany's military resources, but this was not yet apparent. To panzer commanders such as Guderian, though, such matters were of secondary importance. Since 22 June the panzer divisions had proved that they could outflank, outfight and destroy entire Soviet armies as they advanced east. The two panzer groups had advanced so quickly that they had shattered Soviet command and control of the units in their path. Telephone lines were severed and Soviet commanders lost track of their units. For example, on 25 June the 7th Panzer Division sat astride the main highway between Moscow and Minsk, severed the rail line and telephone trunk line between those cities and thus severed the main communications and transportation network between the capitals of White Russia and the Soviet Union.

As well as territorial gains, Guderian's panzers had also scored another victory, in many ways one far more important: a psychological triumph. The Red Army was unable to cope with the pace, violence and scope of the panzers' operations. The orders to formations to resist to the "last cartridge" were evidence of this, as was

◀ **A supply convoy travels across a pontoon bridge beside a destroyed bridge. The Luftwaffe did an excellent job of destroying bridges and railways to prevent the Soviets from transporting reserves to the front, but then army engineers had to erect makeshift bridges to facilitate the Blitzkrieg's advance.**

▲ A group of Panzer IIIs pause during the advance. During Barbarossa German panzer crews became acquainted with a number of unusual Soviet antitank tactics. These included explosives strapped to the backs of dogs, which were trained to run under German tanks. After a few nasty surprises, panzer crews shot all dogs that came near.

the plethora of uncoordinated attacks from all directions that almost always ended in great slaughter. To Guderian, all that was required to bring ultimate victory was to maintain a ruthless drive – against Moscow.

Hitler, however, was already beginning to show a preference for conquering the Ukraine before taking Moscow and Leningrad. In any case, he stated on 8 July that he intended to raze both Moscow and Leningrad to the ground – something that he considered could be done by aircraft without affecting the ground operations – and that for the moment the Second Panzer Group, on the southern wing of Army Group Centre, should continue its eastward advance. In this way the Moscow direction would be covered if it was later necessary for part of Army Group Centre to turn south. Thus he shelved a decision for the moment.

On the same day, Halder presented to him a highly optimistic intelligence assessment, claiming that 89 of the 164 known Soviet divisions had already been destroyed, and that of the remainder, 18 were on secondary fronts, the state of 11 was unknown, and only 46 were still considered combat-worthy.

Hitler, though pleased with the figures, was contemplating the seizure of Kiev and an advance down the west bank of the Dnieper. Von Brauchitsch objected that this was impossible because of supply difficulties, and Hitler conceded that first of all the strength of the opposition at Kiev would have to be ascertained. And there, for the moment, the matter was allowed to rest in the capable hands of von Rundstedt. Despite excellent German gains, the troublesome Soviet Fifth Army remained at

Korosten, resulting in a Soviet salient into German-controlled territory between Army Groups Centre and South. Its presence continued to dim the glittering prize of Kiev. Something would have to be done about it, and the matter was raised with Hitler on 17 July.

The Führer became fixated with Kiev, as the historian and Soviet expert David M. Glantz states: "Hitler began to seek targets that were still within reach before winter came and that would convince the world that Germany was in fact victorious. He was particularly anxious to seize Soviet industry and crop lands, as well as to push the defenders beyond bomber range of the precious Romanian oil fields. He therefore continued to insist that taking Moscow was far less important than securing the industry of Leningrad and the industrial and agricultural heartland in the Ukraine."

The outcome was OKW Directive No 33 of 19 July. This ordered that after completing the encirclement operations at Smolensk, the Second Panzer Group and the infantry of the Second Army should turn southeast to destroy the Soviet Twenty-First Army (which was opposite the right wing of Army Group Centre) and then, in cooperation with Army Group South, should destroy the Soviet Fifth Army. At the same time, a concentric attack by Army Group South was to drive across the rear of the Soviet Sixth and Twelfth Armies and destroy them as well. The remaining panzer forces of Army Group Centre (the Third Panzer Group) were to move northeastwards to assist Army Group North, leaving the advance on Moscow to be continued by the infantry armies of Army Group Centre only.

▼ A German panzer column advances towards Soviet positions in the distance that are under Luftwaffe attack. Note the swastika draped over the tank on the right. Such measures avoided friendly fire incidents. The latter were more of a threat than the Red Air Force, which was reduced in places to dropping nails on the Germans!

This decision was tantamount to abandoning the decisive operations against the main Soviet forces in the centre – Adolf Hitler had saved the bulk of the Red Army before Moscow. The collapse of Soviet units in the northwest and southwest would force the Red Army to continue retreating, but there would be no more major encirclements in the centre.

Two days later Hitler, paying his first visit to his armies in the East, appeared at Army Group North headquarters, where he explained some of his decisions. It was essential to take Leningrad soon, Hitler argued, in order to stop the Soviet Baltic Fleet interfering with iron-ore shipments from Sweden to Germany. The Third Panzer Group would therefore assist Army Group North by cutting the Leningrad–Moscow railway in order to hinder the transfer of Soviet forces to or from the area. This task must be undertaken as soon as the Third Panzer Group was available – that is, in about five days time. The Soviet capital did not concern Hitler, who said, "Moscow for me is only a geographical concept." He believed that "Because of the general situation and the instability of the Slav character" the fall of Leningrad could bring about a complete collapse of Soviet resistance.

A change of plan

On 23 July another conference took place between Hitler, von Brauchitsch and Halder, at which Halder reported that the Red Army forces now facing Germany numbered 93 divisions, 13 of which were armoured. None of the participants seem to have commented on the fact that in the 15 days since his previous report – 15 days of hard but successful operations by the Wehrmacht – Soviet forces had apparently almost doubled. But clearly, as Halder's own diary shows, the fierceness of the Russian resistance was beginning to make an impression. Despite Hitler's talk two days earlier of the possibility of an imminent Russian collapse, a note of uncertainty began to creep into the conversation. Halder reported that the combat capability of the German infantry divisions was around 80 percent, but that the panzer divisions were down to 50 percent; that Army Group South would be over the Dnieper by mid-August; that very strong resistance was to be expected in the Moscow area; and that the operations of Army Group North seemed to be a failure.

Von Brauchitsch and Halder were not happy, and they wrote a minute, in which they set out their views. To attack Moscow with infantry alone would be difficult but possible, provided quick results were not looked for, they stated, but a decisive offensive against the capital would require the Second and Third Panzer Groups, neither of which would now be available until early September. Thus Hitler's plan would present the enemy with a month's grace in which to collect new forces and build and occupy new defence lines. Moreover, the large Soviet group

▼ Light vehicle and horses on the road to Moscow. Guderian's panzer group included the 1st Cavalry Division, which took part in the battles along the Beresina, patrolled the Pripet Marshes and undertook flank protection for the group during the later encirclement battles around Kiev. It was disbanded on 3 November 1941.

◀ An officer leads his company through the remains of a Russian town. The retreating Soviets did not hesitate to burn down their own cities and towns. In this way they almost completely annihilated Vitebsk and Smolensk. Anything that could be of use to the Germans was either evacuated or destroyed.

of forces in front of Moscow constituted a threat to the flanks of the other army groups and would require a dispersion of forces to guard against it as long as it remained in being. As to the idea of destroying Moscow from the air, there was no immediate expectation that the Luftwaffe would acquire bases near enough to operate on the necessary scale.

OKH asked once again for a re-examination of the tasks set for Army Group Centre, while at the same time admitting that there might be decisive economic factors unknown to them (Hitler was frequently given to saying that his generals knew nothing about economics). Naturally OKH would do what it was told, but it had great misgivings about the possible consequences as the Soviet objective was clearly to last out until the winter. If they succeeded, then the next spring Germany would have to face new armies and be involved in the war on two fronts, which it had hoped to avoid. Surely, OKH argued, the best way out would be to attack Moscow. The Soviets would have to stand and fight there, so there would be no question of their armies escaping again. If Germany won the battle she would possess the Soviet seat of government, an important industrial centre and the heart of the Russian rail system. Russia would be cut in two. An aim as important as this must take precedence over smaller operations designed to cut up part of the Red Army, it argued.

The minute was firm and cogent, though deferential, and argued its case well. General Alfred Jodl, OKW's Chief of Staff, even tried to strengthen its arguments by remarking that since the Soviets would inevitably stand and defend it, an attack on Moscow would be merely an expression of the Führer's own dictum that the enemy's "living force" must be attacked wherever it could be found.

▶ German horse-drawn artillery of Army Group Centre. Though summer was the best time for operations in the Soviet Union, any movement in the dry conditions threw up clouds of dust which made concealment very difficult. A panzer division on the move covered 17.6sq km (11sq miles), which created much dust.

But the minute was never sent. Even as the German High Command was debating whether it could kill the Soviet bear in the next two months or would have to be content with crippling it, Marshal Timoshenko hurled several newly raised armies into a counteroffensive in the centre, attempting to relieve the large pocket of forces surrounded at Smolensk. All thoughts of Moscow, Kiev and Leningrad had to be put aside for the time being, and swift improvisation became the order of the day.

The Russian attacks failed to achieve their immediate objective – to wrest the initiative from Army Group Centre and relieve the trapped Soviet Sixteenth and Twentieth Armies. Russian units were ill-prepared, and there were still too many futile frontal attacks, with new forces committed piecemeal – probably because Timoshenko was not aware of the degree to which the Germans were stretched, and thus was led to overestimate the immediate danger to Moscow. But the mere readiness to attack and the appearance of large numbers of new formations intensified still more the divisions of opinion among the German High Command, and led to a further diversion of effort.

The first fruit of the Soviet counteroffensive was a meeting of army commanders of Army Group Centre at Novy Borisov on 27 July. Guderian arrived expecting to be ordered to push on to Moscow – or at least Bryansk – but found instead a memorandum from von Brauchitsch explicitly ruling out either possibility and stating that the first priority was destruction of the Soviet forces in the Gomel area, that is, the Soviet Fifth Army. Again, by continuing to exist in the rear of their main forces, the Fifth Army had succeeded in making the Germans look backwards and divert their attention from the glittering prospects in front of them.

Guderian was astounded. He was being asked to turn in his tracks and advance backwards towards Germany, to finish off forces which he had long left behind and which he maintained should be dealt with by infantry units. Von Brauchitsch was, of course, merely implementing Hitler's cautions about ambitious encirclements mentioned in discussion of Directive No 33, but Guderian knew nothing of this except for what he gleaned in a disjointed fashion from officers at army group headquarters

He suspected the influence of Field Marshal von Kluge, commander of the Fourth Panzer Army, to whom Guderian was uneasily and reluctantly subordinate. It is unlikely that Guderian realized the full extent of the debate, or all the factors involved in it, and he left the conference in a mood of wounded pride, only partially offset by the fact that the Second Panzer Group was renamed Army Group *Guderian* and placed under the command of Field Marshal von Bock himself.

This new freedom from the restraints imposed by Kluge – a man of some guile,

◀ During Barbarossa the Germans were continually surprised at the destruction left by the Russians. Colonel von Luck, 7th Panzer Division, entered Smolensk after its fall: "Smolensk looked as though it had been abandoned. Destruction in the industrial quarters and of the bridges over the Dnieper was immense."

known in the army as *Kluge Hans* ("crafty Hans") and not one to inspire loyalty in his colleagues – was used by Guderian to distort and wilfully misinterpret the directions he had been given at Novy Borisov. He was convinced that the main threat to Army Group Centre was not the Soviet Fifth Army in his deep rear, but the forces assembling on his right flank north of Roslavl, and he continued to believe this irrespective of any decisions Hitler might now take.

This threat which he perceived took the form of a grouping described by *Stavka* as the "Group of Forces of the Twenty-Eighth Army", under the command of Lieutenant-General Kachalov, which had been assembled to help relieve the Smolensk Pocket. Guderian proposed to von Bock that Roslavl be captured, on the grounds that its seizure would give mastery of routes to the east, south and southwest (thus making available a number of possibilities for continuing the offensive).

The necessary preparations took some days, and during this period Guderian received several visitors. On 29 July, Hitler's chief adjutant, Colonel Schmundt, arrived, ostensibly to present Guderian with the Oak Leaves to his Iron Cross, but really to discuss his plans with him. He indicated that Hitler had not yet decided between Leningrad, Moscow and the Ukraine.

There is no evidence as to whether Schmundt was being particularly discreet or stupid, since Hitler had in fact been indicating his lack of interest in Moscow for some time and was the very next day to issue Directive No 34, which ordered Army Group Centre to cease its advance and go on to the defensive.

Guderian took advantage of the opportunity to urge a direct push on the Soviet capital and also to put in a bid for new tanks and tank engines. On the 31st, the OKH liaison officer, Major von Bredow, turned up to report that "OKH and the Chief of General Staff are engaged in a thankless undertaking, since the conduct of all operations is being controlled

▲ A Sturmgeschütz (StuG) III assault gun moves through an abandoned Russian village. Armed with a short-barrelled 75mm gun, the first StuG IIIs were designed to support infantry. Their periscopic sights, capable of twice the magnification of panzer sights, combined with a low silhouette, made them good tank killers.

from the very highest level. Final decisions on the future course of events have not yet been taken." Put more simply, this was a complaint about the Führer's interference and a tacit invitation to Guderian to influence the decisions not yet taken by his own actions of the present and immediate future.

Guderian realized that the Moscow objective was rapidly fading in importance in the Führer's mind. He subsequently wrote: "Hitler designated the industrial area about Leningrad as his primary objective. He had not decided whether Moscow or the Ukraine would come next. He seemed to incline towards the latter target for a number of reasons: first, Army Group South seemed to be laying the groundwork for a victory in that area; second, he believed that the raw materials and agricultural produce of the Ukraine were necessary to Germany for the further prosecution of the war."

The attack of the Soviet Twenty-Eighth Army went in, and was a disaster. Guderian, once again displaying a mastery of armoured warfare, cut the Soviets to pieces. On 4 August the Twenty-Eighth Army had signalled to Western Front Headquarters: "Twenty-Eighth Army fighting superior enemy forces, encircled in area Yermolino, Samodidino, Lyslovka, Shkuratovka, Ozeryavino. Formations making their way in a southeasterly direction, one group through Roslavl, another to the east. Assignment to break through to River Oster. Formations suffering massive losses, unfit for combat. Request air support, particularly fighters."

Having shattered Kachalov's army (Kachalov himself was killed in the fighting), Guderian proceeded to launch his own assault, and within a week he had sliced through the Gomel–Bryansk–Moscow rail link, and had reached Starodub and Pochep.

These gains so alarmed Stalin that he ordered Lieutenant-General Yeremenko, commander of the new Bryansk Front, to destroy Guderian's panzer group. For this venture Yeremenko had the elements of four armies: the Fiftieth, Thirteenth, Third and Twenty-First. However, many units were below strength due to losses in previous battles. Nevertheless, at least he had substantial air assets at his disposal: 230 bombers, 179 fighters and 55 ground-attack aircraft, which constituted the combined air strength of the Reserve, Central and Bryansk Fronts, the 1st Reserve Aviation Group, and units of the Long-Range Bomber Force.

Yeremenko attacked with confidence, and for eight days his units battled on the Desna. Once again, however, the German panzer crews showed their skill. The Soviet Third and Twenty-First Armies were torn apart, while the latter was forced back on to the Desna and separated from the main force of the Bryansk Front. Far from destroying Guderian, the Soviet Bryansk and Southwestern Fronts had been torn apart by the beginning of September.

▲ It is seldom realized that the clothing worn by the average German soldier during the summer of 1941 in Russia was too heavy for warm-weather campaigning. This resulted in men perspiring, becoming very thirsty and being caked in dirt. To add to their woes, the hard-packed dirt roads quickly cut boot soles to pieces.

And yet, for all his successes, Guderian was denied his assault on Moscow. On 23 August, Hitler had decided that the main effort of the German Army was not to be Moscow – which was barely 320km (200 miles) from the lead elements of Army Group Centre's panzers – but rather Leningrad and the Ukraine.

The drive south by Guderian's panzers would help bring about one of the Red Army's greatest disasters – the Kiev Pocket – but it effectively saved Moscow from capture and thus Soviet defeat. From the start of Barbarossa Army Group Centre had proved that it could smash anything the Red Army could field against it. By 31 July, for example, having lost the great battle at Smolensk and all other encirclements having been brought to an end, the Soviets gathered their reserves to protect Moscow. For their part, Panzer Group *Guderian* and the Second Army regrouped and prepared for an expected advance on Moscow. *Stavka*, desperate to save the Soviet capital, launched no less then 13 poorly coordinated armoured and infantry attacks against the German salient around Yelnya. The only element of the Red Army assaults to cause the Germans any concern were the artillery units. However, all the attacks were beaten off with relative ease.

By maintaining the momentum German units achieved much. The 7th Panzer Division, for example, part of the Third Panzer Group, had advanced 340km (212 miles) east in only four days after the start of Barbarossa. Though its troops were exhausted and many of its vehicles were in need of repair, it had lost few men or tanks to enemy action. Some four days later, having been engaged around Minsk in heavy fighting, it had taken heavier casualties but had time to repair its vehicles. The result was that it had 149 tanks ready for action.

The failure to inflict casualties on the invading divisions is a damning indictment of Soviet equipment and training. Mention has already been made of the unimaginative Soviet infantry tactics; their tank tactics also left a lot to be desired. General Erhard Rauss, who fought on the Eastern Front as commander of a panzer army, had this to say about Soviet tank tactics: "The training of the individual tank driver was inadequate; the training period apparently was too short, and losses in experienced drivers were too high. The Russian avoided driving his tank through hollows or along reverse slopes, preferring to choose a route along the crests which would give fewer driving difficulties ... Thus the Germans were in most cases able to bring the Russian tanks under fire at long ranges, and to inflict losses even before the battle had begun. Slow and uncertain driving and numerous firing halts made the Russian tanks good targets."

By September 1941, the panzers could have pushed on to Moscow with the advantages of good weather, strong Luftwaffe support, and against an enemy composed largely of reserve formations with little or no combat experience. The odds of success would have been high. Hitler, however, ordered Guderian south. By the time his panzer divisions were finally allowed to launch an offensive against Moscow, the strategic situation was less favourable.

▶ Army Group Centre had achieved some staggering victories by the middle of August 1941. However, as this image of a *Das Reich* soldier shows, both men and machines had been pushed to the limits of their endurance. Whether they could have gone on to capture Moscow as autumn approached will never be known.

Target Leningrad

The task of Field Marshal von Leeb's Army Group North was to advance from East Prussia, annihilate Red Army forces in the Baltic and then capture the city of Leningrad, which Hitler regarded as the cradle of Bolshevism.

By the Barbarossa directive issued by the Army High Command (OKH) on 31 January 1941, Army Group North received the following order: "Of destroying the enemy forces fighting in the Baltic theatre and by the occupation of the Baltic ports and subsequently of Leningrad and Kronstadt of depriving the Russian fleet of its bases. Timely cooperation with the strong and fast-moving forces of Army Group Centre will be ensured by OKH."

Army Group North, commanded by Field Marshal von Leeb, had been allotted an initial advance of 800km (500 miles). However, this distance was increased by more than 50 percent stretching to the Gulf of Finland. Leeb's command was the smallest of the three army groups: two infantry armies and a panzer group. These

▼ Infantry of Army Group North search for Russian soldiers during the drive to the Baltic. The soldier nearest the camera is armed with a 9mm-calibre MP 40 submachine gun, which had a 32-round magazine and a cyclic rate of fire of 500 rounds per minute. The main users of this weapon were mechanized infantry units.

◀ **General Erich Hoepner (centre), commander of the von Leeb's Fourth Panzer Group, with General Georg-Hans Reinhardt (right), commander of XLI Panzer Corps. Hoepner's first task was to reach the Dvina as quickly as possible below Daugavpils and secure crossing points for a further advance towards Opochka.**

units comprised the Sixteenth Army (General Busch) made up of eight infantry divisions; the Eighteenth Army (General von Küchler) made up of seven infantry divisions; the Fourth Panzer Group (General Hoepner) comprising three panzer divisions, three motorized infantry divisions and two infantry divisions; and the Army Group Reserve, comprising three infantry divisions which were to support the Sixteenth Army. The total strength of Army Group North thus amounted to 20 infantry divisions, three panzer divisions and three motorized infantry divisions.

Von Leeb not only had the smallest of the army groups, potentially he also had the most difficult task. The Soviet deployment in the recently occupied Baltic states represented a defence in depth, with reserves stretching back into Soviet territory and a concentration of armour to the east of Pskov. Though a strategy of encirclement appeared to be unfeasible, von Leeb still hoped to destroy enemy formations piecemeal by the use of speed and mobility. However, such a strategy relied on precision timing and thus von Leeb decided to place his armoured units in the centre of his front and keep the panzer group under his direct command. It would move between the two infantry armies, through Daugavpils (Dvinsk) and Pskov, and on to Leningrad.

There could be no dispersion of effort if Leningrad was to be reached before winter. This meant leaving flank protection to the infantry armies, who would hopefully take advantage of the armoured advance to gain ground as rapidly as possible.

The Sixteenth Army, positioned on the southern wing, would strike for Daugavpils, while the Eighteenth Army would be deployed

▶ **As usual the Luftwaffe was clinically effective. Naval bases were targeted in the preliminary phase of Barbarossa. This photograph of the Soviet battleship *Marat* under attack at Kronstadt naval base was taken from a Stuka dive-bomber. The Soviet Baltic Fleet withdrew to Leningrad on 28 August when the German Army neared Tallinn.**

▲ **The initial German attacks were successful at all points. General Erich von Manstein, commander of the Fourth Panzer Group's LVI Panzer Corps, stated that in the first few days his corps' advance was so rapid that it had neither the time nor the manpower to round up prisoners.**

▼ **Cavalry pass the remains of shot-up Soviet vehicles. The Red Army response in the north was poor. XLI Panzer Corps, for example, simply bypassed the Soviet III and XII Mechanized Corps, both of which suffered 90 percent losses in seven days.**

on the left flank and would drive along the Baltic into Lithuania, Latvia and Estonia.

Von Leeb stressed the importance of speed in his first Army Group Order of 5 May 1941. Referring to Leningrad as the ultimate objective of the operation, it stated: "Forward! Don't stop for anything. Never let the enemy consolidate, once he has been thrown back." The main attack of Army Group North was to be delivered from the centre of its front in the northern part of East Prussia, directed at the River Dvina near Daugavpils. The first objective of the Fourth Panzer Group was the River Dvina – 296km (185 miles) east – and the second was the Ostrov-Pskov area – another leap of 248km (155 miles). Von Leeb's instruction to the Fourth Panzer Group stated: "The Fourth Panzer Group will create the preliminary conditions for a wide and rapid thrust towards Leningrad. To reach the final objective it is essential to move forward at every opportunity as far as time and place allows, and thus to give the opposition no time to create any new defensive positions deep in the operational area."

The infantry's role

The infantry armies, moving at a slower pace, were to liquidate the chief centres of Russian resistance on the flanks. Thus the Sixteenth Army would take Kaunas and the Eighteenth Army would seize Riga. The "quick" thrust of the panzer group, quick in comparison with the slower attack of the following infantry, at least had to take full advantage of surprise if it was to fulfil its instructions.

Daugavpils, with its two bridges over the wide River Dvina, was the first objective of the Fourth Panzer Group and was entrusted to LVI Panzer Corps on the right. From its start point to the south of Memel it had the advantage of good roads and a relatively short distance to travel. XLI Panzer Corps, on the left of the panzer group's advance, was to achieve freedom of movement by a northward strike and then an advance northeast to the Dvina. Throughout Hoepner reserved the right to alter the direction of his command's advance to maintain the all-important aspect of speed.

Together with the rest of the army group, the Fourth Panzer Group crossed the East Prussian frontier at 03:05 hours on 22 June 1941. The Soviet defences opposite Army Group North may have been arranged in depth, but the speed and ferocity of the German attack buckled their Eleventh and Eighth Armies. And the Soviet dispersal gave von Leeb's forces numerical superiority at the key assault points. The fate of the Eleventh Army's 125th Division was typical: within hours of being attacked it had lost all its tanks, most of its antiaircraft guns and was suffering an acute shortage of hand grenades. It was shot to pieces by the German divisions.

An easy advance

The only active Soviet resistance encountered by the Germans was near Taurage, but the area was only garrisoned by special police border troops, and by the evening of the first day the spearhead of LVI Panzer Corps had advanced 59km (37 miles) eastwards.

The Soviet response to the attack was slow and indecisive, though even if the Special Baltic Military District had managed to react quickly it would have had difficulty in deploying its ground units effectively – its aircraft had largely been destroyed on the ground by the Luftwaffe.

Soviet units that engaged German formations were destroyed piecemeal. At Raseynyay, for example, forward Soviet elements had engaged the 6th Panzer Division of XLI Panzer Corps (which allowed LVI Panzer Corps to make an advance on Daugavpils). On the evening of 23 June, the commander of the Fourth Panzer Group ordered LVI Panzer Corps to continue its thrust while XLI Panzer Corps was given the job of destroying enemy units in front of it. The latter was the reinforced Soviet

▲ The infantry divisions could not keep up with the panzers. Nevertheless, their slow speed did divert Soviet attention away from the panzer spearheads. This was especially true of LVI Corps' 290th Infantry Division, following the 8th Panzer Division, which received many Red Army attacks.

▼ A StuG III on the edge of a burning town. Sixteenth Army's II Corps and XXVIII Corps had a number of StuG III batteries. StuG batteries usually had six vehicles (tank companies had up to 22 tanks), and a StuG battalion had three batteries.

▲ German soldiers searching for isolated Soviet troops. The speed and ferocity of the attack by Hoepner's panzer group shattered the frontier positions in its path. Follow-on infantry units were forced to comb the Lithuanian forests for stragglers. This was tiring, dangerous and time-consuming work – but necessary.

2nd Armoured Division. On 24–26 June, the latter was surrounded and liquidated by XLI Panzer Corps northeast of Raseynyay – not one of the 200 Soviet tanks escaped.

This victory was exploited by LVI Panzer Corps. During the afternoon of 24 June, its 8th Panzer Division reached the main road from Kaunas to Daugavpils near Ukmerge and advanced along it without a pause. Pressing hard on the heels of a retreating Soviet troops, a special fighting group from the division forced its way into the city in the early morning of 26 June and captured the two bridges in the face of heavy resistance. It looked as if the Soviets would retake the bridges, but the arrival of tanks of the 8th Panzer Division secured the river crossings. By the end of the day the Germans had secured the whole of the city. Lieutenant-General Sergei Akimov had attempted to hold the city, but stated afterwards: "Our attack was smothered. Individual units penetrated the city from the north and northwest, but when the enemy's reserves appeared, they were thrown out. The reasons for our failure lay in our absence of tanks, insufficient artillery (we had only six guns) and weak air cover."

Having recognized the Soviet weakness on the Dvina, General Hoepner launched XLI Panzer Corps on a wide front over the river below Daugavpils. On 30 June, bridgeheads were established near Livani and Yekabpils, and by the evening of 1 July a wide bridgehead with a depth of up to 29km (18 miles) had been established. Soviet resistance was largely feeble, though the Twenty-First Armoured Group did put in a sizeable effort at Daugavpils, but it was first stopped and then chewed to pieces. Despite

▲ A Waffen-SS light armoured car moves towards the front. The *Totenkopf* Motorized Division was part of the Fourth Panzer Group's reserve, and was described by von Manstein thus: "The division always showed great dash in the assault and was steadfast in defence ... it was probably the best Waffen-SS division I ever came across."

lengthening supply lines, by 2 July the Fourth Panzer Group was ready to proceed towards the Ostrov-Pskov area.

On the morning of 2 July, Hoepner's tanks resumed their advance northwestwards on a wide front. Two days later, the 1st Panzer Division, on the north wing, captured Ostrov. To the south the 6th Panzer Division penetrated part of the "Stalin line" on either side of the Daugavpils–Ostrov road, about 29km (18 miles) south of Ostrov. By the evening elements of LVI Panzer Corps had reached the old Latvian/Russian border.

The Soviets had expected that the main German attack would occur along the highroad to Ostrov via Rezekne, but when this failed to materialize their High Command was unsure how to proceed. This meant that the Soviet tanks waiting to the east of Pskov were not thrown in until 5 July, when they recklessly attacked at Ostrov and ran into the 1st Panzer

▶ A squad takes cover while artillery pounds Soviet positions during Army Group North's advance. The Soviet frontier defences were no match for field artillery or the Luftwaffe. For example, it took less than a day for the 8th Panzer Division, XLI Panzer Corps, to break through enemy fortifications north of Memel on 22 June.

◀ **Infantry equipped with cycles tackle an incline during the drive to Leningrad. It was a great shock to the invading Germans to discover that most roads in Russia were dirt tracks, which in the summer heat turned into dust traps. A greater shock was the discovery that many of the maps issued to the German divisions were inaccurate.**

Division. The result was the destruction of 140 Red Army tanks for no gains. Soviet armoured reserves were now exhausted and the Germans drove on towards Pskov.

At this stage of the campaign geography was more of a hindrance to the Germans than the Red Army. LVI Panzer Corps ran into terrain so marshy and impenetrable that an intended advance towards Opochka had to be abandoned – the bulk of the corps was diverted northwards towards Ostrov.

The unexpectedly rapid advance of the Fourth Panzer Group towards the Pskov area had created something of a problem for von Leeb. Although, beginning on 4 July, the mass of the infantry had begun to cross the Dvina on a wide front, the distance between them and the panzers was widening. However, Soviet forces were in such confusion that audacity was to be encouraged, and General Hoepner took the view that the fast thrust could be continued right up to Leningrad itself.

The panzer drive continued, with the two panzer corps advancing along the only two routes suitable for heavy vehicles: LVI Panzer Corps from Ostrov via Porkhov, Novgorod and Chudovo on the right; and XLI Panzer Corps from Pskov via Luga and Kingisepp on the left. Two factors now combined to slow the German advance. First, the terrain was becoming unfavourable for tank movement. Second, Soviet resistance was stiffening as the German advance slowed and gave the Red Army time to reorganize. Open country was giving way to forests and marshland, in which small units could hold up whole divisions. This terrain also reduced the effectiveness of superior German firepower and speed. The result was that the rate of advance slowed to infantry speed, and then threatened to peter out altogether.

▶ **As the Russian road network was sparse, and those roads that did exist lacked any sort of good foundations, continuous maintenance of roads was essential to the German advance. This was a large drain on manpower. Among the first assignments of the *Totenkopf* Division, for example, was the repair of damaged main roads.**

▲ Mail is distributed to a German infantry section. The metal canisters hanging from the rear of each man's belt are carrying cases for gas masks. On their feet they wear one of the best-known items of German military clothing: the jackboot, or "marching boot" to give it its correct title. The boots were made of black leather.

General Georg-Hans Reinhardt, commander of XLI Panzer Corps, therefore proposed that German forces should head north via the lower course of the River Luga to reach the better terrain on the southern shore of the Gulf of Finland. Once there, the panzers would be able to operate more effectively and the Blitzkrieg could continue. But Reinhardt's plan involved moving the panzer group through 1600km (1000 miles) of sandy and marshy tracks through rough forest, plus changing OKH's plan to advance on Leningrad from the southeast.

To maintain momentum, Hoepner diverted XLI Panzer Corps to the lower Luga, and by the evening of 14 July the corps stood on the lower Luga, and in face of weak resistance established two bridgeheads over that river near Sabsk and Porietchye. By 20 July, having resupplied, Reinhardt was ready for the final push on Leningrad. The great prize was now only 96km (60 miles) away. Though the corps had been forced to leave the 269th Infantry Division on the main road to Leningrad – where it became pinned down by enemy action 40km (25 miles) south of Luga – the speed of the panzer group's advance had exceeded all expectations. This, despite the fact that LVI Panzer Corps was held up in front of Soltsy, some 50km (31 miles) southwest of Lake Ilmen.

Operations on the right wing of the Sixteenth Army, though, were giving cause for concern. The reduction of the Bialystok and Minsk Pockets sucked in divisions of Army Group Centre, which resulted in large parts of the Sixteenth Army's II Corps being drawn into a battle developing between the zones of Army Groups North and Centre in the Nevel area.

▲ Red Army troops taken by Army Group North. Any Russian stragglers who feigned surrender, then fired on their would-be captors, were dealt with harshly. A regiment of the *Totenkopf* Division had this experience on 6 July – the Waffen-SS soldiers responded by shooting all 200 enemy soldiers, even those who genuinely wanted to surrender.

The result, though of benefit to Army Group Centre, was to weaken Army Group North, because by mid-July the centre of gravity of the Sixteenth Army was located on its southern wing. Its two other corps – XXVIII and X – were widely separated to the northeast. There was a further shift to the southeast on 14 July, when X Corps had to help XXVIII Corps to reduce enemy forces in the Novorzhev area. The end result of all these movements was the creation of a sizeable gap between the panzer group, situated on the lower Luga, and the Sixteenth Army.

The advance of Army Group North seemed to have been fatally compromised – but there was still the Eighteenth Army to the north. In Estonia its advance was making good progress, but could it continue with the loss of one of its two corps? If it could, its I Corps could be combined with XXXVIII Corps (south of Lake Peipus) to reinforce the panzer group. Even if the army stalled, a decisive victory at Leningrad would seal the fate of all Soviet forces farther west in Estonia anyway.

With this in mind, I Corps, located south of Pskov, was moved eastwards through Porkhov in the direction of Lake Ilmen, while XXXVIII Corps was moved via Pskov northwards along the east bank of Lake Peipus to Narva. Both formations were put under the command of the panzer group.

By mid-July there was still a chance of a daring thrust to Leningrad succeeding. Before this could take place supplies had to be brought up, which required all the road construction capacity of the panzer group. However, the High Command of Army Group North was becoming more and more hesitant concerning a final dash to Leningrad. This resulted from a combination of OKH issuing a warning against over-committing fast units as a result of unpleasant experiences suffered by Army Group Centre, and recent changes in the Soviet High Command (Marshal Kliment Voroshilov now opposed Army Group North). The Germans believed the latter would result in a more resolute defence and the deployment of fresh Soviet units.

The panzer group's window of opportunity began to close. The northward advance of LVI Panzer Corps was dependant on satisfactory developments to the south. Thus I Corps was ordered to crush enemy forces still holding out east of Porkhov, then turn to cross the River Shel on both sides of Soltsy and advance to Lake Ilmen in conjunction with armoured units. The two corps took Soltsy on 22 July, but then the advance ground to a halt 19km (12 miles) west of Lake Ilmen. Exhaustion now entered the equation: German troops, especially the infantry, were worn out by a month of constant fighting and forced marches, often in great heat.

Von Leeb became more and more inclined to exploit any success on his right wing, specifically by LVI Panzer Corps, after the fighting in the Nevel and Novorzhev areas had been brought to a successful conclusion. Since 21 July, advanced infantry units had been moving northwards, and their arrival in the Lake Ilmen area was expected at the beginning of August. Thus the plan for a "switched attack" on Leningrad by Army Group North was born.

For the panzer group this meant the end of the scheme for the surprise capture of Leningrad. For those who had fought so hard and so bravely for its achievement, this was a

▼ Troops of the German Eighteenth Army march through Narva in August 1941. The Soviet Eighth Army had pulled back through the town earlier after the Germans had shattered the so-called Luga Line. Some of the Soviet regimental and battalion commanders and staffs had suffered 100 percent casualties.

▶ **One of the reasons for von Leeb's rapid advance was the capture of vital river crossings intact. The viaduct crossing over the River Dubissa at Airogola, for example, was captured by a reconnaissance detachment of the 8th Panzer Division in a rapid advance that caught the defenders completely by surprise.**

bitter disappointment. The reality was, however, that XLI Panzer Corps had been held in its two bridgeheads in any case – the window of opportunity had closed.

The unforeseen gap in the deployment of the Sixteenth Army had led to the adoption of a slower and surer solution involving infantry participation. Army Group North's next attack would involve XXVIII Corps and 4.5 infantry divisions from the Sixteenth Army. For its attack through Novgorod, the latter had under its command I Corps, with 3.5 infantry divisions, and XXVIII Corps, with two infantry divisions and one motorized infantry division. On the left of the Sixteenth Army, the Fourth Panzer Group was to attack in two groups: LVI Panzer Corps, with two infantry divisions and one motorized division, was to advance on either side of the Luga–Leningrad road; XLI Panzer Corps was to strike at the enemy from the Luga bridgehead 96km (60 miles) to the northwest. The objective of both corps was to be Krasnogvardeisk. Hoepner had a stroke of good fortune when von Brauchitsch gave him the 8th Panzer Division, which was deployed behind XLI Panzer Corps.

The new attack began during the early morning of 8 August in pouring rain, when the German divisions sprang from the Luga bridgeheads. Soviet resistance was strong, especially opposite the left-hand bridgehead where the Red Army had positioned strong artillery and launched determined counterattacks. Few gains were made for heavy losses, but it was decided to resume the attack on the following day.

On the right wing the attack met with success, but in the centre and on the left fighting was heavy until 12 August, when the German attacks finally succeeded. The three fast divisions of XLI Panzer Corps turned east in the direction of Leningrad, while the 1st Infantry Division

◀ **The remains of a Russian train strafed by the Luftwaffe. As with damaged roads, the repair of sections of track consumed much time because men and materials had to be transported by rail to the affected areas. The damage, combined with the few railroads, had a serious effect on the flow of supplies.**

turned northwest in the direction of Narva to support XXXVIII Corps.

After reaching open country the 8th Panzer Division had reinforced XLI Panzer Corps, and its four fast divisions were heading for Leningrad. LVI Panzer Corps, however, had still made no headway. After an initial advance, the two infantry divisions were held up by a new and well-fortified Soviet position south of the Luga. Its 3rd Motorized Infantry Division was covering the right flank, for XXVIII Corps had not yet arrived from the south.

On 15 August, von Leeb visited his panzer group and informed Reinhardt that he had agreed to his reinforcement of the 3rd Motorized Infantry Division. However, in the afternoon an order was transmitted from Army Group Headquarters that LVI Corps, with the 3rd Motorized Infantry Division, was to proceed at once to join the Sixteenth Army. The war diary of the panzer group had the following to say of this development: "Thus the Panzer Group for the second time has been prevented by Army Group from reaching its objective. The first occasion was on July 18, when it was stopped from following up the capture of the Luga bridgeheads. This time, after breaking through the enemy lines, it is stopped from exploiting its success."

▲ In the German Army horse-drawn transport was divided into two main types: battle transport and supply transport. As the above arrangement is a six-horse limber with a rider on each offside horse, it would appear to be attached to an artillery unit. During the war in Russia the German Army lost an average of 1000 horses a day.

▼ The great advances took their toll on the invaders' resources. The poor quality of the roads had caused a high incidence of mechanical breakdown. By late July, for example, around 65 percent of Army Group North's transport vehicles were out of action due to mechanical problems. The infantry walked – as usual.

The problems encountered by X Corps in the Staraya Russa area south of Lake Ilmen had compelled von Leeb to send it essential reinforcements. And though the Staraya Russa position was retrieved soon afterwards, the Soviets were given a respite of about three weeks. Army Group North was forced to mount a fresh offensive against Leningrad.

The attack beginning on 10 August made slow progress at first, against a Soviet defence in depth. However, on 16 August Novgorod was taken and a bridgehead thrown across the River Volkhov. As the bulk of the Soviet forces had escaped eastwards across the river, the German troops began to advance more quickly along the road to the north. On 20 August, Chuduvo fell – the Germans were now only 80km (50 miles) from Leningrad. Soviet resistance was fierce, though, and soon only XXVIII Corps was continuing to make progress; on 28 August it finally reached Lyuban.

At this point in the offensive, the leading elements of XXXIX Panzer Corps reached the front, having been detached from the Third Panzer Group at Hitler's order to join the right wing of Army Group North. Because of the very difficult terrain southeast of Leningrad, though, its leading 18th Motorized Infantry Division soon had to be diverted east to secure the flank on the River Volkhov. But the 12th Panzer Division had little difficulty in reaching Ishora, 18km (11 miles) southeast of Leningrad, on 28 August. The 20th Motorized Infantry Division following it turned north to the River Neva, to secure the flank extending north to Lake Ladoga. The panzer corps was now overstretched, though, and had a vulnerable east flank along the Volkhov.

The advance of XLI Panzer Corps from the southwest had been equally successful, and by 20–21 August had reached the line Krasnogvardeisk–Krasnoye Selo but did not have the strength to push on any further.

At this juncture, the Fourth Panzer Group ordered any battle-ready units on the frontline and flanks of XLI Panzer Corps to undertake a southward thrust into the rear of the Soviet forces around Luga. It might have been possible

▼ German machine gunners gaze across the River Neva towards Leningrad, September 1941. On 4 September, German long-range artillery opened fire on Leningrad from locations north of Tosno. As they did so Reinhardt's XLI Panzer Corps approached the city, and on the 11th seized the Duderhof plateau that overlooked it.

▲ Hitler's declaration that he wanted to avoid the loss of human life and material to be expected from fighting in built-up areas against a hostile population, resulted in the halting of Army Group North at the gates of Leningrad. He hoped to starve the city into surrender. For the troops of Army Group North (above), a long siege ensued.

to take Krasnogvardeisk and Krasnoye Selo, but it made sense to clear the high road from Luga and thus help the advance of L Corps.

On 21 August, the 8th Panzer Division resumed the advance from the area south of Krasnogvardeisk. Th division linked up with L Corps on 31 August, 24km (15 miles) north of Luga. The result was the trapping of the Soviet XXXXI Corps in the so-called "Luga Pocket". This took 14 days in early September, and at the end 20,000 prisoners entered German captivity.

Thanks to this success the investment of Leningrad could now be undertaken. Von Leeb's plan was to attack from the southeast with XXXIX Panzer Corps, XXVIII Corps from the south and the Fourth Panzer Group from the southwest. From the north would come the Eighteenth Army. Farther north, XVI Corps of the Eighteenth Army was to deal with the remnants of the Soviet Estonian forces. Estonia itself was completely cleared of Soviet forces by the end of August.

The attack started on 9 September. By the 11th the Duderhof plateau, which commanded a view of the city, had been taken by XLI Panzer Corps, and five days later XXXVIII Corps took Uritck and reached the shore of the Gulf of Finland to the west of it. On 17 September, the encirclement of Leningrad on the southwestern side was completed with the occupation of Dyetskoye Selo. To the southeast, XXVIII Corps could make no headway, due to prior battle losses and the absence of XXXIX Panzer Corps. The latter had been diverted east against an enemy force attacking. XXXIX Corps, fighting in difficult, tangled terrain, got into such dire straits that von Leeb reluctantly decided to withdraw

◀ While the panzer divisions consolidated their positions around Leningrad, the infantry marched towards the city on foot. By 16 September OKH was announcing that the Sixteenth Army and LVI Panzer Corps had destroyed nine enemy divisions and shattered nine more in a month of combat, but Hitler saved Leningrad from storm.

8th Panzer Division from the successful southwestern attack, in order to support XXXIX Panzer Corps.

By this time, though, fighting in the Army Group North area was dying down, for all the armour (apart from XXXIX Panzer Corps) had to be withdrawn on 17 September to bolster the Moscow offensive. On that day, the Fourth Panzer Group handed over command of the Leningrad operations to the Eighteenth Army.

The Leningrad campaign is especially significant in that one panzer group, under the command of its army group, was given the opportunity of delivering the main blow at the objective, and that its task was carried through to the goal. The possibilities, capacities and the failures of armoured units can be clearly seen in this offensive. Time and again, it was the tanks that brought the initial successes, which enabled a high degree of mobility to be maintained, and which ensured the final victory.

The initial thrust, in which the spearhead of the Fourth Panzer Group covered 752km (470 miles) in three weeks and reached the River Luga's lower course only 100km (62 miles) from Leningrad, is proof of the importance of tanks in the plans of Field Marshal von Leeb. Daugavpils, Ostrov and Pskov were victories won by the expert use of fast-moving vehicles, while the tank battles of Raseynyay and Ostrov were won by clever concentrations of superior firepower against an enemy deployed in depth. The success won by the tanks was exploited by the infantry on the flanks, which, like their counterparts in the other two army groups, maintained the German advance by their forced marches.

Panzer thrusts

Could the high-speed thrust have been continued over the last 100km (62 miles) to Leningrad? General Hoepner thought so, though only by employing all his mobile divisions. This would have meant abandoning the thrust to Lake Ilmen. The task of I Corps on the right should therefore have been purely defensive, pending the arrival of units from the Sixteenth Army. Large-scale Soviet counterattacks were not to be expected at that particular juncture, as in all probability the Soviets would be continuing their retreat beyond the Rivers Lovat and Volkhov, on both sides of Lake Ilmen.

A thrust from the southwest by the Fourth Panzer Group on or about 25 July would very probably have resulted in the occupation of Leningrad. The Soviet leaders in the city were quite unprepared for defence, and even if the capture of the city had not been achieved a close investment would had been possible six weeks earlier than it was actually effected.

The reason why the final thrust was not in fact attempted in July was due to interference

▶ Drawing water for man and beast. The horses and men of Army Group North were fortunate that in northern Russia almost every inhabited place had a well, from which cool, good-quality water could be drawn. In the south, many wells and cisterns dried up in summer, and the overall water quality was poor.

with Army Group North by Hitler himself. The clearest example of this is seen in the transfer of the main point of the attack by the Sixteenth Army from the north (as originally planned) to the south in order to assist the operations of Army Group Centre. The plans of Army Group North, based on quick thrusts, were in the process ruined.

Despite the original aims of Barbarossa, the attack against Leningrad petered out somewhat. Not only were units directed away from the city towards the south, but the Finns were unhelpful in that Mannerheim refused to cooperate directly with Army Group North. Hitler, of course,

▼ German troops in the suburbs of Leningrad. Conditions for the defenders were far from satisfactory, as the large number of refugees, plus the troops who had retreated to the city, were using up food stocks. On 12 September, for example, there was enough flour in Leningrad to last for only 35 days.

did not push the assault with any great vigour. Obsessed as he was with inflicting a cruel fate upon the city, he was quite content to see it encircled and starved into submission. Indeed, he wished to see the cradle of Bolshevism suffer grievously, hence his orders to pound the city into oblivion.

For its part, the Soviet command never had the slightest intention of yielding Leningrad to the Germans, though ironically it had neglected its defences. Therefore, as Army Group North advanced towards the city up to 500,000 Soviet men and women worked frantically on field fortifications around Leningrad to meet the German invaders. At the end of August, Stalin placed the Soviet Northwestern Front and the newly created Leningrad Front directly under the control of *Stavka*.

The German panzer commanders of Army Group North were naturally bitter about the ending of the campaign. They had fought well, only to see victory snatched from their grasp. Erich von Manstein, one of Germany's finest panzer commanders during the war, led LVI Panzer Corps during Operation Barbarossa. His later writings on the campaign illustrate the frustration felt by many in the armoured arm. During August, for example, in conjunction with X Corps, his corps had shattered the Soviet Thirty-Eighth Army near Lake Ilmen by rolling

▶ **The Germans soon discovered that earth roads turned into mud quagmires after heavy rains, which brought transport to a halt. One solution was the construction of so-called corduroy roads, whereby logs were placed side by side to facilitate movement by vehicles. Rigid road discipline also reduced the influence of mud.**

up its flank. His own command took 12,000 prisoners, 141 tanks, 246 guns and several hundred small arms and vehicles. The subsequent indecision regarding where LVI Corps should be allocated – "we ourselves were told on 12th September that we would shortly be moved south with 3 Motorized Division to come under command of Ninth Army in Central Army Group. Even as a corps commander one could make neither head nor tail of all this chopping and changing, though I did form the impression that it was all ultimately due to the tug-of-war evidently going on between Hitler and OKH over whether the strategic aim should be Moscow or Leningrad" – did nothing to facilitate a speedy end to the campaign. In addition, at the end of August heavy rains had begun to turn the roads to mud, which slowed the advance to a trickle and at times stopped it altogether. In the event Manstein's corps continued to fight alongside the Sixteenth Army.

The resumed advance brought fresh victories against the Soviet Eleventh, Twenty-Seventh and Thirty-Fourth Armies, but the bitterness of the army group's panzer commanders was apparent by this stage of the campaign. Manstein again: "We still failed to find any real satisfaction in these achievements, however, for no one was clear any longer what the actual aim of our strategy was or what higher purpose all these battles were supposed to serve. Whatever else might happen, the period of sensational advances of the kind we had made on Dvinsk [Daugavpils] was at an end."

◀ **Nothing prepared the Germans for the muddy conditions they encountered. The historian James Lucas states: "The whole story of the German Army's experiences in Russia is dominated by stories concerning mud ... stories of jackboots being sucked off a wearer's foot are commonplace."**

▶ **In the siege lines around Leningrad. The city had been divided into seven military defence districts, and much use was made of natural obstacles such as canals (even the sewers doubled up as communications trenches if needed). Outside the city were kilometres of anti-tank ditches, mines, bunkers and pillboxes.**

It is true that by mid-September the ring began to close around Leningrad – from the Duderhof heights German artillery had a clear view of the city – but a German attempt to cross the Neva at Porogi failed, and von Leeb's troops could make no further effort on the defences which the Leningraders had so urgently erected.

Army Group North had advanced 921km (570 miles) and had conquered much land, but to achieve a strategic victory it needed to take the city. Hitler intended this to happen through a combination of bombing and starvation. The first large-scale bombing raid against the city was launched on the night of 8 September, when some 6000 incendiary and 50 high-explosive bombs were dropped mainly on the south and southwest areas of the city. This was the beginning of real terror and hardship for the two-and-a-half million people who remained in Leningrad (over 700,000 had been evacuated from the city up to the beginning of September).

Stalin was determined that the city would not fall, and he sent representatives such as Molotov and Malenkov, the latter the head of the NKGB – People's Commissariat for State Security – with special instructions. The two individuals responsible for running Leningrad on a daily basis were Andrei Zhdanov, Communist Party Chief of the City, and Aleksei Kuznetsov, Secretary of the City Party Committee. Rationing was introduced in August 1941, and in September the bread ration was cut twice.

As German troops dug in around the city, it appeared to Hitler that the annihilation of Leningrad was only a matter of time. However, Army Group North was faced with a long siege at the end of very long and very vulnerable lines of communications, with partisan bands operating in its rear. In addition, some 300,000 German troops were now tied down around the city, and winter was approaching. Though conditions would deteriorate for those trapped inside Leningrad, the Germans would be sucked into a long war of attrition which would also sap their manpower and morale. The cradle of Bolshevism remained an unattainable goal for Army Group North.

Drive to Kiev

The German Army achieved some of its greatest victories of World War II in the Ukraine, killing or capturing 765,000 men during the annihilation battles of Uman and Kiev. But in doing so Hitler delayed the assault on Moscow.

Army Group South's campaign was south of the Pripet Marshes. Its order of battle at the start of Barbarossa, from north to south, was as follows: the Sixth Army, First Panzer Group, Seventeenth Army, Third Romanian Army, and Eleventh Army of Colonel-General Ritter von Schobert. The Hungarian Army Corps and Fourth Romanian Army were committed later. The Hungarians and Romanians were largely equipped with old or captured French equipment and were given secondary tasks.

The army group's tasks were as follows: the Sixth Army was to create a hole through which the First Panzer Group would pour towards the River Dnieper below Kiev, then south along the river bank. The Seventeenth Army was to make for Vinnitsa and then continue southeast to link up with the First Panzer Group. When this happened all Soviet forces west of the Dnieper would be annihilated. In the south, the Eleventh Army, the Romanians and the Hungarians

▼ German infantry march into the Ukraine in June 1941. On the first day of the campaign Army Group South's 56th and 62nd Infantry Divisions, both of XVII Corps, crossed the Bug and ran into immediate and heavy resistance, but overcame it and managed to advance 14km (8.75 miles) into Soviet territory.

◀ Field Marshal Gerd von Rundstedt, commander of Army Group South. A naturally cautious leader (it was upon his advice that Hitler issued the controversial "stop order" to the panzers outside Dunkirk on 26 May 1940), his army group had only one panzer group. His total tank strength was just under 600 vehicles.

would initially protect the Ploesti oil fields, before advancing and capturing the southwest Ukraine. In this way all the Ukraine west of the Dnieper would fall to the Germans.

Gerd von Rundstedt's army group would then be in a position to take Kiev, third largest city in the Soviet Union, the centre of Slav Christianity and the capital of the Ukraine. It was also the key to the huge Kharkov industrial region, a major source of Soviet heavy industry, coal and oil.

When the attack began Soviet formations were shattered or brushed aside. The Germans had made no plans to operate in the Pripet Marshes, which they considered, quite reasonably, unsuitable terrain for a modern army.

There was, therefore, a broad gap between Army Groups Centre and South, and when the First Panzer Group swept the Soviet Fifth Army aside, elements of the latter took refuge in the marshy areas, threatening the northern flank and rear of the German Sixth Army. This action alarmed the Sixth Army's commander, General Walther von Reichenau. His fears were not ungrounded. On 10 July, for example, Stalin ordered the Fifth Army south, from Korosten towards Novograd Volynski. At the same time, the Soviet Sixth Army attacked northwest from Kazatin. The objective was to surround the First Panzer Group west of Kiev.

It was a good plan – on paper. But the Germans simply formed defensive fronts to north and south, then counterattacked. Between Zhitomir and Berdichev six understrength Red Army tank corps fought the First Panzer Group for several days, allowing the Soviet Sixth, Twelfth and Twenty-Sixth Armies to withdraw from threatened encirclement. But the losses in

▶ Each of the armies in Army Group South had specialist engineer regiments attached to facilitate the crossing of water obstacles. The Germans found that many bridges across rivers were unsuitable for heavy vehicles. One over the Dnieper, for example, broke under the first tank to cross.

◀ **Infantry of General von Stülpnagel's Seventeenth Army during the first days of Barbarossa. This formation encountered immediate heavy resistance. In IV Corps' sector, for example, at the end of the first day, there was a dangerous 10km (6.25-mile) gap between the 24th and 262nd Infantry Divisions.**

tanks were enormous, and the First Panzer Group was still rolling east.

Some Soviet units had been newly equipped with the T-34 tank, which outclassed anything the Germans had and made something of an impression on Wehrmacht antitank gunners. But the Red Army did not have enough to reverse the tide of defeat, and crews were not fully trained. Though the Germans found their 37mm antitank guns were useless against the T-34, they improvised by using the heavier 88mm gun. Although designed as an antiaircraft gun, it had been discovered to be very effective against tanks and had already been used in that role in the deserts of North Africa.

With the Soviet counterattack broken, the Soviet Fifth Army retreated once more to the marshes around the Korosten fortified region, and continued to molest Reichenau's left flank, which was to have important consequences later.

The failure of the Soviet counteroffensive had now placed Kiev in danger: on 11 July the 13th and 14th Panzer Divisions had reached the River Irpen, less than 16km (10 miles) from the city. There they halted, for the panzer group's commander, General von Kleist, would not sanction their use for street fighting. Moreover, the Soviets were fortifying the city: in addition to a militia of 29,000 men, defence lines were being built to supplement those constructed in the early 1930s. For his part, von Rundstedt believed that towns should be outflanked, not fought over. To draw Soviet forces into the open, where they could be destroyed, he informed the First Panzer Group that "A *coup de main* against Kiev can only come into question when the local commander believes himself to have a favourable opportunity to exploit".

To compound the problems the Soviets were having, the Romanians began their advance on 10 July, together with the German Eleventh

◀ **A StuG III assault gun equipped with a short-barrelled 75mm StuK37 L/24 gun. The following Sturmgeschütz Abteilungen (assault gun battalions) began Operation Barbarossa with Army Group South: 190th, 191st, 197th and 243rd. Commanders of infantry divisions tended to assign each of their regiments a StuG battalion.**

Army. Their opponents, the Soviet Ninth and Twelfth Armies, already in danger of being outflanked to the north, were ordered to fall back to Uman. The commander of the Southern Front, General Tyulenev, complied but found that his task was made more difficult by the fact that the Zhmerinka–Odessa railway line had already been disrupted and that heavy rains had turned the roads to mud.

The port of Odessa, now under threat, was placed under the command of Lieutenant-General Golden Party Badge G.P. Sofronov under the grand title "Coastal Group of Forces". Odessa would be turned into a "Black Sea Tobruk", capable of holding out under siege even if completely isolated from the main front. The choice of title would be appropriate, though not in the way the Soviets hoped.

On 17–18 July, *Stavka* ordered Budenny to hold a line from Belaya Tserkov to the mouth of the Dniester in front of Odessa, hoping thus to block the threat of encirclement of the inner wings of their Southwestern and Southern Fronts, and hopefully restore a continuous front-line. Tyulenev's force at Uman was to be used as a strategic reserve, to block any dangerous gaps which might develop.

At this time *Stavka* believed that Moscow was the main target for the German invaders. It therefore decided to concentrate its main forces opposite Army Group Centre, on the grounds that this would not only provide frontal protection for Moscow itself, but would also limit German opportunities for major offensives in the north or south in two ways. First, it would limit the forces available to them by forcing Army Group Centre to maintain strong forces. Second, any German attempt at deep penetration in the north or south would find large Soviet forces threatening their flanks. A strong defence should therefore be combined with

▼ A Soviet aircraft burns on the steppe. Despite its massive initial victories, the Luftwaffe lost many aircraft during Barbarossa. From the beginning of the campaign until 27 September, the total number of German aircraft damaged or destroyed was 2631 – almost equal to the number committed on 22 June 1941.

counterattacks aimed at the exposed flanks of German forces and at the many junctions between them.

Stavka had grasped the nature of the problem and the potential for exploiting gaps between the panzer spearheads and the slower-moving German infantry divisions. *Stavka*'s task was to sever the one from the other. The question was whether, after their mauling on the frontiers, the Red Army's soldiers could carry out the mission set them.

The attack by the Soviet Fifth and Sixth Armies on 10 July had been an attempt at severing the First Panzer Group from the Sixth Army (see above). The Soviet Fifth Army, operating out of the gap between Army Groups Centre and South against the north flank of von Kleist's panzers, attacked from the north, while the Soviet Sixth Army was meant to strike from the south. The operation had caused the Germans some scares, and its failure had not removed the threat presented by the Fifth Army, which had merely retreated back to its start line. It proves that Red Army units and commanders were more than willing to launch counterattacks against the invaders, but the prerequisites for success were missing on many occasions. In the south, as elsewhere, the Luftwaffe ruled the skies. This meant Red Army formations had to move to their assembly areas under constant threat of air attack. A general lack of antiaircraft weapons meant vehicle columns did not have the means to combat Luftwaffe aircraft when they did attack. Laying aside the aerial threat, Soviet mechanized units lacked spares, fuel and ammunition, and many tank crews possessed only the most basic training. There was a chronic lack of radio communication, which made coordination in battle all but impossible. Finally, and perhaps this condemned Soviet mechanized units to defeat more than any other single factor,

▼ Troops of the Romanian Third Army in the Ukraine. This force consisted of two infantry divisions, a mountain infantry division and a reconnaissance cavalry division. Commanded by General Dumitrescu, the Romanians lacked training, had poor officers and much of their weapons and equipment was obsolete.

▲ Personnel of the German 68th Infantry Division, which was part of XXXXIX Corps, Seventeenth Army, check their map during the drive along Rollbahn 2 (one of the few modern main highways in Russia). Note the destruction – German artillery and dive-bombers were effective as ever – and the destination the Germans would never reach.

personal initiative was stifled at every command level. Orders were obeyed blindly even when there was no hope of success, for to do otherwise would inevitably result in interrogation by the NKVD for disobeying orders, with the possibility of loss of rank and even execution.

As Army Group South continued to advance farther east, Hitler was already beginning to show a preference for conquering the Ukraine before Moscow and Leningrad (on 8 July he stated that he intended to destroy Moscow and Leningrad by air power alone – the failure of the Luftwaffe to do this to London a year before, with more bombers and fighters, seems to have been conveniently forgotten by the Führer).

Guderian's Second Panzer Group, on the southern wing of Army Group Centre, was left alone to continue eastwards. But Guderian was labouring under false illusions – the Moscow direction would still be covered, but part of Army Group Centre would soon be ordered to turn south – the Führer was becoming obsessed by the Ukraine.

On the same day, Halder presented to him an assessment of Soviet losses to date: 89 of the 164 known enemy divisions had been destroyed; of the remainder, 18 were on secondary fronts, 11 unknown, and only 46 known to be still combat-worthy. Von Brauchitsch then advocated turning von Kleist's First Panzer Group south into the rear of the Soviet Sixth and Twelfth Armies. But Hitler wanted nothing less than the capture of Kiev and the annihilation of all enemy forces west of the Dnieper.

Von Brauchitsch was horrified, and stated that in any case it would be impossible due to supply difficulties. For once Hitler yielded the

▼ A Romanian cavalry column. General von Manstein, who commanded the Romanians in the Crimea, had the following to say of Germany's allies: "One final drawback regarding the use of Romanian troops on the Eastern Front was their terrific respect for 'the Russians'. In difficult situations this was liable to end in a panic."

▲ **German infantry moves past a dead Russian soldier. The commander of the Southwestern Front, General Kirponos, marshalled his armies with skill at the start of Barbarossa, but tactics at lower levels were poor, such as the use of mass infantry attacks. One German described them as "a machine gunner's dream target".**

point, leaving von Rundstedt to carry on his campaign. He unleashed von Kleist against Kazatin, which was captured on 15 July. This severed the Southwestern Front's main railway link, forcing Budenny to pull his units back into the Dnieper bend.

The Soviet Fifth Army, though battered, was still at Korosten, and its presence continued to cast a shadow over the capture of Kiev. It would have to be destroyed, which was raised with Hitler on 17 July. The result was OKW Directive No 33 of 19 July. This ordered that after completing operations at Smolensk, the Second Panzer Group and the infantry of the Second Army should turn southeast to destroy the Soviet Twenty-First Army (at that time opposite the right wing of Army Group Centre) and then, in cooperation with Army Group South, should destroy the Soviet Fifth Army. At the same time, a concentric attack by Army Group South was to drive across the rear of the Soviet Sixth and Twelfth Armies and destroy them as well. The remaining armoured forces of Army Group Centre – the Third Panzer Group – were to move north eastwards to assist Army Group North. This meant that the advance on Moscow would be left to the infantry armies of Army Group Centre.

Turning point of the campaign

On 23 July yet another conference took place between Hitler, von Brauchitsch and Halder, at which the latter reported that the Red Army forces now in the field numbered 93 divisions, 13 of which were armoured. This highlights the dismal failure of German intelligence concerning the number of Soviet divisions. Despite massive losses, the number of Soviet units seemed to be increasing!

At this point it would be useful to say something about the Soviet replacement system. In the face of massive losses, *Stavka* issued a circular on 15 July 1941 that eliminated the corps level of command, and instead created smaller field armies of 5–6 rifle divisions, 2–3 tank brigades, 1–2 light cavalry divisions and attached artillery regiments. In addition, the rifle divisions were simplified by giving up their anti-tank, antiaircraft, tank and artillery units. In this way the strength of a rifle division fell from 18,000 to 11,000 (though in fact the strength of many divisions was far less, prompting their redesignation as separate brigades).

The same circular abolished the mechanized corps, which existed only on paper as most of their tanks had been lost (such were tank losses in the second half of 1941 that the largest new armoured units formed were tank brigades). In addition, and to partly offset the dearth of tank units, there was a massive expansion of cavalry units: the creation of 30 new light cavalry divisions of 3447 horseman apiece.

As Barbarossa progressed, the German High Command was continually baffled by the seemingly never-ending supply of enemy divisions. In part this was due to wrong intelligence assessment, but it was also due to the Red Army's ability to create new forces from scratch and rebuild shattered units quickly. This stemmed from the idea of cadre and mobilization forces: units that had few active soldiers during peacetime, but would be filled with reservists and volunteers in wartime. The strength of this system in the latter half of 1941 became apparent, as the historian David Glantz states: "prewar Soviet theory estimated that the army would have to be completely replaced every four to eight months during heavy combat. To satisfy this need, the 1938 Universal Military Service Law extended the reserve service obligation to age 50 and created a network of schools to train those reservists. By the time of the German invasion, the Soviet Union had a pool of 14 million men with at least basic military training. The existence of this pool of trained reservists gave the Red Army a depth and resiliency that was largely invisible to German and other observers."

Nevertheless, stunning though this achievement was, the Germans still held the initiative in July 1941 and still had the opportunity of

▼ Troops of one of Army Group South's light divisions (it had the 97th, 99th, 100th and 101st). Originally designed as highly mobile, semi-mechanized units, light divisions were a cross between an infantry and mountain division. Note jäger arm badge – three oakleaves and acorn – and the metal version on the cap on the right.

▲ German artillery pounds Soviet positions in the Uman Pocket, July 1941. The jaws around the Soviet Sixth, Twelfth and parts of the Eighteenth Armies closed at the end of that month. Desperate Soviet attempts to break out of the pocket largely failed due to the supreme efforts of the German infantry divisions.

bringing the war in the East to a successful conclusion. This seemed all the more likely when the Germans won another battle of encirclement at Uman.

The Führer ordered the closing of the Uman Pocket on 24 July. Von Kleist had wanted to encircle Kiev from the south with one corps, and send two other corps into the rear of both the Soviet Southwestern and Southern Fronts, but he was overruled. On 30 July, the First Panzer Group smashed into the columns of Red Army troops withdrawing from the pocket, wheeled towards the southwest, and on 3 August linked up with the forward elements of General Karl-Heinrich von Stülpnagel's Seventeenth Army near Pervomaisk, trapping the Soviet Sixth and Twelfth Armies and part of the Eighteenth, a total of 15 infantry and five armoured divisions. As ever, Soviet efforts to break out of encirclement were relentless, and for a while the thin screen of panzer and motorized divisions on the eastern side of the pocket were under great strain before the infantry divisions arrived.

By 5 August Soviet forces in the pocket had been herded into an area 20km (12.5 miles) wide and 20km (12.5 miles) deep southwest of Uman. Hemmed in on every side, the Russians began to surrender in droves. On 7 August OKH released a special bulletin: "On the southern flank, the army group, under the command of Field Marshal von Rundstedt, has overcome particularly difficult terrain and weather obstacles and a numerically superior enemy ... Current totals for this combat sector exceed 150,000 prisoners, 1970 tanks and 2190 guns.

▲ **Waiting for the next Soviet attack out of the Uman Pocket. The MG 34 machine gun (shown here) was probably responsible for killing more Red Army soldiers during Barbarossa than any other German infantry weapon. In Russia, machine-gun teams went through many barrel changes (barrels had to be changed after 250 rounds of burst fire).**

▲ **Moving forward to "squeeze" the Uman Pocket. Before the pocket was sealed the Soviet Twenty-Sixth Army had attempted to halt the German advance and thereby save the Sixth and Twelfth Armies. The attack failed, while inside the pocket Soviet resistance, at first fanatical, suddenly collapsed as units began to surrender.**

The participation of the air fleet of General Loehr had a prominent effect on the successful development of this operation. They had shot down or destroyed on the ground 980 aircraft of the Soviet Air Force."

Though some of the Soviet formations succeeded in fighting their way out, resistance in the pocket ended on 8 August. About 100,000 prisoners were taken (note the difference between actual numbers and German claims), together with the commanders of the two trapped armies – Generals Muzychenko and Ponedelin – 317 tanks and 1100 guns.

At the southern end of Army Group South's operations, where the main weight was to be carried by the Romanian Third and Fourth Armies, advances had been slower than in the north, and the progress that had been made was as much the result of deliberate Soviet withdrawals as of actual gains. Yet, the withdrawal of Soviet forces into the Uman Pocket had left the far south vulnerable, and by the beginning of August the port of Odessa was accessible to the

▼ **Some of the 100,000 Red Army soldiers capture at Uman. General Erhard Rauss fought on the Eastern Front, and had this to say of the Russian soldier: "As inexplicable as the fanatic resistance of some units, was the mystery of mass flights, or sudden surrender. The reason may have been an imperceptible fluctuation in morale."**

Red Army only by sea. The Romanian Third Army settled down to invest it on 5 August, thus allowing the German Eleventh Army to continue the advance east. The Uman disaster, plus the beginning of the 73-day siege of Odessa, made *Stavka* realize that the Soviets' Southwestern Front was on the verge of collapse.

Stavka also realized that it was useless allocating reserves piecemeal, especially in futile attacks against panzer and motorized infantry divisions. Therefore the new divisions – 10 to the Southwestern Front, 12 to the Southern Front, and two into the Front Reserve – were deployed to prepare a defensive line along the east bank of the Dnieper, and to help remove industrial equipment. (The achievements of the Soviets in shipping their industry east was truly amazing: in all, 1523 factories, including 1360 related to armaments, were transferred to the River Volga, Siberia and Central Asia between July and November 1941.)

Scorched earth

Stalin announced that a scorched earth policy would be fully implemented in the Ukraine. He stated: "In case of forced retreat ... all rolling stock must be evacuated, the enemy must not be left a single engine, a single railway car, not a single pound of grain or gallon of fuel. The collective farmers must drive off all their cattle and turn over their grain to the safe keeping of the states authorities for transportation to the rear.

▲ The rich industrial and agricultural lands of the Ukraine had always obsessed Hitler. Their conquest was not only to provide Germany with resources but also to deny the Soviets raw materials and food supplies. Hitler's decision to halt the drive on Moscow ensured the Germans a large harvest of Ukrainian agricultural produce.

All valuable property, including non-ferrous metals, grain and fuel that cannot be withdrawn must be destroyed without fail. In areas occupied by the enemy, guerrilla units ... must set fire to forests, stores and transports."

The results of this instruction were the shipping of six million cattle from the Ukraine, 550 large factories, thousands of small factories and 300,000 tractors. Among the things sabotage by the Soviets as they retreated were the Dniprohes Dam on the Dnieper, the largest hydro-electric dam in Europe, dozens of mines and major industrial factories, and, in a particularly vindictive act, the Dormition Cathedral in Kiev, which had been built in 1073.

◀ After the Ukraine had been conquered, the Nazis' racial policy could be implemented. Reichsführer-SS Himmler: "Like the skimmed fat at the top of a pot of bouillon, there is a thin intellectual layer on the surface of the Ukrainian people: do away with it and the leaderless herd will become an obedient and helpless herd."

▲ Junkers Ju 52 transport aircraft fly towards the front. When mud made road transport difficult, the Germans experimented with flying ammunition to units in transport aircraft. However, the cost in terms of fuel and aircraft lost proved prohibitive. The Luftwaffe began Barbarossa with 210 Ju 52s.

West of the Dnieper, delaying actions would be fought to gain time for removing or destroying the factories. The Red Army was already painfully aware of the contribution being made by Western European industry to the German war effort, and its leaders were determined that Germany should derive no such benefit from captured Soviet industry. What could be moved would be set up again in the Urals or Siberia. Even if it rusted away in railway sidings or open fields (and much of it did), it would not be used to kill its owners. Much sabotaged equipment left behind was later repaired by the Germans, but at least the time it was out of action helped the Red Army.

The Red Army itself took measures to ensure that mass surrenders would become a thing of the past. The Head of the Political Propaganda Directorate, Army Commissar First Rank L.Z. Makhlis, issued two directives. First, he ordered political commissars to emphasize that surrounded units must either fight their way out or, if that proved impossible, must operate against the enemy rear for as long as they could. Second, he exhorted Communist Party and Communist Youth League members to set an example and provide leadership. For his part, Stalin still did not believe that the professional soldiers could be trusted to do their best (the military disasters suffered in June and July had reinforced his negative views about professional officers; the fact that he had contributed to the inherent weaknesses of the Red Army did not enter his thinking), and he had already restored the political commissars in the forces to a position of equality with their unit commanders, in effect making them responsible for the reliability of the professional military.

In fact, Stalin at this time was turning on the Red Army with a particular vengeance. He did not see heroic counterattacks against an enemy that was militarily and technically superior, he saw only treachery. The result was the *Stavka* Order No 270, dated 16 August 1941. It talked of "inadmissible clumsiness" and "despicable

▲ Another Russian village burns as the Ukrainian advance continues. One of the advantages the Germans had during Barbarossa was excellent intelligence provided by the Luftwaffe to ground units (more than a quarter of the entire Luftwaffe force committed to Barbarossa consisted of reconnaissance types).

cowardice" and stated: "Can cowards who go over to the enemy and give themselves up, or such commanders, who at the first sign of difficulties at the front, tear off their insignia of rank and desert to the rearward areas, be tolerated in the ranks of the Red Army? No, that is impossible ... Cowards and deserters must be destroyed." It stated that the families of commanders and political officers who surrendered were to be arrested as "families of perjurers and treacherous deserters". As the historian Heinz Magenheimar records: "Stalin's hostile and pitiless attitude towards all Soviet soldiers who had preferred captivity to death on the battlefield also explains his refusal to accord soldiers who had fallen into German hands that status of prisoners-of-war. According to official doctrine, there were no such prisoners."

Hitler also had problems with his commanders, though in his case they sprang from the options that became available as a consequence of military victory. Army Group Centre, for example, especially Guderian, hypnotised by Moscow, was openly thwarting the directives it received from OKH (Guderian was stubbornly trying to keep his panzers in positions from which they could resume the eastward march to the Soviet capital). But while he was doing this, most of Hoth's Third Panzer Group was busily redeploying, as ordered, to assist Army Group North in its advance against Leningrad. It must have appeared to Hitler that Hoth was the only senior officer in Army Group Centre who still believed in doing what he was told!

While Guderian was finding reasons why he should not go back to Gomel to deal with the Soviet Fifth Army (see Chapter 3), and was submitting plans to take Moscow, Army Group South ground to a halt in front of Kiev.

The commander of the German Sixth Army, General Walther von Reichenau, was concerned about his left flank. He had good reason to be: between him and the Second Army of Army Group Centre was a gap of 240km (150 miles). His 56th Infantry Division was covering some 96km (60 miles) of this, but the troublesome Soviet Fifth Army still had several divisions. Von Reichenau had been ordered to press ahead with a direct attack on Kiev, but in the circumstances he objected to von Rundstedt. OKH refused to give a clear lead in the matter, and so, on 9 August, von Rundstedt called off the offensive in the Kiev-Korosten area. The Sixth Army remained on the defensive.

On 10 August OKW made its decision on the next stage of Barbarossa. While agreeing that the main enemy forces were in front of Army Group Centre, and that the most important task was to destroy them and seize Moscow, it decreed that enemy forces facing the other two army groups constituted a threat to Army Group Centre's flanks. This being the case, the

▲ One of Army Group South's supply columns halts for a rest. Even dry mud roads could become heavily rutted by heavy usage. German-made trucks were not rugged enough for Russian roads.

▼ A Panzer III, truck, motorcycle and car of a panzer division on the road. Each panzer division was liberally equipped with motorcycles (each one had a motorcycle battalion), but motorcycle riders were always vulnerable to small-arms fire.

▲ Part of an artillery detachment on the way to Kiev. During Barbarossa German artillery regiments expended massive quantities of ammunition. Between 22 July and 7 August 1941, for example, the 25th Infantry Division's artillery regiment fired 20,135 105mm shells, while its antitank battalion used 6643 37mm rounds.

decisive attack on Moscow must be preceded by operations with limited aims against the Soviet forces in the north and south. It was assumed that the destruction of these forces would take two weeks, thus an offensive against Moscow, with infantry armies in the centre and a panzer group on each flank, could begin at the end of August. Anticipating Red Army movements, OKH believed the enemy would be engaged and destroyed in the Bryansk and Vyazma area.

Regarding Army Group South, its Seventeenth Army would be employed in forcing the Dnieper between Kiev and Kremenchug, thereby breaking up large Soviet forces forming up on the east bank of the river. When the Dnieper line had thus been forced, part of Army Group South would turn north into the rear of the Soviet Fifth Army, annihilating this formation once and for all. The whole scheme was an object lesson in compromise.

But OKH had failed to take into account the thoughts of Hitler, who on 12 August again emphasized that the precondition for all future operations was the destruction of all enemy forces on the flanks of Army Group Centre, and in particular those in the south – the Soviet Southwestern Front.

Stavka, however, was just as obsessed by Moscow as was Army Group Centre. For example, the movement of Guderian's Second Panzer Group southwest, behind Gomel and Starodub, was interpreted as a manoeuvre to exploit the large gap which had opened between the Reserve and Central Fronts, after which the Germans would turn east, break through at Bryansk and outflank Moscow from the south.

Marshal Budenny, commander of the Southwestern Front, saw things differently, and correctly. He asked permission to withdraw the Fifth Army and XXVII Independent Corps from the Korosten Fortified Region, thus blocking any German drive across the rear of his front. In this way Guderian would be unable to link up with von Kleist's First Panzer Group advancing

▼ Men of the 1st Gebirgs (Mountain) Division, part of the Seventeenth Army's XXXXIX Corps. Each mountain division had an average strength of 13,000 men, divided between a headquarters, two rifle regiments, an artillery regiment and divisional support units. Each division had a large quantity of mules and horses.

north from Kremenchug and complete a massive encirclement of the Kiev region. *Stavka* refused, and instead ordered the formation of the Bryansk Front, at first with responsibility only to fill the gap between Central and Southwestern Fronts and prevent a German breakthrough to Moscow.

The commander of the new front was General Andrei Yeremenko. Stalin gave him the following order: "You, Comrade Yeremenko, are appointed commander of the Bryansk Front. Tomorrow you will go there and organize the Front at top speed. Guderian's tank group is operating on the Bryansk axis, and there will be some heavy fighting. So you will have your wish. You will meet the mechanized forces of your 'old friend' Guderian, whose methods should be known to you from the Western Front."

His attack against Guderian was a disaster, and did not stop the panzer general from driving south to link up with von Kleist. With an exposed left flank (which the Soviets failed to

▲ German cars and motorcycles somewhere east of Uman, August 1941. Though the German Army requisitioned many civilian cars prior to Barbarossa, many were two-wheel drive and had poor performance.

▼ There were never enough trucks to keep the troops supplied. In one 16-day battle, for example, the 25th Infantry Division fired 1,155,000 rifle and machine-gun rounds, and used up 10,290 hand grenades.

exploit), Guderian's panzers seized the vital crossing over the Desna at Novgorod Severski on 26 August. To the south, von Kleist's panzer divisions captured the city of Dnepropetrovsk the day before. The fall of the city immediately prompted *Stavka* to deploy more divisions to the Dnieper Front in the belief that the Germans would strike even farther east. However, the German units at Dnepropetrovsk were to provide flank protection for the approaching encirclement battle of Kiev.

The German jaws were closing in on the capital of the Ukraine. On 16 September, at Lokhvitsa, 160km (100 miles) north of Kremenchug, von Kleist's panzers linked up with those of Guderian, while during the following days Wehrmacht infantry divisions of both panzer groups moved up to close the gaps in the armoured cordon. Behind them, the Seventeenth Army on von Kleist's left, and the Second Army advancing south on Guderian's right increased the pressure on the pocket. Von Reichenau's Sixth Army, meanwhile, marching east from Uman, constricted the pocket along its western edge. And overhead, the Luftwaffe pounded Red Army units incessantly.

Marshal Budenny informed Stalin that Kiev must be abandoned, which resulted in Budenny being replaced by Marshal Timoshenko. The new commander of the Southwestern Front, General Kirponos, would not evacuate Kiev without confirmation from Moscow, which arrived on 17 September. By that time it was too late.

Inside the pocket were five Soviet field armies – Fifth, Twenty-First, Twenty-Sixth, Thirty-Seventh and Thirty-Eighth – and they were doomed. The panzer divisions simply

▼ Because German horses on the open steppes suffered from respiratory complaints brought on by low night-time temperatures, as the campaign wore on Wehrmacht units tried to get hold of as many of the native *Panje* horses as possible. The latter were immune to most diseases, could resist low temperatures and were tireless.

chewed the enemy to pieces. The following account is from a soldier serving in the 3rd Panzer Division, Second Panzer Group: "After a three-hour trip, the first town emerged on the left. A Russian transport column was on the road. As the German vehicles approached, the Soviets abandoned their horse carts and fled into the nearby field of sunflowers. As we moved on, the enemy supply wagons crossed the road. The machine guns spoke again. We advanced further. It was the Soviets already. This time it was an enormous column of batteries, supply trains, construction battalions, guns, horse carts, and tractors, with cossacks and two combat vehicles riding in between. The machine guns howled anew, shooting a passage through the Russian column, and the tanks raged with great speed into the middle of the stream."

▲ Dust created many problems for the invading Germans. This was particularly so in the panzer divisions, as most tanks were not fitted with dust filters. Dust was sucked into engines, which rendered tanks unserviceable. In addition, the abrasive action of dust reduced engine efficiency and thus increased fuel consumption.

Futility

Inside Kiev, Kirponos ordered his armies to break out of the encirclement. Short of ammunition, artillery and devoid of air cover, it was a hopeless task. The Twenty-Sixth and elements of the Thirty-Eighth Armies attempted an attack towards Lubny, only to be shot to pieces. Stalin may have forbidden surrender, but inside the cauldron Russians began to surrender in droves. Their morale would suddenly collapse after being bombed and strafed for days, or after having been thrown back by German artillery and machine guns.

Some units managed to break out of the cauldron, but 665,000 Red Army soldiers fell into German hands, along with 884 tanks and 3718 artillery pieces. Many thousands lay dead, including Kirponos. A surgeon in the 3rd Panzer Division recorded the scenes in the Kiev Pocket after the Soviet surrender: "Chaos reigns. Hundreds of trucks and cars, interspersed with tanks, are scattered over the land. Often the occupants were overcome with fear when they tried to get out and they hang from the doors, burned into black mummies. Thousands of

▼ StuG IIIs on the edge of the Kiev Pocket in August 1941. By the time the fighting at Kiev had ended on 19 September, the Soviet Fifth, Twenty-First, Twenty-Sixth, Thirty-Seventh and Thirty-Eighth Armies had been annihilated – 665,000 prisoners fell into German hands. The Southwestern Front had virtually ceased to exist.

▲ Farther and farther east. German troops on the road to Kharkov, September 1941. The Soviet Southwestern Front's losses between 7 July to 26 September amounted to a staggering 8543 troops a day. But the Russians were still fighting.

▼ The Germans also suffered casualties. By 31 July they had suffered 213,301 casualties on the Eastern Front – around 15 percent of their total invasion force – which began to worry senior commanders.

corpses lay around the vehicles." The battles around Kiev came to an end on 24 September.

By any measure the Uman and Kiev Pockets had been military triumphs on a grand scale. At Kiev no less than five Soviet armies – 50 divisions – had been annihilated. The Red Army was forced to rebuild Southwestern Front from the 15,000 men who had escaped encirclement.

Hitler was elated, and called Kiev the "greatest battle in the history of the world", while Halder termed it the "greatest strategic blunder of the eastern campaign". It is true than two months had been lost before an assault against Moscow could be launched, but it was the Führer who turned the Kiev decision into a blunder. Having captured the capital of the Ukraine, the Führer could have turned military triumph into political victory by winning over the Ukrainian populace. However, Nazi racial ideology precluded such a prudent move, and the Germans set about alienating and exterminating those Ukranians who occupied the land earmarked for *Lebensraum*. Hitler had reminded everyone of his intentions on 16 August: "Fundamentally our policy is to cut the gigantic cake with skill, so that it can be first mastered, secondly administered, thirdly exploited ... it is wrong to induce any subjected people into rendering us military assistance, even though it may appear more convenient at first sight ... Naturally, the vast territories have to be pacified as soon as possible; this can only be achieved by shooting everybody who shows a wry face."

The first to suffer from this viewpoint were Soviet prisoners, of which there were four million taken between June 1941 and February 1942. Herded into open camps, with little food and water, and many with untreated wounds, they began to die in their thousands: over 500,000 were to die between November 1941 and February 1942 alone.

Further victories

The Soviet defeat at Kiev also threatened other sectors of the Russian front farther south. The Romanians had reached Odessa on 5 August, and there they established siege lines around the city. But it would take until 16 October, at a cost of 100,000 casualties, before the port fell. After its fall it was incorporated into Romania as the capital of the new Romanian province of Transniestria.

The German Eleventh Army, now under the command of General Erich von Manstein (who had been transferred from LVI Panzer Corps), was to advance as far as the neck of the Crimean peninsular, which threatened to turn all the Soviet defences of the Donets and Don. The terrain was more suitable to panzer operations, and in von Manstein Germany would have one of the finest panzer commanders of the war. He would have to wait for his tanks, though, as he stated: "After the forest tracts of northern Russia in which I had last had to operate with a tank corps unsuited to that type of country, I now found myself in the vast expanses of the steppes, which were almost entirely devoid of natural obstacles, even if they did not offer any cover either. It was ideal tank country, but unfortunately Eleventh Army had no tanks."

▲ General Walther von Reichenau, commander of the German Sixth Army. He issued a "severity order" which encouraged acts of "vengeance" against the Russians.

▼ The fall of Kiev allowed Army Group South to enter the industrial basin of the River Donbas in late September 1941, while the First Panzer Group raced for the River Don and the Caucasus.

▶ **Vehicles of Guderian's Second Panzer Group on the way north after helping to reduce the Kiev Pocket. His units had been given a foretaste of the power of mud in early September, when the 3rd Panzer Division was reduced to an effective strength of 10 tanks after heavy rains.**

The commander of Army Group South, von Rundstedt, argued that the German armies in the East should halt on the Dnieper line for the winter and should not attempt a final push towards the Soviet capital. The Führer refused to countenance it, however, since it would involve a general retreat in the centre of the front. And commanders such as Guderian and Hoth were not to be denied their chance of taking the Soviet capital.

Stalin was understandably alarmed by the Kiev disaster. In a message to British Prime Minister Winston Churchill at the beginning of September, when the Ukrainian situation was developing ominously, he had requested that Britain and the United States send him 30,000 tons of aluminium by the beginning of October, plus a minimum monthly aid of 400 aircraft and 500 tanks. He ended the message: "without these two kinds of aid the Soviet Union will either be defeated or weakened to the extent that it will lose for a long time the ability to help its Allies by active operations at the front against Hitlerism."

Even if such aid was immediately available, which it wasn't, the Red Army would have had to fight the Wehrmacht with its own resources in front of Moscow. At the end of September 1941 these resources east of Moscow were as follows: Western Front (General I.S. Konev) comprising the Twenty-Second, Twenty-Ninth, Thirtieth, Nineteenth, Sixteenth and Twentieth Armies; Reserve Front (Budenny) comprising the Twenty-Fourth and Forty-Third Armies; Supreme Commander's Western Reserve made up of the Thirty-First, Forty-Ninth, Thirty-Second and Thirty-Third Armies; and Bryansk Front (Yeremenko) of the Third, Thirteenth and Fiftieth Armies.

The three fronts had a total strength of 800,000 men, 770 tanks and 364 aircraft, which at the time constituted almost half the Red Army manpower and artillery strength on the

◀ **Of all the vehicles employed by the German Army on the Eastern Front, the halftrack (right) was perhaps the most useful. It was steered by two front wheels (instead of changing the speeds of each track as in tanks), and its cross-country performance was only marginally less than a fully tracked vehicle**

entire Eastern Front, and one-third of its tanks and aircraft. By this time the average strength of a Soviet infantry division was around 7000 men, though many were as low as 5000.

The outlook for the Red Army seemed gloomy, but as September ended another factor entered the strategic equation: the weather. The summer heat had reduced river levels and made both tracked and wheeled movement relatively easy. But as the autumn approached the weather began to change. Heinz Guderian, during his panzer group's advance south to take part in the Kiev encirclement, experienced at first hand the effect adverse weather conditions could have on operations: "During the night it poured with rain. My drive ... on the 11th [September], therefore, proved very difficult. I had covered 100 miles in 10 hours. The boggy roads made any faster progress impossible. These time-wasting drives gave me sufficient insight into the difficulties that lay ahead of us. Only a man who has personally experienced what life on those canals of mud we called roads was like can form any picture of what the troops and their equipment had to put up with, and can truly judge the situation at the front and the consequent effect on our operation."

Hitler and OKH had taken good weather for granted, though Guderian was far from convinced: "It [the attack on Moscow] all depended on this: would the German Army, before the onset of winter and, indeed, before the autumn mud set in, still be capable of achieving decisive results? Was there still sufficient time to succeed?" For the victorious German Army, all the weeks of bloodshed, manoeuvres, decisions, blunders and victories came down to one thing: would there be enough time? Or would General Winter halt the Blitzkrieg?

▼ Hauling a stranded Wehrmacht vehicle through the mud. The Germans suffered high losses in tanks and motor vehicles of all kinds during the autumn muddy season in 1941. In addition, artillery units found that the effectiveness of their fire was much reduced by mud, which dampened the splinter effect of shells.

Finnish revenge

Hitler and his generals thought Finland would be a willing participant in Barbarossa, and would be eager to avenge territorial losses in 1940. This was true, up to a point, but Finland proved to be a disappointment to Berlin.

Notwithstanding the peace treaty signed in Moscow in March 1940 at the end of the Winter War, it was not surprising that the Finns and Soviets should start fighting each other again after their conflict of 1939–40. The Soviets had subsequently followed a policy of pressure and harassment against Finland, which only served to confirm the belief of the latter that a Red Army attack on Finland would occur sooner rather than later. Thus when, in August 1940, Germany requested transit rights for her troops in northern Norway to travel through Finland as part of Operation Barbarossa, the Finns readily agreed. To expedite the agreement, the Germans offered to sell arms to Finland at

▼ A Finnish field telephonist. Though the Finnish Army was small and was essentially an infantry formation, the quality of its officers and men was high. An average Finnish infantry division had three infantry regiments and a field artillery regiment.

◀ Finnish infantry move through wooded terrain. The Karelian Isthmus consists of virgin forest, swamps, moors and loose rocks and is unsuited to operations involving large formations. Small units are more suitable, which gave the Finns an advantage over the Red Army.

the same time. It was a small price to pay, for under cover of these transit agreements the Germans were able to establish a base system, well-placed strategically, in northern Finland.

These German troop movements did not go unnoticed by the USSR, but in November 1940 Hitler rejected Molotov's demand to reduce Wehrmacht activity in Finland. The Führer, as ever with economic considerations uppermost in his mind, had two immediate aims for his troops in Finland. First was the seizure of the vital nickel deposits of northern Finland (code-named Operation Reindeer). Second was the establishment of bases for a possible German attack on Murmansk and its railway (code-named Operation Silver Fox).

The Germans revealed their plans to the Finns in May 1941, which included moving troops into northern Finland shortly before the start of Operation Barbarossa. The Finns were asked to cooperate in Operation Silver Fox, with their main army threatening Leningrad from the north. Though no formal agreements were made, this was tacitly agreed during conferences in Helsinki held in early June. On 8 June 1941, German troops began to disembark in Finland, while general Finnish mobilisation began eight days later, eventually leading to over 400,000 men being made available for the campaign.

The Finns did not immediately join Barbarossa (troop concentrations were not complete by 22 June), but if there was any doubt over their participation it was ended on 25 June with Russian air raids against the country.

▶ The River Tuloma, and beyond the ice-free waters that lead to Murmansk. The port and its railway was the lifeline for Allied supplies to the Soviet Union, and *Stavka* launched a number of attacks against German and Finnish forces in 1941 to prevent the fall of both. *Stavka* kept the railway line and port open throughout the war.

▲ Finnish troops behind a temporary barricade during a summer exercise. The Finnish Army trained its men to fight effectively in wooded and arctic terrain. This produced soldiers who were good trail readers and could move through woods silently without becoming separated from their comrades.

Since March 1940 Finland's armed forces had been undergoing a reorganization, and in June 1941 consisted of 16 infantry divisions with three brigades of elite troops, a cavalry brigade and two Jäger (rifle) brigades. Field artillery units had adequate supplies of ammunition, but little in the way of heavy pieces. The bulk of the army still depended on horses for moving guns and supplies, but so did most armies in World War II. Some tank units had been formed, and were equipped with captured Soviet vehicles from the Winter War. Radio communications had been introduced, but most army units remained reliant on field telephones and runners for communication. The Finnish Air Force had been modestly expanded and modernized, but had no heavy bombers and so had a limited offensive capacity. But the Finnish attack was not executed with the same determination as shown in the Winter War.

The Finnish-German front was divided at the opening of hostilities by a line running east from Oulu. To the north of this line, operations were conducted by the German Norway Army under the command of General von Falkenhorst. On the Arctic Ocean was Dietl's Gebirgs Corps (Mountain Corps) – two mountain divisions – facing Murmansk. Deployed in the centre was XXXVI Army Corps, comprising the 169th Division, SS Panzer Division *Nord* and the Finnish Sixth Division, at Rovaniemi.

Dietl's right was covered by the Finnish III Corps, though this formation had only one division. South of the line, Marshal Mannerheim commanded 13 divisions and three brigades, plus the German 163rd Division. His forces faced southeast.

Soviet forces opposing the Germans and Finns compromised the following: General Gerasimov commanded the Twenty-Third Army (four divisions) covering the direct approach to Leningrad from the north. General Meretskov commanded the Seventh Army (five divisions) and covered the frontier from Lake Ladoga to Yhta. In the far north was the Fourteenth Army (five division, including one armoured) covering the approaches to Murmansk and the White Sea. And on the Gulf of Finland was the Russian base of Hanko, which had a garrison of 27,000 men and which could not be ignored.

The nature of the theatre's terrain dominated military considerations. In von Falkenhorst's sector, who had basically three routes across the border, it affected supply and communications. First, along the coast of the Arctic Ocean. Second, along the railway from Kemijärvi to Kandalaksha. Third, via the poor road to Louhi and Kem. Communications were better for the Russians, who had the advantage of the Murmansk railway behind their front, with spur lines and roads heading west towards the border.

The chances of success for the Finns and Germans were poor. Not only did the terrain favour defence, the attackers (with a superiority of only three to two) had to divide their forces between three separate sectors which were essentially cut off from one another. The Russians, on the other hand, could concentrate at the vital points to fend off attacks. The result would be frustration all along the line.

▼ One advantage the Finnish Army enjoyed was being commanded by Marshal Mannerheim, who once remarked: "I must be cautious, because the Finnish Army is so small, the theatre of war so gigantic, and the losses suffered thus far are so high."

▲ **German ski troops of General Eduard Dietl's Gebirgs Corps in the wastes of northern Norway. The Germans found that operations in the far north were best conducted by small units, as every piece of equipment had to be carried.**

▼ **In many ways the terrain north of the Arctic Circle was unsuited to a mechanized formation like the German Army. No German tanks or self-propelled guns were used north of the Arctic Circle. The Germans did employ unusual tactics, though, such as using seismological instruments to detect Red Army night-time patrols.**

Dietl's attack went in on 29 June with three successive advances towards Murmansk. But Soviet command of the sea meant his men failed to capture the Rybachiy Peninsula, and were forced to dig in on the line of the River Litsa in September. XXXVI Corps had more success and cleared the Salla area, but was then held just beyond the 1939 frontier. The Finnish III Corps, attacking on the right, was stopped in early September just short of its first objective – Yhta – while a second attack was blocked near Kestanga in November.

Mannerheim's strategy

Marshal Mannerheim, under pressure to recover the areas ceded by Finland in 1940, intended to advance farther in Soviet Karelia up to the line of the River Svir-Lake Onega-Lake Segozero to form a deep buffer zone which would have a short, and defensible, front. Having been informed by his allies that Army Group North would capture Leningrad and link up with his troops on the River Svir, he decided to attack north of Lake Ladoga (his resources would only allow an attack on one sector at a time), and thus on 28 June he formed the Karelian Army under General Heinrichs. This was in accordance with German requests and his own wish not to approach Leningrad until the Germans were much closer.

His plan was to drive down to Lake Ladoga from the northwest to pin Russian units against the lake, allowing his forces to clear the area north of it up to the 1939 frontier. The attack opened on 10 July. The Finns, enjoying a superiority of two to one and aided by the mistaken Soviet tactic of stubbornly clinging to frontier defences and thereby inviting their flanks to be turned (there were no reserves to plug gaps in the line) reached Lake Ladoga on 16 July and advanced southeast. The Soviet front had been split in two.

Russian units put up their usual dogged resistance, but were pushed back steadily against

▲ Finnish troops on the Mannerheim line drag an antitank gun into position. This defensive line was constructed before the Winter War, and consisted of a lightly defended forward area along the border, behind which were two belts of field fortifications, minefields and barbed wire, all linked to rivers and lakes.

the lake. An attempt to relieve them by a fresh Russian division coming up from the Karelian isthmus failed at the end of July. By 7 August parts of two Russian divisions were trapped, and seven days later three Finnish divisions moved in for the kill. But this was not to be a battle of annihilation like the ones waged to the south of Leningrad. The Soviets were able to extract their men by boat – proof that the Finnish Army was not the Wehrmacht.

The Karelian Army also performed poorly, notwithstanding the involvement of the German 163rd Division. By the end of July it had been halted, less than halfway to its objectives. Again the Soviets fought a skillful campaign, which they kept up right through August. On 25 August, the Finns launched a final drive, involving a brilliant flank march through the wilderness and reached Mannerheim's stop-line by 1 September. The Russians proved the importance they attached to this sector by their first use on this front of T-34 tanks, against which the Finnish antitank guns were useless. The Karelian Army now had a few days in which to prepare the second stage of its advance.

The T-34 has, since the end of World War II, entered military legend. Excellent though its design was, its use during 1941 is shrouded in myth. The tank became available to Red Army units in late 1940, however due to poor training (T-34 crews were trained on outdated T-26s) and a lack of trained mechanics it had less effect on the conduct of the campaign than many commentators would have us believe.

At the beginning of the war, Soviet factories had built a total of 1225 T-34s. However, there is no evidence to suggest that all these vehicles

▲ A Messerschmitt Me 109 supplied to the Finnish Air Force. By providing such aid, Hitler hoped that the Finns would become staunch allies and willing participants in Barbarossa. In the event, Helsinki had no interest in taking part in an ideological crusade, and effectively halted military operations once Finnish aims had been met.

were deployed to fighting units. By 1 June, the Leningrad, Baltic Special, Western Special, Kiev Special and Odessa Special Districts had 832 T-34s between them. Some 68 more were in the rear military districts – Moscow, Kharkov and Orel. In the Baltic, only III Mechanized Corps had the vehicle, and it only had 50 in January 1941. It is a sobering assessment that in the western military districts, of the total Soviet tank force of 12,782 vehicles, only 7.5 percent were T-34s.

When hostilities broke out on 22 June, most T-34s were deployed poorly (far from the front), and there was a shortage of crews and spares. When mechanized corps began their drives to meet the German panzers, the inexperienced crews produced many broken gearboxes and burnt-out clutches. Tanks couldn't be repaired on the spot, and there was a general lack of recovery vehicles. To make matters worse, it often required two or three tractors to tow one T-34. Nevertheless, when it did appear in combat, the T-34 caused a scare, especially when Axis antitank rounds bounced off its hull.

While some of his troops were fleeing from the Soviet tank, Mannerheim focused on cutting Soviet communications with Leningrad. He intended to do this by an attack north of the River Vuoksi and a second assault on Viipuri, He would use his heavy artillery for each attack, as the Russians were strongly dug in.

The attack started on 31 July with two Finnish divisions with powerful artillery support, followed by a third division on 4 August. This resulted in the Soviet 198th and 142nd Divisions being trapped against Lake Ladoga. A counterattack to relieve the two Russian divisions was defeated on 11 August, and Finnish forces then swept forward to the Vuoksi and formed a bridgehead at Vuosalmi. Despite the whole north bank being cleared by 23 August, the Soviets were able to evacuate their trapped force around the lake by boat.

The attack against Viipuri was to begin on 22 August, but it was anticipated by the

Russians, who began to withdraw, apparently intending to abandon the city due to the threat from the direction of Vuosalmi. But when the Finns attacked on 23 August, two Soviet divisions were launched against them and the retreat from Viipuri was halted. It took two days of fighting to defeat the Russian attacks and resume the advance, but by 27 August the Finns had cut the main road and railway to Leningrad, effectively trapping three Russian divisions.

But Mannerheim didn't want to approach the city; instead, he directed three divisions to advance to the 1939 frontier. The Red Army saw its chance. Launching a counterattack on 29 August, two of the trapped Soviet divisions escaped, and most of the others reached Koivisto island, and were later evacuated by sea. Nevertheless, Red Army units in this sector had lost most of their equipment and were thoroughly disorganized.

The Finns followed without meeting much organized resistance, to be halted by Mannerheim just in front of the pre-1939 fortifications of Leningrad. The Finnish troops had reached all of their objectives by 9 September. The previous day, the Germans had cut Leningrad off by land when they captured Schlüsselburg, to the extreme south of Lake Ladoga. Total victory seemed to be at hand.

On 22 August, OKW requested Mannerheim to attack Leningrad by thrusting down behind the city to link up with the Germans on the River Neva. Mannerheim procrastinated until 27 August, when he launched nothing more than light attacks in front of Leningrad. He did, though, express a willingness to renew the attack north of Lake Ladoga to link up with the Germans on the River Svir. Stating that the Finnish people had no wish to take part

▼ Troops and transport of Army Group North advance towards Leningrad. Berlin hoped that the city would be crushed between the two pincers of von Leeb and the Karelian Army, but by 1 September 1941 the latter had halted in front of Leningrad's defences – it would advance no farther for the rest of the war.

◀ German troops in the Salla area, where German divisions suffered many losses in 1941. As a result morale plummeted, prompting one German officer to remark: "The German soldier is anxious to leave these never-ending Karelian woods; with half the losses, the Finns will accomplish twice as much here as the Germans."

in an attack on Leningrad, he also reminded the Germans that he lacked the heavy artillery and dive-bombers necessary to break through the fortifications. OKW was mortified, and on 4 September dispatched Field Marshal Wilhelm Keitel, chief of OKW, and General Alfred Jodl, Chief of Staff of OKW, to Mannerheim's headquarters to convince him to make an immediate attack on Leningrad. Mannerheim still refused.

Mannerheim's decision, undoubtedly political, reflected the Finnish people's lack of interest in Leningrad. The Finnish government had no real wish to be a part of Hitler's crusade against Bolshevism: the regaining of territory that had been seized by the Soviets in the Winter War was the ultimate aim of Helsinki.

The Karelian Army, rested and reorganized, resumed its offensive against the Soviet Seventh Army. The Finns concentrated their heavy artillery on the shore of Lake Ladoga, while a motorized force, commanded by Colonel Lagus, waited behind the front. The attack opened on 3 September, and by the 6th Lagus' troops had captured Olonets and reached the River Svir the next day. They cut the Murmansk railway at Lodenoe Pole on the 8th and consolidated their positions around the Svir.

Learning the hard way

To the north, the Finns began their attack along the main railway to Petrozavodsk, the capital of Soviet Karelia, on 2 September. Ten days later they were joined by comrades from the Svir Front, who attacked from the south. The Soviets conducted an orderly withdrawal: evacuating the inhabitants and installations from Petrozavodsk well in advance of the Finnish Army, which didn't take the city until 1 October.

Finnish tactics were initially unsophisticated and involved costly, and unsuccessful, frontal attacks, but eventually they reverted to sending flanking columns through the swamps and forests. The Soviets, having few reserves, had to retreat or face encirclement.

By early October the Finns had cleared the area north of the River Svir, but Mannerheim wanted a substantial bridgehead along its eastern bank. The subsequent fighting to achieve this aim lasted from 6–23 October, when the line was stabilised. By this stage in the campaign all was not well with the Finnish Army. Some Finnish units mutinied and refused to cross the river. Though they were eventually persuaded to resume fighting, it was a sign that the Finnish soldiers saw no point in further advances. This should have come as no surprise to the military hierarchy, which had been sending out the same signals to the Germans.

An interesting footnote to the campaign is the appearance of the Soviet 114th Siberian Division, which required heavy fighting to stop – an ominous foretaste of the later intervention of the Siberians before Moscow.

The remaining task for the Karelian Army was to secure its northern flank along the short line from Maselskaya to Medvezhegorsk, at the top of Lake Onega. However, deteriorating weather, growing battle-weariness, poor communications and stiffening Soviet resistance (the Soviet High Command was rightly concerned about the railway junction at Belomorsk, through which Murmansk was still connected with the interior of Russia and which, increasingly, the Finns seemed to threaten) combined to present the Finnish Army with problems. To make matters worse, the Soviets brought up two fresh infantry divisions.

▲ Well-wrapped German Gebirgsjäger in Finland in 1941 (note the edelweiss badge on the cap). Stick grenades, such as the ones tucked into the belts of these German soldiers, were found to be unsafe in the Arctic – they caught on trees and rocks.

◀ Finnish troops in foxholes. All Finnish troops were well equipped for cold-weather operations, being issued with fur caps featuring ear and neck protectors, warm underwear, woollen scarves, fur gloves and warm footwear. Frostbite was unknown among Finnish troops.

The Finns deployed only one additional division, and in his haste to bring the campaign to an end General Heinrichs decided not to halt for reorganization but to launch an immediate offensive. The result was poorly coordinated and improvised Finnish attacks.

The Finns moved forward slowly throughout late October from the south and the west, enduring many casualties as they progressed. By 7 November, though, they had been stopped in all sectors. A general advance was resumed on 21 November, but not before a number of units had again mutinied or had not pressed their attacks. With this in mind it was amazing that the Finns had reached Maselskaya by the end of November, and that all the approaches to Medvezhegorsk had been cleared. But thereafter the offensive ground to a halt.

The fighting on this sector of the front was not over, though. Following reorganization, the Finns attacked again on 5 December. By this time the weather was extremely cold – so cold that the tank turrets froze immobile – which affected military operations.

The Finns did manage to break through Soviet defences, taking Medvezgehorsk on 6 December and advancing to Povenets to the southeast. Two Soviet divisions were trapped south of Medvezhegorsk, where they were totally destroyed (possibly a deliberate sacrifice by the Soviet High Command to hold up a Finnish advance towards Belomorsk). The Finns had finished mopping up by 12 December and went onto the defensive. In fact, this was their last major offensive of the war.

▼ Axes and saws were essential items for Finnish soldiers. Whenever there was a pause of several days, the Finns built barrack-like huts from logs with amazing speed. In addition, Finnish tents were made of plywood and could be heated.

◀ Germans troops fire a 81mm mortar, which the Germans found effective in deep snow. German submachine guns could jam in low temperatures, so Dietl's troops tried to get hold of Russian models. In addition, it was impressed upon troops that strict fire discipline was essential to conserve often scarce ammunition supplies.

Mannerheim had achieved all his original objectives, and thus he ordered his forces to fortify their lines. Having abandoned any notion of a future strategic offensive, he even demobilized some of his troops. His victory had not been bought cheaply: the Finns had lost around 25,000 dead and over 50,000 wounded. Red Army casualties are unknown, but the Finns did take 47,000 prisoners. Mannerheim thought about a further operation against Belomorsk in early 1942, but that is outside the scope of this study, and in any case it came to nothing.

There is no doubt that Finland's lukewarm attitude and limited offensives in the far north frustrated the Germans. However, they could do little about it. The Wehrmacht was fully occupied in the Soviet Union throughout 1941, and therefore had no strategic reserve available to reinforce the Finnish war effort (or provide physical coercion if Helsinki continued to dither). There were also no other sanctions Berlin could use to enforce its wishes. In effect, Finland was de facto free to chose its own course in the war. And she showed clearly she was not interested in assaulting the city of Leningrad, or of participating in its reduction by a process of starvation and terror.

▶ T-34 tanks on the way to the front in Leningrad. Finnish reluctance to take part in a direct assault against the city disappointed Berlin, and made Army Group North's task more difficult. It also contributed to Leningrad's ability to hold out, as the Soviets were able to maintain a tenuous lifeline across Lake Ladoga.

First defeat

Army Group South drove into the eastern Ukraine after its victory at Kiev. But von Rundstedt's divisions were suffering from attrition, the weather was getting worse and the Red Army was still fighting. And then came defeat at Rostov.

Despite its great victories at Uman and Kiev, Army Group South was in a weakened state as its divisions pushed east towards Rostov and the Ukraine. Von Kleist's First Panzer Group, for example, was down to only 300 tanks, while von Rundstedt's other formations – the German Sixth, Eleventh and Seventeenth Armies, the Hungarian corps, the three divisions of the Italian Expeditionary Force, and the Slovak Light Division – were in an equally depleted state. Of course Axis morale was high, but as they advanced to conquer the industrial area of the eastern Ukraine, the divisions began to encounter the sapping effects of having to trudge through thick mud as the autumn rain fell. But what of their Red Army opponents?

For the remnants of the Soviet's Southern and Southwestern Fronts, the outlook was grim indeed. They defended a region that produced

▼ A German motorcycle reconnaissance team watches as a Russian village burns. The second stage of Army Group South's conquest of the Ukraine began well when the First Panzer Group smashed its way east from Novomoskovsk in September.

◀ **A German medical company pauses for a rest. The constant fighting produced a never-ending stream of wounded who had to be treated. The 125th Field Hospital, for example, treated a total of 1654 wounded between 23 July and 7 August 1941 alone. Notwithstanding Nazi racial policies, surgeons also treated wounded Russians.**

60 percent of the USSR's coal, 30 percent of its iron and 20 percent of its steel. Of every four electric power stations in the Soviet Union, three were situated in the eastern Ukraine, as was three-fifths of the Soviet rail system, including the main line that transported oil from the Caucasus. It was therefore crucial that this vital region should be held by Soviet troops. At the very least, the Red Army had to buy time – time to evacuate the factories and reorganize the shattered Soviet armies that had suffered so much since the end of June.

The commander of the Soviet Southwestern Front, Marshal Timoshenko, had seven armies with which to hold back Army Group South. He had a daunting task, but at least the German effort was being dissipated by a number of diversions. First, until 16 October, the Fourth Romanian Army was busy besieging Odessa. Second, from the end of September the German Eleventh Army was engaged in invading the Crimea, being joined thereafter by the Romanian Fourth Army following the Soviet evacuation of Odessa.

Von Manstein, the commander of the Eleventh Army, gives the reasons for the Crimean invasion: "One reason for this was the favourable effect the capture of the peninsula was expected to have on the attitude of Turkey. Another even more pressing one was the threat of the enemy's Crimean air bases to the Romanian oil fields, so vital to Germany."

At this stage of the war a Soviet army was much smaller than its German counterpart, and Timoshenko's armies were nowhere near full

▶ **Germans surrender to Red Army soldiers. Being captured was one of the greatest fears among German soldiers, especially after advancing German units in the first weeks of Barbarossa had discovered the mutilated corpses of German soldiers captured by the Russians.**

▲ **Once again the Luftwaffe air protection proved invaluable in aiding ground units, particularly the Junkers Ju 88, which could operate as a dive-bomber, fighter and reconnaissance aircraft.**

▼ **German troops examine what appears to be the upside-down turret of a T-34 tank lying in a river. The autumn rains had already begun to fall, swelling rivers and creating large areas of mud, when von Rundstedt's offensive opened on 1 September.**

strength. In the middle of July 1941, *Stavka* reorganized its field forces, which included creating smaller field armies composed of five or six rifle divisions plus one or two tank brigades, one or two light cavalry divisions and several attached artillery regiments. Timoshenko's armies were well below these figures. General Feklenko's Thirty-Eighth Army, for example, had two infantry divisions, a tank division and an ad hoc regiment of 7000 men. One of the infantry divisions had barely a third of its authorized strength – and only four field guns – while the tank division had just one tank (authorized strength around 250 tanks)! Most of Timoshenko's other armies were in a similar state.

The German plan for the conquest of the eastern Ukraine was simple. The First Panzer Group would break out of its bridgehead on the Dnieper and Samara Rivers between Dnepropetrovsk and Novomoskovsk, then drive south towards the shore of the Sea of Azov. In this operation of encirclement, the Soviet Ninth, Twelfth and Eighteenth Armies, which made up the Southern Front, would be surrounded and then annihilated. It was a bold plan, especially

so given the time of the year and the autumn rains. Nevertheless, if von Kleist's 300 tanks could reach the sea – a 192km (120-mile) dash – they would link up with the Eleventh Army and trap 100,000 Soviet troops.

Stavka had no time to organize a defensive belt, as on 30 September the First Panzer Group dashed from its bridgehead at Novomoskovsk and headed for the main Soviet lateral supply route: the Kharkov–Zaporozhye railway. Despite the efforts of an armoured train, the line – the only all-weather route by which Soviet troops, supplies and equipment could be transferred quickly between the various sections of the front – was reached and cut by 1 October. Lieutenant-General Cherevichenko, the commander of the Southern Front, was a worried man. However, the autumn rains had already begun, which would slow the movement of each side.

As far as von Kleist was concerned it was business as usual. The right wing of the Soviet Twelfth Army had been shattered, and now the coast beckoned. However, on 5 October

▲ A Pak 38 antitank gun engages Russian tanks on the open steppe. Introduced in 1941 to replace the inadequate 37mm gun, in the panzer divisions it provided flank defence. It had a muzzle velocity of 1200m/sec (3940ft/sec) and could penetrate 56mm (2.2in) of sloped armour at a range of 914m (3000ft).

Cherevichenko swung his whole line 45 degrees to the east, pivoting on the coast, and presenting a new front to the Germans. He abandoned Zaporozhye, but his tactic at least offered a hope of halting the panzers. It was a good idea, but it came too late.

The German panzers broke through the Twelfth and Eighteenth Armies as they were attempting to establish the new line. Then, on 6 October, von Kleist's forward elements linked up with von Manstein's Eleventh Army, thus trapping the Soviet Ninth and Eighteenth Armies between Orekhov and the small port of Osipenko. The battered Soviet Twelfth Army

▲ **German troops on the outskirts of Kharkov in October 1941. Trapped between the Sixth and Seventeenth Armies, the city was encircled by the 24th. The Soviets had already shipped Kharkov's tank engine plant east to prevent its capture.**

▼ **German troops in Kharkov at the end of October 1941. The city fell relatively easily to the Sixth Army of Army Group South due to the inadequate state of Red Army units defending it, which were withdrawn to prevent their annihilation.**

managed to retreat to the north. For their trapped comrades, however, their was no escape.

Soviet resistance in the pocket was its usual fierce self, but in view of the loss of leadership (the commander of the Ninth Army, Major-General F.M. Kharitonov, had been evacuated by air, while the commander of the Eighteenth, Lieutenant-General Mirnov, had been killed while attempting to escape the pocket) it was uncoordinated. Some of the Ninth Army's right flank units managed to fight their way out and part of the Eighteenth Army was able to blast a corridor through to Donetsk. But when the pocket had been reduced the Germans had taken 212 tanks, nearly 700 guns and 106,000 prisoners. The Eleventh Army was sent south to invade the Crimea, leaving the First Panzer Group to continue the advance on Rostov.

The Germans believed that they had destroyed four Soviet armies, but in fact the Sixth and Twelfth Armies, though they had been mauled, were far from being finished. In addition, the pocket at Orekhov had not been watertight, and some Soviet formations had escaped and were now reforming.

In particular, the "destroyed" Ninth Army was rapidly reconstituting itself, absorbing reinforcements of infantry and cavalry and settling down to block the approaches to Rostov. Even more ominous for the Germans was that *Stavka* was no longer desperately plugging gaps. It was trading space for time and planning an eventual counteroffensive.

Stavka, seeing the danger in the south, ordered a withdrawal to a shorter line, thereby releasing 10 infantry divisions and two cavalry corps into the reserve. At the end of October 1941 they formed the cadre of a new army – the Thirty-Seventh – deployed around Krasnodon, northeast of Rostov. Its mission was to launch a counterattack into the flanks of any German force attempting to encircle Rostov.

To the north, the three armies of the Soviet Southwestern Front deployed ahead of Kharkov – Twenty-First, Thirty-Eighth and Fortieth – were in a weakened state. The Red Army in this sector was scraping the barrel. At Dergachi, north of Kharkov, for example, a regiment was formed from lieutenants and political officers who had been attending courses. It had one rifle for every two or three men, and its total heavy

▲ As German troops consolidated their position in Kharkov, *Stavka* realized that its defence west of the city had been a failure, notwithstanding a massive mine-laying operation that had been undertaken.

▼ The German occupation of Kharkov. By the end of October 1941, the Donbas – the "Soviet Ruhr" – had been overrun despite some desperate measures, which included the mobilization of 100,000 Soviet miners to fight the Germans.

◀ A German mortar crew in action. The Germans developed no less than 12 types of mortar ammunition during the war, including high-explosive rounds, target markers and smoke-producing bombs. Wehrmacht mortar crews were well trained and quickly gained a reputation for accuracy and a high rate of fire.

▼ An infantry section watches Stuka dive-bombers reduce a Red Army position. The soldier second from the left carries the 7.92mm PzB 39 antitank rifle. By 1941 this weapon, which could penetrate only 25mm (.98in) of armour, was obsolete, and could only knock out lightly armoured or soft-skimmed vehicles.

equipment was four field guns and six mortars. Hundreds of thousands of weapons had been lost in the battle of the frontiers in June, and so the Soviets had to disarm transport and supply troops in order to issue their weapons to the infantry. This made the unarmed rear service personnel extremely apprehensive whenever the Germans were reported as being nearby.

The citizens of Kharkov responded marvellously to the impending danger: 90,000 of them volunteered for the militia. But no amount of enthusiasm could make up the desperate shortages being experienced: the supply of rifles, for example, was bolstered by scouring the battlefields and taking them from dead soldiers.

The German Sixth and Seventeenth Armies were advancing, but their units were feeling the effects of struggling through the mud. As an artilleryman noted: "Overnight we sank into mud, we could not move forward, and we also lost contact with the enemy. The vehicles were stuck fast, the wheeled guns were pulled out of the mud by our artillerymen with difficulty, and they were covered in mud up to the ammo boxes. A few days later, a cold wave struck overnight, and it chilled everything. With difficulty, we overcame this new inconvenience. We didn't move any faster than before – we crawled. This is the way it went, day in, day out."

▲ A German infantry section rests during the advance towards Rostov. As the autumn unfolded, infantry divisions found that the wet and muddy weather took a heavy toll on uniforms, which became matted and then fell apart. In addition, rain and mud got into the working parts of small arms, rendering them useless.

Von Rundstedt wanted to bypass large towns, as he had done at Uman and Kiev, and then encircle them. However, his panzer group was in the south, and there were no tanks to encircle Kharkov. However, he believed that he could still entice the Red Army to give up the city. He ordered the left wing of the Seventeenth Army to seize a bridgehead over the River Uda, only 8km (five miles) south of the city, while the Sixth Army pushed units to the north and south of Kharkov. Stalin, realizing the futility of trying to hold the city with the meagre forces available, issued orders for the main forces to pull out of Kharkov. Von Rundstedt had his victory, but when the German Sixth Army entered the city on 24 October they captured very few prisoners.

▼ An MG 34 machine-gun team in action east of the Dnieper. In the autumn of 1941, many German troops went without rations for days as the mud made the transportation of supplies problematic. Priority was given to ammunition, which was needed in massive quantities. The MG 34, for example, could fire up to 900 rounds a minute.

▲ Typical scene in the Ukraine in the autumn of 1941. The Soviet scorched earth policy, combined with German bombing and artillery, reduced many Russian towns and cities to rubble. The fate of the inhabitants concerned neither Stalin (Soviet collectivization in the 1930s killed an estimated seven million Ukrainians) nor OKH.

The Red Army had learned its lesson, it seemed, and it retreated in good order as the German divisions followed.

The First Panzer Army (the First Panzer Group renamed) was making steady progress against the Soviet Southern Front: the weather was fine and the panzers were achieving relatively fast speeds. However, the speed was much less than the heady days of June and July. There were two reasons for this. First, von Rundstedt had been careful to preserve his panzer strength, as armoured-warfare expert Kenneth Macksey states: "Among the military virtues practised by the Germans in all their earlier campaigns, was the discipline of minimizing casualties: where opposition was likely to be heavy they were reluctant to follow – the more so as they increasingly realized that Russian resistance might be a force beyond their strength. Rundstedt would not permit panzer divisions to charge into Kiev or into the Pripet Marshes. Instead he kept his mechanized forces moving freely in the plains where they dominated."

The second reason for the slowing pace was the change in Soviet tactics. The Soviet Ninth Army, responsible for the protection of Rostov, constructed four belts of defences, one behind the other. These belts utilized interlocking fields of fire between each strongpoint. Prepared dug-outs protected the crews of field, antitank and machine guns. In addition, large numbers of dummy dug-outs were constructed to confuse German artillery spotters. The field fortifications themselves had been constructed to allow a 180-degree gun traverse, and there were also alternative positions to which the guns could be moved quickly if necessary.

The Soviets had made use of the civilian population (including women and children) to create these defences. Infantry trenches were very narrow so they would not collapse when

▲ The German Army enters Rostov. This was no easy mopping-up operation, but rather a costly frontal assault, in which fierce street battles were the order of the day. The heavy assault on the city by III Panzer Corps was preceded by the first prolonged and heavy snowfall of the winter – a foretaste of things to come.

panzers passed over them. The occupants would then be free to deal with the follow-on German infantry (interestingly, these same tactics were used by the Germans when they had lost the strategic initiative after 1943).

Additional antitank defences including tank traps were dug, though the shortage of land mines made complete mining of approach roads impossible, but all road junctions were mined. The Red Army tended to favour wooden-box mines, which could not be detected by standard mine detectors.

▶ "We are working our way forward from the end of the bridge and firing at the fleeing Russian trucks. In the middle of all this, a railroad train bursts out of the city. It is full of Russians and equipment. We immediately open fire on the locomotive." (Waffen-SS soldier fighting in Rostov, November 1941)

Each of the four defensive systems had a depth of 2.4km (1.5 miles), with excellent fields of fire in front of each zone. The distance from the front of the Ninth Army's to the rear was nearly 80km (50 miles), which included the fortified town of Novoshakhtinsk to the northeast, where army headquarters was set up.

Rostov itself was extensively booby trapped, with explosive charges attached to abandoned vehicles, field kitchens, tombstones, doors, windows, stoves and even corpses (following fighting). Pressure mines were laid under stairs and floors. In addition, the Soviets made use of radio-controlled mines to blow up entire blocks of houses as soon as anyone entered.

The assault on Rostov

When the First Panzer Army's offensive towards Rostov began on 1 November, the Soviets' Ninth Army had finished only three of the four defensive belts around the city. However, assisted by the poor state of the roads, these defences proved effective. As a result the battle developed into a slogging match fought in mud and ice. It was not until 12 November that the First Panzer Army was able to report a daily advance of as much as 8km (five miles).

On the 14th the Germans reached the south bank of the River Tuzlov, near the coast, which did not fall within the Ninth Army's defence

area, but was being held by the hastily raised Fifty-Sixth Independent Army. This scratch force presented no major problems, but von Rundstedt had to call a two-day halt to the main attack on Rostov (an outflanking blow to envelop the city from the north). His northern flank force was beginning to appreciate the presence of the Thirty-Seventh Army, which, as mentioned above, was being assembled north and northeast of the city. Timoshenko had at his disposal 22 rifle divisions, nine cavalry division and five tank brigades available for his defence of Rostov. Even so, each of these units was understrength.

German units by this time were also suffering from the strains of continuous combat and fighting in deteriorating weather conditions. Frontline units were suffering from dysentery, bronchitis and other lung infections. Among infantry divisions, there was a shortage of marching boots, which had literally been worn out during the course of tramping across 1600km (1000 miles) of Russian terrain. Service personnel in rear areas were contracting typhus, though frontline troops also caught it, especially when they occupied captured enemy positions and then slept on the lice-infested straw they found in the dug-outs and other shelters.

The evacuation of wounded German soldiers was also a major problem in the adverse weather conditions. It took hours for a four-man stretcher team to carry serious cases through knee-deep mud to medical aid stations. Further evacuation by ambulances to hospitals could take just as long – one 48km (30-mile) trip could take 6–8 hours – and so many ambulances broke down that wounded had to be transported in trucks.

▼ German soldiers keeping watch for Red Army units near Rostov. The German soldier on the left carries a Flammenwerfer klein verbessert 40 flame-thrower. Its distinctive doughnut-shaped tanks can be seen clearly. It weighed 21kg (47lb), making it easily manportable, though at a cost of reduced fuel capacity.

▲ When the fighting in Rostov was over, III Panzer Corps' "Order of the Day" listed 10,000 prisoners, 159 artillery pieces, 56 tanks and two armoured trains captured. It was a fair haul, though far short of the great victories of July and August. Nor was it a complete victory, for the Red Army was about to launch a counterattack.

Von Rundstedt was forced to amend his plan. He ordered a covering force to be left behind to guard against a Soviet counterattack by the Thirty-Seventh Army, and regrouped the First Panzer Army on the River Tuzlov, opposite the Fifty-Sixth Independent Army. For this attack Army Group South was forced to undertake a frontal assault. The spearhead of the assault would be General von Mackensen's III Panzer Corps (the 13th and 14th Panzer Divisions, 60th Motorized Infantry Division and the SS *Leibstandarte* Motorized Division).

The offensive began on 17 November. The weather was poor – snow covered the landscape and a numbing blizzard was blowing – but despite this the German troops carried out the offensive with efficiency. The northern edges of Rostov were reached after only two days of fighting. However, on the very day that the coastal offensive began, the troops left behind to guard the northern axis reported that they were under attack – Timoshenko's offensive had begun.

The Soviet Thirty-Seventh Army had been ordered forward – now the Germans were forced to face an enemy attack prepared and launched after adequate advance planning, rather than mounted as a desperate attempt to stave off impending disaster. That said, as usual Soviet formations were denied adequate air cover and were rather slow in getting off the mark. Interestingly, Major-General von Mellenthin, a panzer commander on both the Western and the Eastern Fronts, believed that air power was not a decisive factor on the Eastern Front: "In the western campaigns of 1940 and 1944–45 air power had a great effect on the armoured battle, but on the vast plains of Russia, tank armies were the main instrument of victory. Air support could only be secured locally and for restricted periods and never attained the degree of efficiency achieved in the western theatre by the Germans in 1940 and by the Anglo-Americans in 1944–45."

As Red Army troops poured into Rostov from the west, the First Panzer Army continued to push into Rostov. A member of the *Leibstandarte* Division described the scene in the city: "The city is in uproar, numerous tracks of fleeing Russians, vehicles, horses, civilians and a great confusion. All leading in the direction of the Don bridges. Russians on foot with guns are still posted in front of public buildings. The enemy doesn't realize that soon we will be at the bridges." But on the 19th, even while they were clearing its northern suburbs, the SS *Wiking* Division (which had started the campaign as part of the First Panzer Group) began to give ground to the northeast. On the 21st Rostov fell to III Panzer Corps, but its defensive screen to the north was falling back. A dangerous gap had opened between the First Panzer and the Seventeenth Armies. Timoshenko was determined to exploit it to surround and then annihilate III Panzer Corps.

Elements of the Thirty-Seventh Army were joined in the attack by parts of the Ninth Army. These formations were already nearing the Tuzlov line, threatening the German flank and rear. The Germans, having lost the initiative on their northern and northeastern flanks, could not break out in those directions. A breakout to the south of Rostov was also out of the question, since all bridges had been destroyed and Fifty-Sixth Independent Army was now holding firm.

Could the commander of Southern Front, Cherevichenko, copy von Kleist's earlier manoeuvre and sweep on to the sea and trap the Germans? Both he and *Stavka* believed so. However, at the front the Red Army was still desperately short of mobile formations, and its

▼ Fighting on the outskirts of Rostov. The vehicle on the right appears to be a German sIG33 self-propelled infantry gun mounted on a Panzer I tank chassis. Only a total of 38 of these vehicles had been constructed by February 1940, though it is known that several were still in service in 1943. It was armed with a 150mm gun.

▲ **A German Panzerjäger self-propelled anti-tank gun advances down a burning Rostov street. Armed with a 47mm gun, it first saw service in Belgium in 1940. During Barbarossa the First Panzer Group had in its ranks the 670th Panzerjäger *Abteilung* (Antitank Battalion), which was equipped with these vehicles.**

infantry divisions, especially those of the Ninth Army, were much below strength. It was decided, therefore, to take the safe route and settle for the recapture of Rostov, coupled with a drive along the coast to Taganrog.

Despite their lack of armour and manpower, the Red Army divisions had fought well. A member of the German 297th Infantry Division, XXXXIV Corps, remembered the severe fighting encountered by his unit at this time: "On the same day, the firing positions of the 6th Battery were again occupied. However, soon after, strong Soviet elements again attacked, and artillerymen, who had to defend themselves by firing directly into the attacking Soviets from a distance of 100 metres, had to finally withdraw after destroying their howitzers."

The recapture of Rostov

Soviet counterattack plans around Rostov were quickly made: the Fifty-Sixth Independent Army would attack the southern sector in three groups, while the Thirty-Seventh Army would move in from the northwest, the Ninth Army from the northeast.

On the night of 27/28 November the operation began. A company of the 33rd Motorized Rifle Regiment crossed the frozen Don on the ice to seize a small bridgehead on Theatre Square accompanied by two battalions of the Rostov militia, seizing the cement factory and two adjoining streets. Only light weapons could be brought across – the ice was too thin to bear artillery or tanks – but the bridgeheads were held through the night, and mortar troops crossed over in the morning. Simultaneously, a fierce assault was mounted along the entire Tuzlov line. The First Panzer Army succeeded in holding a corridor open, using all its reserves, and Rostov was hastily abandoned before the Soviet Thirty-Seventh Army had even arrived. For the first time in the East, the panzer divisions held off the enemy to give the rest of the army time to escape.

With Soviet forces pursuing him, von Rundstedt decided to fall back to the more easily defended River Mius, abandoning Taganrog in the process. Knowing Hitler would oppose the withdrawal, he did not bother to notify the High Command until he had set it in motion. As expected Hitler promptly ordered him to cancel the withdrawal and stand fast, whereupon the commander of Army Group South resigned on the spot – Hitler accepted his resignation. Von Reichenau took his place.

For the first time since the beginning of Barbarossa, the Red Army had dictated the course of events in a major battle. The German positions were exposed as the flanks of their forces occupying the industrial area between Kharkov and Rostov were vulnerable to attack from the south. There were wider ramifications of the Rostov victory: Soviet morale among both civilians and the armed forces received a badly needed boost, and in the international arena the saving of the Caucasus had indicated the Soviet ability to at least survive the winter. In addition, with the continued resistance of Sevastopol and the victory at Rostov, Turkey would be less eager to join the Axis camp.

For their part, the Germans were experiencing severe problems on the Eastern Front. On 1 December, OKH issued another assessment of what it believed to be current Red Army strength. It did not make for pleasant reading. Despite the stunning victories of the summer, and that German armies stood before Leningrad and Moscow, OKH estimated that the Germans were faced by 200 infantry divisions, 35 cavalry

▲ The German occupation of Rostov was to be brief. The Soviet counteroffensive began on the night of 27/28 November. After fierce fighting the SS *Leibstandarte* Division was forced out of the city, prompting a general German withdrawal.

▼ "There is no battle line, no outposts, no reserves. Just small groups of us depending upon each other to hold defended points. We have to strip the fallen, theirs and ours, for warm clothing." (Diary of a member of the SS *Leibstandarte* Division)

▲ German troops of the First Panzer Army (the First Panzer Group renamed) pull back westward. Von Rundstedt recognized that he could not hold Rostov. Hitler was furious and accepted von Rundstedt's resignation, replacing him with von Reichenau – who would die of a heart attack on 17 January 1942 while flying to Germany.

divisions and 40 armoured brigades. Elsewhere in the Soviet Union were a further 63 infantry divisions, 6.5 cavalry divisions and 11 armoured brigades. An unknown number of additional divisions was also being formed.

Amazingly, despite the hundreds of thousands of prisoners taken, the Red Army now appeared to be over twice as strong as OKH had estimated it to be on 23 July. Of course, many Red Army units were understrength and lacked experienced leadership and equipment. Nevertheless, OKH was alarmed, the more so since Hitler, as Halder noted, "refuses to take any account of comparative figures of strengths. To him our superiority is proved by the number of prisoners taken".

Von Rundstedt was understandably bitter about his treatment. He stated: "I had previously asked for permission to withdraw this extended spearhead to the River Mius, about 100 kilometres west of Rostov. I was told that I could do this and we began to withdraw very slowly, fighting all the way. Suddenly, an order came to me from the Führer: 'Remain where you are, and retreat no farther,' it said. I immediately wired back: 'It is madness to attempt to hold. In the first place the troops cannot do it, and in the second place if they do not retreat they will be destroyed. I repeat that this order be rescinded or that you find someone else.' That same night the Führer's reply arrived: 'I am acceding to your request,' it read, 'please give up your command.' I then went home."

As soon as he had taken up his new command, von Reichenau, seeing the hopelessness of the situation his troops were in, requested he be allowed to withdraw his divisions – it was granted on 1 December. Halder noted: "We have arrived where we were yesterday evening. Meanwhile we have lost energy and time, and von Rundstedt."

▼ As Army Group South pulled back, its new commander could take stock of its condition. On average, each division had a shortfall of 2000 men (each infantry division had a full strength of 16,854 men), while the First Panzer Army was suffering a total shortage of 20,000 men, 200 tanks and 100 artillery pieces.

The battle for Moscow

Finally, Army Group Centre was allowed to begin the offensive against Moscow. Three panzer groups – a total of 1500 tanks – were earmarked to storm Stalin's capital. But could Moscow be taken before the weather broke?

By superhuman efforts the Soviets had established a defence line in front of Army Group Centre. This comprised a system of deep defences in echelon and in several zones, one behind the other. Although some of these fortifications were still under construction, the Germans would have to smash through them in order to reach Moscow.

German intelligence estimated that six Soviet armies – 55 divisions, under the command of Marshal Timoshenko, with his advanced headquarters at Vyazma – were deployed along the Smolensk–Moscow road. It was also believed that to the south, between Pokshep and Glukhov, General Yeremenko was organizing a new front with three armies of some 30 divisions, while to the rear there were between 10 and 15 reserve divisions.

In fact, Konev had replaced Timoshenko as commander of the Western Front, and the force actually consisted of the Sixteenth, Nineteenth, Twentieth, Twenty-Second, Twenty-Ninth and Thirtieth Armies. Reserves comprised Marshal Budenny's Reserve Front: the Twenty-Fourth, Forty-Third, Thirty-First, Forty-Ninth, Thirty-Second and Thirty-Third Armies. Although seemingly impressive, Konev had only 479 tanks.

The Germans marshalled their forces. At Smolensk, General Hoepner (Fourth Panzer Group) and General Hoth (Third Panzer Group) stood ready. To the south, at Glukhov, was Guderian (Second Panzer Group). The latter would attack from Glukhov via Orel towards Tula. It would have been better if Guderian had been farther north, and thereby closer to Moscow, but his participation in the Kiev encirclement ruled this out.

◀ A Czech-built Panzer 38(t) light tank in Russian mud. The German panzer divisions had fielded a total of 625 of these vehicles when Barbarossa began. The 7th Panzer Division, for example, was equipped with 167 out of a total tank strength of 265. Armed with a 37mm gun, it was no match for the Soviet T-34.

On 24 September, plans were discussed at the headquarters of Army Group Centre at Smolensk. Present were Field Marshal von Bock, army and panzer group commanders, plus the Commander-in-Chief of the Army, von Brauchitsch, and Chief of Staff Halder. Orders were issued two days later.

Von Kluge's Fourth Army and the Fourth Panzer Group would attack along the Roslavl–Moscow road, and General Adolf Strauss' Ninth Army would advance on the north side of the Smolensk–Moscow road. The two armies would then swing in and trap the enemy to the east of Vyazma. To the south, the Second Army would attack north of Bryansk, while the Second Panzer Group would advance northeast, link up with Second Army units and thereby trap enemy units around Bryansk. Guderian would then push on to Tula to secure the flanks of his comrades farther north. Army Group South was ordered to advance in the direction of Oboyan, while units belonging to Army Group North were to move up to the Ostashkov lakes. This was the plan for the capture of Moscow, codenamed Typhoon.

▲ It was unfortunate for the German Army that the winter in European Russia in 1941–42 was particularly severe. These Wehrmacht infantry troops are reasonably well equipped for the winter.

▼ One advantage of winter weather was that it made frozen roads surfaces passable, often better than in summer. A major problem, however, was that the rutted roads were particularly hard on suspension systems, especially springs.

▲ Horses in German use died in their thousands in mud on the road to Moscow. Pulling artillery pieces through mud led to death through overexertion, and shortages in feed led to death through starvation.

▼ In the muddy season, the best vehicles were those with high ground clearance, light weight and low ground pressure. Unfortunately, German trucks, such as these, had low ground clearance.

Army Group Centre mustered 44 infantry divisions, 14 panzer divisions, eight motorized infantry divisions and one cavalry division. In the air, II and VIII Fliegerkorps of Luftflotte II were assigned to support Typhoon.

Von Bock chose 30 September for the attack of the Second Panzer Group, and 2 October for the general attack. But now success depended more on the weather than the fighting ability of the army's divisions.

When Typhoon opened it did so in sunny weather, and five days later the spearheads of the Fourth and Third Panzer Groups trapped large parts of five Soviet armies – Thirtieth, Nineteenth, Twenty-Fourth, Forty-Third and Thirty-Second – in the Vyazma area. Guderian charged towards Orel while diverting some of his panzers to Bryansk. The latter was taken on 6 October, and his men linked up with the Second Army on the 9th. This trapped two more Soviet armies – the Third and Thirteenth – while to the north of Bryansk the encirclement of the Soviet Fiftieth Army began.

Units were not to be wasted in mopping up the pockets – the momentum towards Moscow was to be maintained. Von Bock ordered the Second Panzer Army (the new term for Guderian's command) to take Tula on 7 October, and then drive on to the southern outskirts of Moscow. The Fourth Panzer Group was to strike for Mozhaysk, 96km (60 miles) from Moscow.

It appeared that the Soviet capital would be taken with ease, but then heavy rain set in on 8 October which severely slowed all movement. To the south, moreover, Guderian was engaged in the fighting on both sides of the Bryansk Pocket. This, combined with the weather and fuel shortages, prevented the advance on Tula. The reduction of the Bryansk Pocket ended on 20 October, but once again large numbers of enemy troops escaped into the forests, later to reappear as partisans. More promising for the Germans was the fighting at Vyazma, which ended on 14 October.

The double battle of Vyazma/Bryansk had yielded a rich haul: 673,000 prisoners, 1242 tanks and 5412 artillery pieces. Eight Soviet armies of 86 divisions, 13 of them armoured, had been destroyed.

Hitler became confident that Moscow would at last be conquered. On 12 October, OKW issued the following order: "The Führer has reaffirmed that the surrender of Moscow will not be accepted, even if it is offered by the enemy ... Everyone who tries to leave the city and pass through our positions must be fired upon and driven back ... It would be utterly irresponsible to risk the lives of German soldiers to save Russian towns from fires or to feed their populations at Germany's expense."

▼ "In the autumn of 1941, when frontline troops were already stuck fast, the German High Command still believed that mud could be conquered by main force, an idea that led to serious losses of vehicles and equipment." (General Erhard Rauss, who commanded the 6th Panzer Division and then a panzer army on the Eastern Front)

The Second Panzer and Fourth Armies and the Fourth Panzer Group closed in on Moscow. In the capital the mood was grim: the government and diplomatic corps were evacuated to Kuybeyshev on the Volga on 16 October, though Stalin himself remained in the Kremlin and declared a state of siege three days later.

The second half of October was characterized by thick mud, into which the German Army sank. Roads became almost impassable, and the movements of units were slowed down or brought to a complete standstill. Overnight the amount of fuel being used by German vehicles trebled as they tried to force their way through the quagmires.

Vehicles began to break down and horses died in their hundreds through overwork and starvation. Guns and heavy transport ground to a standstill and the only transport still capable of movement were the tracked recovery vehicles. Guderian wrote: "The roads became nothing more than canals of bottomless mud, along which our vehicles could advance only at a snail's pace and with great wear to the engines ...

▲ The onset of heavy snowfalls brought vehicle columns to a complete halt. In such conditions the Germans were forced to deploy one battalion every 48km (30 miles) for snow-clearance duties. In addition, civilian labour was also used.

▼ The German armies were often lashed by strong winds during the advance to Moscow, causing snowdrifts which blocked all traffic. In such circumstances shovelling was futile, as the roads quickly became covered again.

The next few weeks were dominated by the mud. Wheeled vehicles could advance only with the help of tracked vehicles. These latter, having to perform tasks for which they were not intended, rapidly wore out." The panzer general noted bitterly that Hitler was living in a "world of fantasy" when he talked of fast-moving units.

The whole front ground to a halt. T-34 tanks, appearing in increasing numbers, added to the Germans' woes. Communications were also affected, as reconnaissance vehicles could not report to their headquarters, which made strategic leadership impossible. Reinforcements reached the frontline at a trickle, if they reached it at all. Fuel, which had to be transported to the front by vehicle, began to run out, thereby further diminishing the strike power of the motorized units.

At the end of October 1941, the condition of the German Army in the Soviet Union was grim. The 101 infantry divisions in the East had a fighting strength equivalent to 65 divisions at full strength, while the 17 panzer divisions had been reduced to a fighting strength of the equivalent of six at full strength. Guderian, who had earlier been so enthusiastic about attacking Moscow, argued that his "army" was incapable of achieving its objectives. One of his panzer corps, for example, had only 50 tanks left out of a full establishment of 600!

The onset of the cold weather in November brought even greater hardship to the troops. Guderian again: "The icy cold, the lack of shelter, the shortage of clothing, the heavy losses of men and equipment, the wretched state of our fuel supplies, all this makes the duties of a commander a misery, and the longer it goes on the more I am crushed by the responsibility I have to bear."

▼ As the advance continued the weather got colder. A problem for the Germans was the lack of antifreeze – Glysantin – though even that was inadequate to prevent water in radiators from freezing, and so engines had to be left idling, especially at night.

Requests by frontline officers for winter uniforms and protective clothing for their men came to nothing because there was no transport to move them from rear supply depots, and those railways that were working were earmarked for ammunition and fuel.

The Soviets, on the other hand, were well prepared and equipped to deal with the adverse weather. That said, the Red Army had suffered massive losses and was in a depleted state. It did not yet have the reserves to launch a substantial counterattack. It therefore concentrated on small-scale operations to slow down the weakening German panzers. These often consisted of nothing more than using tank obstacles and other improvised methods.

The advance continued at an agonizing pace. The Fourth Army reached the River Oka at Naro-Fominsk. The Ninth Army, following severe fighting around Kalinin, established a defensive front north of Rzhev and made contact with the southern wing of Army Group North near Ostashkov. But the weather was getting worse every day.

▼ A knocked-out Soviet KV-1 heavy tank. This vehicle spread alarm among German troops in 1941. Impervious to their 37mm antitank guns, many KV-1s simply ran over the German Pak guns, crushing them and their crews. It was armed with a 76.2mm gun and had a crew of five.

▲ **Soviet BT medium tanks west of Moscow in late 1941. Armed with 45mm guns and crewed by three-man teams, their thin armour plating – 22mm (.86in) – meant thousands were knocked out in 1941.**

▼ **A pep talk before the next attack towards Moscow. This photograph is at the start of Typhoon. The snows are yet to come, but the weather is still cold – note the well-wrapped officer giving his speech.**

Von Bock wrote the following in his diary on 25 October: "Resistance on the Fourth Army front is stiffening. The enemy has brought up fresh forces from Siberia and the Caucasus and is making counterattacks on both sides of the roads leading southwest from Moscow. The southern half of the Fourth Army, which has not yet got up most of its artillery because of the mud roads, is forced on to the defensive. On the northern flank of the army, the left wing of the Fourth Panzer Group is making some progress in the direction of Volokolamsk ... Near Kalinin there are new and fierce attacks by the Russians, who on the west side of the city are pushing southeast across the Volga.

"But if one thinks on larger lines, all this is nothing. It is the dispersal of the Army Group and the frightful weather that have brought us to a standstill. The Russian is winning time to reconstitute his shattered divisions and bolster his defences and it is he who controls the railways and roads that centre in Moscow. It all looks very bad."

Despite Guderian's anguish, he pushed his army on, and by 30 October his spearhead approached Tula, but was not strong enough to

◀ **A German MG 34 machine-gun team rushes forward to set up a fire position to cover an infantry advance. The weapon is mounted on a tripod, which gave the MG 34 a theoretical range of 2000m (6600ft). German infantry firepower was built around the MG 34, which the Germans believed was the equivalent of 20 riflemen.**

capture the city. Then his right flank was attacked by enemy cavalry, which were repulsed at Teploye after a battle lasting several days. But reconnaissance revealed more enemy forces were in the area. The Second Army, now switched to the south, had reached Kursk, but the north wing of Army Group South had been held up at Belgorod, creating a gap of 128km (80 miles) in the German frontline.

The critical stage in the offensive had been reached. On the strategic level the Germans had taken the Donbas, Kharkov and threatened both Leningrad and Sevastopol, and their divisions had breached Moscow's first defence line, barely 80km (50 miles) from the city. To get so close and then withdraw was unthinkable (especially for Hitler), so OKH decided to order the attack on Moscow to continue. As von Bock stated: "… the last battalion will decide the issue."

The Red Army digs in its heels

Then, at the beginning of November, the temperature at last dropped below zero, the roads became firmer, allowing vehicles to move. Despite the mud, German fighting strength had diminished, but not catastrophically so: infantry divisions had 65 percent of their original numbers, and the number of tanks had decreased to 35 percent. More importantly, the fighting spirit of the troops was still good, and their endurance was excellent. As long as they were going forward their morale was maintained, notwithstanding the great hardships they were enduring on a daily basis.

The morale of Red Army troops was also holding, no doubt helped by the appointment of Zhukov as the commander of the Western Front. Soviet resistance was stiffening, and counterattacks were increasing in intensity due to the arrival of fresh troops from Siberia and the Caucasus. In and around Moscow, defences were

◀ **These troops are well equipped with winter clothing, but as Typhoon progressed many divisional commanders became concerned about the general inadequate supply of winter clothing. Medical officers found that frontline troops, under enemy pressure, became mentally numbed in extreme cold conditions.**

being constructed – three belts of inner urban defences under the immediate control of the Moscow garrison.

The measures taken to defend the city were suitably Stalinist: 200,000 Muscovites were conscripted, given 28 days of training and then sent to the front; more than 500,000 old men, women and children were mobilized to work on the defences, which eventually consisted of 1400 pillboxes, 96km (60 miles) of antitank ditches and over 8000km (5000 miles) of infantry trenches. *Stavka* issued strict, unequivocal orders that troops "giving up town after

▲ Advancing through a burning village. Note the soldier carrying a box of machine-gun ammunition on the right. During Typhoon supply problems became critical. The 1st Panzer Division of the Third Panzer Group, for example, nearly had to abandon the thrust towards Kalinin due to severe fuel shortages.

▼ A column of panzers during Operation Typhoon. A major shortcoming of German tanks was the narrow width of their tracks, clearly seen here. This, plus their limited ground clearance, meant they sank into the snow and became stuck. After the first winter on the Eastern Front, the Germans began to use wide, removable tracks.

▲ Cossack soldiers on reconnaissance near Moscow. The Soviet authorities made great efforts in the 1930s to break any nationalistic feelings among the Cossacks. However, during Barbarossa Cossack units played an important part in covering the Soviet withdrawal, as well as undertaking valuable reconnaissance duties.

town" would not be tolerated. Stalin also allocated 100,000 men, 300 tanks and 2000 guns to Zhukov to defeat the German offensive.

Von Bock seized the last chance to take Moscow before 1941 ended, perhaps the last chance to take the Soviet capital ever. The Second Panzer Army, under cover of an assault on Tula, was to occupy Kolomna on the Moskva. In addition, it would also have to secure its eastern flank, as the Second Army was too weak to do so. The Fourth Army was to remain on the defensive, though its northern wing, together with the Third and Fourth Panzer Groups, would advance to the Volga canal. The Ninth Army was to advance to the southeast of Kalinin.

Only after these goals had been obtained would the close encirclement of Moscow itself be undertaken. The official start dates for the attacks would be 15 November for the Ninth Army and Third Panzer Group, and 18 November for the Fourth Panzer Group and Second Panzer Army.

The offensive started according to plan, and at first the Blitzkrieg carried all before it. The Third Panzer Group chewed up Rokossovsky's Sixteenth Army north of Moscow. His men fought well, but after one day of fighting the 17th Cavalry Division had only 800 men left (authorized strength over 9240 men). Zhukov tried to hold Klin, northwest of Moscow, with the Sixteenth and Thirtieth Armies, but they were cut to pieces. Klin fell on 24 November, prompting Zhukov to state: "It gets worse from hour to hour." Rokossovsky's regiments were averaging 150–200 men apiece – they should

▶ **Soviet artillery in action near Istra in November 1941. These guns appear to be 152mm Model 1910 field howitzers, which dated back to Tsarist days – anything that could fire was drafted into use.**

have numbered 2700 each. However, overhead at least the Soviet Air Force was more active than the Luftwaffe, which was paralyzed by the cold and fuel shortages.

Attritional effects

Sub-zero temperatures were now sapping the morale of German troops. Machine guns and engines seized up, but still the Germans advanced. Guderian's army tore into the Soviet Fiftieth Army north of Tula, reducing many of its divisions to ghost units. The 108th Tank Division, for example, started the battle with 2000 men and 26 tanks (it should have numbered 11,000 men and 375 tanks at full strength). By the end of the day it had virtually ceased to exist.

◀ **Marshal Georgi Zhukov, who on 10 October 1941 was appointed commander of the Western Front to save Moscow. He then succeeded in halting the German offensive.**

By the end of November, the right wing of the Ninth Army had reached the River Volga between Kalinin and the dam, and the Third Panzer Group, advancing via Klin and Istra, reached the Volga canal south of Dmitrov. On 27 November, the 2nd Panzer Division was only 32km (20 miles) from Moscow. The next day the 7th Panzer Division pushed a bridgehead over the Volga south of Dmitrov, but could go no further in the face of desperate Soviet counterattacks. On 28 November von Bock reported to Halder: "If within a few days they do not force the front northwest of Moscow to collapse, the offensive must be abandoned. It would merely lead to a soulless frontal struggle with an enemy who apparently still has large reserves of men and material."

To the south, the Second Panzer Army, forced to watch its flank, began to run out of steam. Its 8th Panzer Division reached Kashira on 25 November, but remained there for two days as it was attacked relentlessly. Guderian asked for assistance on 27 November from the Fourth Army, which was asked to attack across the River Oka. It was in no position to do so, and instead instructed him to abandon his attack and consolidate his position near Tula. Meanwhile, the Second Army also ground to a halt in the face of resistance.

The last act of Typhoon was played out on the morning of 1 December, when von Kluge launched XX Corps along the Moscow–Minsk highway. Part of the Ninth Army, the corps was at first successful, breaking through the Soviet Thirty-Third Army to a depth of 3.2km (two miles) in the area from Naro to Fominsk. It looked as though a breach could be made between the Thirty-Third and Fifth Armies, but then Zhukov launched a counterattack which halted and then threw back the German divisions with relative ease. Typhoon was over.

The German High Command, recognizing the futility of further offensive action in 1941, approved von Bock's proposal to withdraw both the Third and Fourth Panzer Groups westwards to the Istra-Klin line. The Second Panzer Army was to be pulled back behind the River Don, while the Fourth and Ninth Armies, consisting mainly of infantry divisions, were already in defensive positions.

The attack on Moscow had been a gamble, one that the Germans had lost, and now they had to suffer the repercussions. Their immediate problem was attrition. On 1 December Halder noted the state of the Axis military effort on the Eastern Front: "total losses on the Eastern Front (not counting sick) 743,112 [since 22 June], i.e.

▼ A Panzer III halts on the road to Moscow. The Germans made strenuous efforts to reach the Soviet capital, despite the weather. The 6th Infantry Division, Third Panzer Group, for example, covered over 400km (250 miles) in just over two weeks, despite fierce combat and poor roads.

▲ **In late October 1941 the Germans were only 80km (50 miles) from Moscow. However, as well as stiffening Soviet resistance, units were suffering severe shortages of ammunition, which affected fighting capability. The 1st Panzer Division, for example, had inadequate ammunition to defeat Soviet forces east of Kalinin.**

23.12 percent of the average total strength of 3.2 million ... On the Eastern Front the army is short of 340,000 men, i.e. 50 percent of the fighting strength of the infantry. Companies have a fighting strength of 50–60 men. At home there are only 33,000 men available. Only at most 50 percent of load-carrying vehicles are runners. Time needed for the rehabilitation of an armoured division is six months ... we cannot replace even 50 percent of our motorcycle losses." It is estimated that at this time the Germans had only 75,000 working trucks on the entire Eastern Front.

Stavka realized the German position and took immediate advantage of their success. The German Army was in a dangerously exposed position, with its battle-weary divisions strung out along a vast front and with no reserves to call on. This was bad enough, but the attack against Moscow had left those armies involved in an exposed salient. Moreover, that salient contained the cream of Germany's panzer divisions, albeit much reduced.

The Führer issued his Directive No 39 on 8 December. Though he accepted that the army should go onto the defensive, he stated that areas "of great operational or economic importance to the enemy" were to be held (with what he did not specify). In addition, the soldiers were to be allowed time to rest and recuperate, though only for the next great offensive: "The main body of the Army ... will, as soon as possible, go over to the defensive along a lightly tenable front to be fixed by the Commander-in-Chief of the Army ... Where the front had been withdrawn without being forced by the enemy, rear areas will be established in advance which

▲ Infantry and a Stug III in the last phase of Typhoon, December 1941. Soviet authorities boasted that "Hitler was beaten by mistaken strategy and our heroic resistance." The weather also helped.

▼ At one point in early December the temperature dropped to minus 35 degrees centigrade (minus 61 degrees fahrenheit), causing the breakdown of hundreds of German motor vehicles.

offer troops better living conditions and defensive possibilities than the former positions ... The frontline must be chosen with an eye to easy quartering and defence, and simplification of supply problems." Hitler also talked of establishing conditions "suitable for the resumption of large-scale offensive operations in 1942."

His armies had come to within a few days' march of Moscow by the end of October 1941. If Typhoon had started in good time, the German Army would have probably occupied Moscow, with its comfortable winter quarters for the troops. The supply problem, which now hung by a thread, would certainly have been easier to solve.

Hitler still talked of a fanatical resistance, and that "willpower" could overcome the crisis that the Wehrmacht in the East faced. Those at the front knew differently. Guderian noted: "We had suffered a grievous defeat in the failure to reach the capital which was to be seriously aggravated during the next few weeks thanks to the rigidity of our Supreme Command [Hitler]: despite all our reports, these men far away in East Prussia could form no true concept of the

▶ Frostbite was endemic among German troops near Moscow in late 1941. In one instance, a German company that spent a day during a thaw entrenching itself lost 65 of its 93 men to frostbite as a result of a sudden night frost. The Fourth Army suffered 2000 frostbite casualties alone.

real conditions of the winter war in which their soldiers were engaged. This ignorance led to repeatedly exorbitant demands being made on the fighting troops."

German frontline divisions had enough to contend with with poor supply and the adverse weather. But the Red Army, which for the past six months had been disorganized and on the defensive, was about to launch its own counter-attack against the Wehrmacht. For the tens of thousands of German soldiers shivering in their foxholes, it was going to be a long, hard winter for survival.

▼ Tank losses during Typhoon had been heavy. The 6st Panzer Division had 60 tanks on 16 October; by 1 December the figure was four. Likewise, the tank strengths of the 7th Panzer Division on the same dates were 120 and 36 respectively.

Red blizzard

Having stopped the German Army at the very gates of Moscow, Zhukov hurled his armies against the overstretched and understrength Wehrmacht and saved the Soviet capital – but then Stalin insisted on a widening of the offensive.

▲ **In the extreme cold German soldiers found it difficult to use their rifles. When they tried to shoot, bolt mechanisms would become jammed, strikers shattered and recoil liquid froze inside the guns.**

In Moscow the people trembled with fear as Hitler's armies had approached the Soviet capital. Stalin remained in the city, from which local trains travelled out to the outskirts carrying the *opolchenie* (home guards) units – civilians from city blocks and factories, men poorly trained and even worse equipped. At the front they were given a brief talk on tactics, a rifle or a few "Molotov cocktails" (in reality nothing more than bottles of petrol with a flaming rag attached).

In mid-November, Stalin telephoned General Georgi Zhukov (commander of Western Front) and asked him: "Do you think we can hold Moscow?" Zhukov thought so, provided he was given two fresh armies and 200 tanks. The armies would be forthcoming – the First Shock Army in the north at Yakharoma, the Tenth Army with its 80,000 men in the south at Ryazan – but Stalin had no tanks to spare.

The Germans were suffering supply shortages because of the poor quality of the roads and the unsuitability of many of their trucks. The Red Army was experiencing shortages because of the number of factories that had either been lost to the enemy or were in the process of being shipped farther east. The output of artillery ammunition plummeted down to a little over three million shells in November 1941 – a consequence of 303 munitions plants being out of commission. The coal mines of the Donbas region and the Moscow basin were gone, resulting in the loss of two-thirds of Soviet coal production, and three-quarters of Soviet iron and manganese production. In addition, less than

▲ **The Spanish Blue Division in retreat in December 1941. The Spanish dictator Franco sent 18,000 volunteers to fight in the "crusade against Bolshevism" in Russia. It became the 250th Infantry Division.**

▼ **Cossack cavalry in the rear of Army Group Centre's lines in late December 1941. It was cavalry units that spearheaded the counteroffensive in the winter of 1941–42, driving deep into German lines.**

half the steel and only one-third of the pig-iron produced in June 1941 was being turned out as the year neared its end.

With the loss of the plants and factories throughout the western and southern Soviet Union went a reduction in Soviet industrial manpower. In November 1941, for example, the number was just under 20 million; it had been 31 million in 1940. Many workers had been captured by the advancing German armies, but most were still on the move to the east.

Soviet losses up to November 1941

By November 1941, the Wehrmacht on the Eastern Front had conquered around 35 million Soviet citizens and, equally as damaging, the second most important component of the USSR, the Ukraine.

By the beginning of December 1941, though, there was a glimmer of hope. Reinforced by men and tanks from the Far Eastern Front as a result of intelligence received from the spy Richard Sorge in Tokyo that the Japanese would not attack the Russians in Mongolia, Zhukov was able to build up his forces. These reinforcements arrived from October 1941 onwards, and totalled 18 divisions, 1700 tanks and 1500 aircraft. To the south Marshal Timoshenko with Lopatin's

▲ Among the vehicles the Germans began to receive as replacements at the front was the Panzer III armed with the long-barrelled 50mm gun. Unfortunately, it was of little use in a frontal engagement with a T-34.

Thirty-Seventh Army and Kharitonov's Ninth Army had forced the Germans out of Rostov. At Tikhvin in the northwest, a number of Soviet rifle battalions supported by T-34 tanks had retaken the ruins, which was all that remained of Tikhvin, and had then pushed German units back to the Volkhov. It was a small but crucial victory, for it prevented the encirclement of Leningrad by the link-up of German and Finnish forces to the east of the city.

The Soviet counterattack before Moscow began on 5–6 December 1941 across a front stretching from Kalinin in the north to Yelets in the south, a distance of 800km (500 miles). Zhukov unleashed the armies of the Kalinin, Western and Southwestern Fronts. The Red Army caught the freezing soldiers of the Wehrmacht by surprise, and individual units struggled to survive. At Klin, for example, the 3rd Panzer Division had only one icy road as an escape route, and that was soon packed with German wounded and heavy equipment. Soviet troops closed in on Klin and Kalinin on 13 December, but the 3rd Panzer Division managed to escape – just. Thus did the Red Army remove the northern threat to Moscow.

Guderian's Second Panzer Army to the south was a tempting target, and so Zhukov launched the Tenth, Forty-Ninth and Fiftieth Armies against it. Soviet divisions struck to the northwest, north and northeast of Tula, while Lieutenant-General Golikov's Tenth Army threatened German escape routes.

The Soviet advance continued until the middle of December, against Kalinin, Klin, Istra and Yelets. Nevertheless, Soviet resources were stretched, however much German commanders felt that they were up against an endless flood of men and machines. Zhukov's three central armies – the Thirty-Third, Forty-Third and Forty-Ninth – had been stripped of every available man for the desperate flank offensives against the Wehrmacht during the defensive fighting in November, and now, with counterattacks being launched to the north and south, they were once again at the bottom of the list for reinforcements. Ammunition and fuel were in short supply, while mechanized and tank units – the spearheads of Zhukov's offensive – were critically short of both tanks and lorries.

Zhukov had called for a "non-stop offensive" to break into the German rear with all possible speed. There were to be no frontal attacks on German rearguards and strongpoints; these were bypassed or outflanked. Zhukov's aim was to smash the German Army Group Centre, but Stalin, buoyed up by the victories in front of Moscow, was already thinking about destroying Army Groups North, Centre and South. To this end, Andrei Zhdanv, commander of the newly created Volkhov Front (under General Meretskov) and two army commanders (Twenty-Sixth and Fifty-Ninth Armies) were summoned to *Stavka* to consider the breaking of the Leningrad blockade. The Fifty-Fourth Army (Leningrad Front) would move from the southern shore of Lake Ladoga to link up with the Fourth Army of Volkhov Front. Simultaneously, the right flank of Northwestern Front would sweep round the lower shore of Lake Ilmen through Staraya Russa and Soltsy and then drive north towards Luga, and the left flank of the Volkhov Front would make for Novgorod. Army Group North would then be annihilated.

The Kalinin and Western Fronts would destroy Army Group Centre, but they would receive assistance from the north. On 17 December, the Volkhov Front was informed that its left flank would attack into the deep rear of Army Group Centre, through Toropets and on

▼ "Many men who had become separated from their units marched westward singly or in groups and, when apprehended, freely admitted that their destination was Germany because the 'war is over'. These men were turned over to the nearest combat unit for rehabilitation." (General Erhard Rauss)

to west of Smolensk. The Southern and Southwestern Fronts would liberate the Donbas region, while the Caucasus Front, supported by the Black Sea Fleet, would relieve Sevastopol and clear the whole of the Crimea.

Unfortunately for the Red Army, Stalin had wildly overestimated its own capabilities. The December counteroffensive which stopped the Germans in front of Moscow was a superb achievement. However, even against an overstretched Wehrmacht Stalin did not have the means to recover all the territory that the Germans had taken since June 1941.

At a full meeting of *Stavka* on 5 January 1942, Stalin formally laid out his plans for an "all-out" attack using nine Soviet fronts against all three German army groups. Zhukov was unhappy. Though Army Group Centre was in some disarray, in the south and around Leningrad the Red Army would come up against well-prepared defences and intact enemy units.

But Stalin had decided. He was supported by Marshal Timoshenko, Beria, head of the NKVD, and Georgi Malenkov, a member of the Committee of the Defence of the State (GOKO) and a close associate of the Soviet dictator. The new offensive began on 7 January.

▲ T-34 tanks in the attack. The only German weapons that could knock out these tanks at long range were Panzer IVs armed with 75mm guns and 88mm Flak guns, both of which were in short supply in Army Group Centre.

At first all went well: the Eleventh Army, Northwestern Front, swept round the southern edge of Lake Ilmen, bypassed the German strongpoint of Staraya Russa and thrusted northwards. The Volkhov Front advanced the same day, but it had great difficulty in moving up both men and supplies: the divisions had only 25 percent of food, fuel and ammunition.

Two so-called "shock armies" – Lieutenant-General Purkayev's Third and Colonel-General Yeremenko's Fourth – attacked on 9 January. The latter was ordered to undertake a deep advance into Army Group Centre's rear. It had the resources to carry out this mission: eight rifle divisions, three rifle brigades, plus tank, artillery and *Katyusha* multiple rocket launcher units. It says much for Red Army resources that the Fourth Shock Army was to replenish its rations when it captured the German base at Toropets! The Third Shock Army made good progress until it encountered stiff German resistance at Kholm. Yeremenko continued to strike southwest, reaching Demidov, less than 160km (100 miles) from Smolensk.

Konev's Kalinin Front attempted to envelop the German Ninth Army between the Rzhev and Vyazma line. Having torn a hole in the German front, the Soviet Marshal sent XI Cavalry Corps into the gap. To the south, Zhukov also headed for Vyazma, feeding units into the "Kaluga gap" between the Second Panzer Army and the Fourth Army. All along the line it was a tale of success: the Tenth Army had encircled the German garrison at Sukhinichi, the main rail link on the German southern wing. By late January, though, the offensive began to run out of steam.

▼ Soviet troops in winter clothing advance during Zhukov's counteroffensive. Their tactics were to isolate and then annihilate German positions, and to this end they employed cavalry, ski troops, airborne forces and partisans.

On Northwestern Front's sector, Staraya Russa remained in German hands, and though seven German divisions of II Corps (Sixteenth Army) were trapped in the Demyansk Pocket, they had to be annihilated before the front could advance farther to the west.

Massive losses

Stalin then started to personally intervene in the situation, which compounded Zhukov's problems. For example, to deal with Sukhinichi he ordered that Rokossovsky's Sixteenth Army be deployed from Zhukov's right and sent to the south. Heavy losses were also taking their toll. By late January, for example, the Kalinin Front was reduced to a total tank strength of 35. The 249th Rifle Division, Fourth Shock Army, began the offensive with 8000 men, by late January it had been reduced to 1400. The five rifle divisions of the Thirtieth Army, Bryansk Front, had a combined strength of just over 11,500 man, while tank brigades on the Western Front were down to 15–20 tanks apiece. In addition, air cover began to dry up as Soviet

▲ **During the withdrawal demolitions were useful for destroying equipment that would otherwise have fallen into Russian hands. The 6th Panzer Division, for example, destroyed its 88mm guns in this way. Note the anti-personnel mine in the foreground.**

▼ **Waffen-SS graves in the snow. Between December 1941 and March 1942, Army Group Centre alone lost 256,000 men, plus 55,000 motor vehicles, 1800 tanks, 140 heavy artillery pieces and over 10,000 machine guns.**

units on the ground advanced beyond the range of bombers and fighters, which could not establish forward airfields.

If Vyazma could be taken, however, then the German Ninth and Fourth Panzer Armies could still be surrounded. Zhukov therefore continued his attacks. By 22 January, 2000 Soviet paratroops had been dropped on Zhelanye, 40km (25 miles) south of Vyazma, where they linked up with Red Army cavalry that had broken through German lines. However, attempts to drop the whole of IV Parachute Corps just south of Vyazma failed when Luftwaffe bombers caught the transport aircraft on their ill-defended airfields. IV Parachute Corps was defeated before it got off the ground. The 8th Parachute Brigade did manage to mount an airborne drop, between 27 January and 2 February, when 2323 men were dropped around Vyazma. On the ground, only 1320 managed to form up into units on the ground. The rest were scattered over a large expanse of marsh near Vyazma.

General Zhukov had written the following prior to the Soviet counteroffensive: "The German Army is extremely powerful, but in that power lies its weakness. The German soldier has been trained to depend too much on the quality

▲ The Germans used explosives to blast temporary shelters in the ground in December 1941. During the retreat from Moscow the Germans had great difficulty in building shelters and emplacements in the hard-frozen ground.

of his equipment. His strength lies in an almost blind faith in his weapons. Our men are self-reliant, they will rather die than give ground. Time and again we have seen how even first-rate German tank and gun crews lose heart when their gods – their tanks and engines – turn out to be vulnerable after all. Victory will be ours if we succeed in smashing the German materiel against which we can operate only after it has been put out of commission." But the Germans were proving they were also adept at hand-to-hand combat. The attack against Vyazma, for example, was beginning to stall. Strong German reinforcements deflected the thrusts from the south and the east. The divisions of the Thirty-Third Army were down to about 2000 men each, some even less.

As Army Group Centre fought desperately to survive throughout January and February 1942, Army Group South was battling to hold Marshal Timoshenko's armies. The so-called "Izyum bulge" extended 96km (60 miles) into German positions from the Donets, and gave the Red Army a springboard from which to launch an attack on either Kharkov or Dnepropetrovsk. If Timoshenko reached Dnepropetrovsk and Zaporozhye he would cut Army Group South in two and take possession of its vital supply lines.

Each side realized what was at stake, and for 70 days savage fighting took place on both sides of the bulge, but Timoshenko's rifle and cavalry divisions broke the German defence. On the Kerch peninsula, meanwhile, the troops of the Crimean Front were forced out of the port of Feodosia and were unable to drive westwards from Kerch into the Crimea.

In the Leningrad sector, Meretskov's Volkhov Front tried to smash its way through the German defences throughout January. The Fifty-Fourth Army of the Leningrad Front joined in

▲ Partisans played a minor role in Zhukov's counteroffensive, but their mere existence caused problems for Army Group Centre. In general, partisan groups operated from swamps and forests in German rear areas, usually close to highways. During large-scale Soviet breakthroughs, partisans were able to coordinate action with regular forces.

these attacks, but in a 72-hour period it only succeeded in using up all its ammunition and had to stand in its tracks. Meretskov continued to batter at the German defences, and at the end of January managed to force a 19km (12-mile) gap in the German defences along the River Volkhov. Through the gap he sent XIII Cavalry Corps and the majority of Second Shock Army. In this way cavalry, ski battalions and tanks advanced westwards, then swung northwest to Lyuban. But south of the town Soviet units came up against strong German defences at Krasnaya Gorka. Throughout February the Second Shock Army tried to advance, and the Fifty-Fourth Army renewed its attacks. But the corridor was too narrow and the attacks failed. In March the Germans counterattacked and closed the corridor that connected the Second Shock Army to Soviet-held territory. The Second Shock Army was then annihilated.

Stalin's great offensive was drawing to a close towards the end of February 1942. His armies were still taking ground (except in the south), but were bleeding themselves white in the process without mortally wounding their opponents. Army Group Centre re-established its front at Rzhev in early February. Vyazma was still in German hands, notwithstanding the massive Soviet effort against it.

Stavka issued revised directives to Zhukov in late March 1942 that he was to push his armies farther to the west, to a line not far from Smolensk. In addition, Vyazma, Rzhev and Bryansk were to be seized by early April. It was all pure fantasy. In mid-March, Marshal Timoshenko was still thinking of a massive offensive involving the Bryansk, Southwestern and Southern Fronts with the aim of retaking Kiev, over 320km (200 miles) to the west. He submitted his proposal for the attack to *Stavka* in mid-March. It was later scaled down to an attack on Kharkov. In late March, the Germans finally succeeded in relieving the Demyansk Pocket, thus dashing Red Army hopes of an annihilation victory that had seemed so certain only a few weeks before.

By this stage the Red Army had been worn down by continuous operations and heavy losses, and its equipment and ammunition were in short supply. Much of the blame must lay with Stalin himself, who had failed to grasp the complexities involved in his grand strategic plans and had been blind to the limitations of the understrength Soviet armies.

The Red Army had failed to destroy the three German army groups, and yet the Soviets had achieved a great victory. For one thing, the myth of the invincibility of the Wehrmacht, built on lightning victories in Western Europe and in the Balkans, was shattered for all the world to see. The Japanese, now engaged in a war against the might of the United States, was unlikely to trouble the Soviets in the Far East. Their mauling at the hands of the Soviets before the

▼ Well-equipped Siberians move towards the front. Red Army ski troops were very effective in the winter of 1941–42, and managed to cut off the 6th Panzer Division, part of the Third Panzer Group's LVI Panzer Corps, west of Moscow in December. As can be seen, though, the brown uniforms of the Siberians were very visible.

▲ **A Red Army infantry unit in the attack. The bipod-mounted machine gun is a 7.62mm Degtaryev, nicknamed the "record player" on account of its top-mounted circular magazine. It was the standard support weapon of a Red Army infantry section. The other troops are armed with rifles and submachine guns.**

war, combined with the Germans' failure to defeat the Soviet Union, would ensure that Stalin would not be troubled by Tokyo's legions. For its part, the Red Army was no longer a defeated force but a determined enemy, as its successes during the counteroffensives had shown. Attacking across 1600km (1000 miles) of front, the Red Army was estimated to have destroyed 50 enemy divisions. On some sectors, the Germans had been pushed back up to 320km (200 miles). The Moscow and Tula regions had been cleared, while parts of the Kalinin, Smolensk, Orel and Kursk regions had been partially cleared. Some 60 towns and 11,000 other smaller centres of population had been freed. And another factor now entered the war: partisans.

The first attempt to organize some sort of partisan movement had been made at the end of June 1941, when Moscow called for the creation partisan detachments for "action against units of the enemy army, for kindling partisan war everywhere and anywhere, for blowing up bridges, roads, telephone and telegraph lines, destroying dumps and the like." Organized through Communist Party officials, the first period of the partisan movement, up to August 1941, was not a great success. This was due to a combination of lack of weapons, administrative breakdown brought on by the rapid German advance, and collaboration with the enemy on the part of the local population in many areas. Nevertheless, as the war progressed a large number of partisan groups were set up behind German lines.

Many groups originated from the massive encirclement battles of 1941, as the historian Alan Clark stated: "Bands of soldiers, cut off from their units, men often who had slipped out of some panzer encirclement at night and found

▲ "The counteroffensive of the winter of 1941–42 was conducted in the difficult conditions of a snowy and severe winter, without numerical superiority over the enemy. We had more armies than he did, but each was barely equal in size and equipment to a German army corps." (Marshal Georgi Zhukov)

themselves impossibly far from their own lines, usually with a good leavening of deserters and local militia who had simply gone to ground in country they knew well, these were the stuff of the marauding groups which roamed White Russia in the summer of 1941, pillaging and looting certainly, but exchanging fire with the Germans only when necessary to save their own skins." Nevertheless, as the war progressed the partisan movement grew, forcing the Germans to devote more military resources to rear-area security tasks, and increasing the savagery of the conflict, as partisan atrocities against the invaders was answered with brutal, and often indiscriminate, reprisals.

Keitel, Chief of OKW, explained the German failure in 1941 thus: "During the summer of 1941 it almost seemed as though the eastern colossus would succumb to the mighty blows inflicted by the German Army, for the first and probably best Soviet frontline army had, in fact, been all but wiped out by that autumn ... One wonders what army in the world could have withstood such annihilating blows, had the vast expanse of Russia, her manpower reserves, had the Russian winter not come to its assistance?"

The Red Army success before Moscow, though, had not destroyed the Wehrmacht's offensive capacity. Hammered though the German Army had been, it would still be able to launch a fresh offensive in 1942, one that would lead to the city of Stalingrad. Though the Red Army had saved Moscow in late 1941, Soviet victory on the Eastern Front was not yet a possibility. Having withstood the winter counteroffensive, the initiative once more passed to the German Army. Hitler's troops had been hard pressed, but they had held.

"Hold fast!"

Army Group Centre's divisions were deployed in a large salient that was exposed and difficult to defend. The army commanders wanted to withdraw, but Hitler insisted on a fanatical resistance in which superior willpower would triumph.

The winter of 1941–42 was a hard time for the German Army on the Eastern Front. Momentum ground slowly to a halt as the temperatures dropped. It is not an overestimation to state that after six months of continuous fighting, mounting casualties, dreadful weather and supply lines which were overstretched, the Wehrmacht was close to collapse at the end of November 1941.

On 5 December 1941, 500,000 Soviet troops launched the Soviet winter offensive. On 8 December, before leaving for Berlin, Hitler, in response to the Red Army offensive, issued a directive to the commander of Army Group Centre, Field Marshal von Bock. While conceding that the severe winter weather and consequent supply difficulties required the troops

▼ The failure of Operation Typhoon lowered the morale of both officers and men in the German Army, who believed that lack of preparation for winter warfare (many troops were clothed like the two below) had contributed to their defeat.

◀ **A German 20mm quadruple Flakvierling prepares for action against the Red Air Force in December 1941. Each gun had a rate of fire of 600 rounds per minute and was effective up to 1829m (6000ft).**

around Moscow to abandon "all major offensive operations and go over to the defensive", he would sanction no withdrawals unless fortified lines could be prepared close by as rallying points. Given the difficulty of erecting such lines in the frozen and forested terrain, the exposed units at the front entertained few hopes of relief.

In fact, the Führer's directive did nothing to stop the crumbling of the German frontline around Moscow. Many units were already falling back when the order came down, and their commanders could do little to halt such retreats without sacrificing their men. In any case, within a few days of issuing his order Hitler was forced to sanction limited tactical withdrawals to prevent exposed units that had held their ground from being surrounded and annihilated.

▶ **The Russian winter was a disaster for German small arms. Both rifles and machine guns malfunctioned because the grease and oil used were not cold-resistant. Light weapons had to be warmed in huts.**

General Schaal, whose tenacity in holding the crossroad at Klin bought precious time for the escape of the main body of the Third Panzer Group, noted that overall German discipline was beginning to crack: "More and more soldiers were making their own way west, without weapons, leading a calf on a rope, or drawing a sledge with potatoes behind them – just trudging westward with no one in command. Men killed by aerial bombardment were no longer buried." For troops who had known nothing but victorious advances up until then, having to retreat was an unpleasant and unnerving experience. Schaal again: "Supply units were in the grip of psychosis, almost of panic, probably because in the past they had only been used to headlong advance." Much German equipment was discarded: artillery, because the horses needed to pull the guns had died of hunger or exposure; tanks and trucks ran out of fuel and were left by the roadside.

The infantry armies were also suffering badly. General Adolf Strauss's Ninth Army, Field Marshal Günther von Kluge's Fourth Army and

General Rudolf Schmidt's Second Army were desperately stretched. On the eve of the Russian counteroffensive, for example, Schmidt's army held a front 288km (180 miles long). This equated to nearly 3.2km (two miles) of front for every 100-man company.

Soviet forces broke through the 45th and 95th Infantry Divisions near the town of Yelets on 8 December. Two days later the gap was 25.6km (16 miles) wide and 80km (50 miles) deep and threatened the critical rail junction at Orel. The High Command was forced to transfer General Wilfred von Oven's 56th Division from the Second Panzer Army, and feed it piecemeal into the yawning gap.

▼ Despite the efforts of field kitchens, like the one shown here, food transported over even short distances to the troops on the frontline turned into lumps of ice. On the other hand, the rations were sufficient to keep the men fit for combat duties.

A German infantryman remembered the nature of the fighting during this period: "Whenever we moved into a village in the evening, we first had to eject the Russians. And when we got ready to move again in the morning, their machine guns were already stuttering behind our backs. Our dead comrades, whom we could not take along, lined the roads together with the dead bodies of horses." One Second Army division – the 45th Infantry – reached safety on 14 December but left behind all of its vehicles, half its guns and 400 dead.

The Soviet thrust toward Orel created a crisis for Guderian's Second Panzer Army farther north, and as the Second Army began to retreat along its front, Guderian had no choice but to do the same to avoid envelopment. Conferring with the Commander-in-Chief, Field Marshal Walther von Brauchitsch, on 14 December, he asked for permission to pull the Second Panzer Army back to a line formed by the River Oka, north of Orel. As this position had been

▲ The German Army introduced a number of measures to try to make the Russian winter roads at least passable. In hilly terrain, for example, sand dumps were set up to increase traction on the roads.

Guderian's frontline in October and was thus partially fortified, it met the criteria of Hitler's directive. At the meeting Guderian also received joint command of the Second Army and Second Panzer Army to coordinate their movements. Guderian had persuaded von Brauchitsch to let him pull back both armies to the October line.

To his dismay, Hitler learned that Guderian was just one of the field commanders urging a deep withdrawal. In the north, General Strauss believed that his Ninth Army could no longer hold Kalinin, the fall of which would endanger the Third Panzer Group and the Fourth Panzer Army unless they too continued to fall back. Therefore von Bock informed von Brauchitsch that his forces would have to retreat en masse to the more defensible line, codenamed the Königsberg Line. This was close to positions they had occupied in October, and ran southwards from Rzhev past Orel to Kursk. This would not only ease von Bock's critical supply situation, but would also leave Army Group Centre in a position to renew the offensive in the spring.

Hitler, who had long contended that willpower was the most decisive factor in all manner of conflict between men and nations, was insistent that the German Army should prove its will in this crisis and root out the "contagion of defeatism". He therefore overrode von Bock and von Brauchitsch and issued a new directive on 16 December 1941 that forbade even limited withdrawals.

Hitler would tolerate no voices of dissent. He placed von Bock on leave – ostensibly for reasons of health – and named von Kluge as the new commander of Army Group Centre. The Führer was convinced he would uphold the stand-fast policy and ignore subordinates who sought to spare their units by retreating. On 19 December, Hitler accepted the resignation of von Brauchitsch, who had stated: "I can take no

▲ Laying a booby trap. In their defence the Germans were aided by the weather: sound travels a great distance over snow and the approach of Red Army units could often be heard well before they were seen.

▼ The soldier on the left is carrying a Teller mine, the German Army's most common antitank mine. In late 1941 and early 1942, such mines were one of the few weapons that could disable T-34 or KV-1 tanks.

more", and assumed full responsibility for operations on the Eastern Front. Hitler informed General Halder, Chief of OKH, that "this little affair of operational command is something anybody could do."

An end to uncertainty

When Hitler's no-retreat order reached the front, it put an end to the mixed signals the troops had been receiving. In the Fourth Army's sector, for example, orders to withdraw had been issued, countermanded, reinstated and then rescinded again. In one area engineers had laid and removed demolition charges on bridges three times in one day.

At least the divisions now knew they had to stand and fight. In fact, few soldiers who had shelter from the cold relished the thought of a long journey to the rear along icy roads; where they would be lashed by freezing wind and buried by snowstorms. One German soldier described life in a dug-out thus: "stale urine, excrement, suppurating wounds, Russian tobacco and the not-unpleasant smell of Kascha, a sort of buck-wheat porridge." But at least it was better than being out in the open.

On 18 December, Guderian was ordered to hold the ground that his men had already conceded. Guderian decided to appeal to the Führer himself for permission to complete the withdrawal of his forces to the October line. On 20 December, he boarded an aircraft that took him to Hitler's headquarters in East Prussia. At the Wolf's Lair, he saw in the Führer's eyes "for the first time a hard, unfriendly expression". Hitler refused to see sense. When he told Guderian that his men must dig in, the panzer leader answered that the ground was frozen solid and could not be pierced by entrenching tools, whereupon Hitler told him to use howitzers!

Eventually, Hitler fell back on his authority as supreme commander, insisting that he was entitled to ask "any German soldier to lay down his life". Guderian then pointed out that the October line offered some protection against the weather as well as the Soviets: "We are suffering twice as many casualties from the cold as from the fire of the Russians. Anyone who has seen the hospitals filled with frostbite cases must realize what that means." In typical Hitlerite fashion, the Führer replied: "You feel too much pity for them. You should stand back more."

Guderian was not long to remain in command on the Eastern Front, however. When the town of Chern fell to the Soviets, he and von Kluge argued over who was responsible for losing the position. Guderian threatened to resign – the next day he was relieved of his command by order of Hitler, who had been persuaded by von Kluge that Guderian lacked discipline.

Though commentators subsequently thought this was ill-advised, at the time Hitler seemed to have made the right choice. By 19 December, for example, both the Third Panzer Group and the Fourth Panzer Army had stopped retreating

▼ The Luftwaffe was ill-prepared for the Russian winter. Aircraft often had to be parked in the open, as here, which meant engines and guns froze solid. This meant that heating devices had to be improvised to get the aircraft in an air-worthy condition.

▲ **By the end of February 1942 the great Russian counteroffensive had effectively run out of steam. The Germans were able to established a continuous front and semi-permanent positions, as here. Despite the scale of the Red Army's offensive, the Germans lost more men to the cold weather than they did to enemy fire.**

▼ **The winter also presented problems for the horses in the German Army. The heavy breeds brought from France were unable to withstand the winter, while others lacked proper winter shoeing which caused them to fall on icy roads.**

and were holding a line above the Moscow–Vyazma highway, approximately midway between those two cities.

The German Ninth Army, though, was in difficulty. The Soviets took Kalinin on 16 December, and subsequently threatened to break through to Rzhev and Vyazma. Hitler insisted that the Ninth Army hold the line at Starytsa, 48km (30 miles) northeast of Rzhev. But Strauss wanted to withdraw to the front that his men had held in October: behind the River Volga running through Rzhev. His pleas to von Kluge to be allowed to do so on 21 December resulted in the Field Marshal assuring Strauss that his army was in an excellent position and would stay where it was!

By the end of 1941 the Ninth Army's front was in tatters. German units became isolated as the Soviets attacked their flanks and rear. Morale was cracking, as one of Strauss' subordinates reported: "The men are just dropping with fatigue. They flop into the snow and die from exhaustion. What they are expected to do is near suicide. The young soldiers are turning on their officers, screaming at them: 'Why don't you just go ahead and kill us?'"

▲ A German 75mm leIG 18 infantry gun is wheeled into position by its crew. Each infantry battalion was equipped with six of these weapons, which were designed to support infantry attacks. The shield for the crew was necessary because it had a maximum range of only 3550m (11,650ft), though combat ranges were often less.

As 1942 dawned, Soviet units were advancing towards the supply depots at Yukhnov and Sukhinichi, only 80km (50 miles) from Vyazma. To the north, the Red Army was on the verge of a major breakthrough on the Starytsa line. As if this was not enough, on the shore of the Black Sea another German army was imperiled.

Hitler had ordered Army Group South to reclaim the initiative and retake Rostov and the Donets Basin. The group was also ordered to capture Sevastopol, the main Russian Navy base on the Black Sea – the only part of the Crimea still in Soviet hands. General Erich von Manstein's Eleventh Army was given the task of taking the heavily fortified port, while guarding the vulnerable Kerch peninsula to the east at the same time. Von Manstein, who would become one of the finest commanders in the German Army, committed six of his seven divisions to the attack, leaving the 10,000 men of the 46th Infantry Division, plus some Romanian brigades, to cover the peninsula.

Von Manstein's attack had broken through the port's outer ring of fortifications by 17 December. The main German attack was launched just north of Sevastopol, but even with powerful support from the Luftwaffe the advance was painfully slow. After five hard days, the 22nd Infantry Division – Manstein's vanguard division at Sevastopol – pushed its way through the second defensive line and was bearing down on the third, within sight of the harbour. But then the Soviets launched a counterattack, supported by shellfire from warships offshore and massive coastal guns in Sevastopol itself. The German attack was stopped.

On 26 December von Manstein learned that Russian troops were coming ashore on the Kerch peninsula – the Red Army was launching its own offensive in the area. But he refused to abandon the assault on Sevastopol, ordering his forward

▲ **The Red Army also lost heavily in war material during the winter fighting. The weapon lying in the snow appears to be a 152mm Model 1910 field howitzer. Snow reduced the lateral fragmentation of artillery shells, and only heavy artillery, such as the German 210mm mortar, remained effective in deep snow.**

units north of the port to redouble their efforts to reach the bay. The 16th Infantry Regiment of the 22nd Division penetrated Fort Stalin, but then the attack faltered again. Von Manstein, his units faltering, had no choice but to send reinforcements eastward.

The 46th Infantry Division was led by Lieutenant-General Hans von Sponeck, a Prussian count who had earned the Knight's Cross of the Iron Cross commanding airborne troops in Holland. At first, Sponeck's task was made easy by poor Soviet tactics. The infantry waded ashore without artillery or vehicles. Their first beachheads around the port of Kerch were sealed with ease by the Germans. However, on 28 December, 5000 Russians came ashore at the Black Sea port of Feodosia, at the western end of the Kerch peninsula. Von Sponeck believed that the 46th Division would soon be trapped on the peninsula. He therefore ordered it to pull back at once to the Crimean mainland. Von Manstein lost radio contact with von Sponeck's headquarters, and the withdrawal continued despite his orders to the contrary.

Von Manstein managed to halt the demoralized 46th Division just west of the peninsula, and he established a defensive cordon with the help of the reinforcements from Sevastopol. This could not disguise the fact, however, that the entire Kerch peninsula had become a Soviet jumping-off point. The initiative was now with the Red Army, as was shown on 4 January 1942 at Yevpatoriya, a Black Sea port 64km (40 miles) north of Sevastopol where a combination of amphibious troops, paratroopers and a partisan uprising in the town established a bridgehead. Nevertheless, a German infantry regiment managed to oust the Soviets after three days of hard fighting. Von Manstein followed up this success by driving the Russians from Feodosia, but his army was unable to retake the peninsula. A stalemate ensued, with the Soviets still holding the Kerch peninsula and Sevastopol.

The loss of the Kerch peninsula enraged Hitler. Von Sponeck, whose unauthorized withdrawal had violated the Führer's stand-fast order was recalled from the front and court-martialled by a special tribunal headed by Reich Marshal Hermann Göring. Von Sponeck was stripped of his rank and decorations and sentenced to death, later commuted to seven years in prison on Von Manstein's request. This sent a clear message to any commander who dared to defy the Führer.

Hitler's stand-fast order did, ironically, prevent a total rout of the German armies before Moscow. The front had stabilized by the end of January in the central sector, the Soviet offensive having exhausted itself (see Chapter 9). Unfortunately, his determination to defend what were known as "fortress areas" in future years, when any strategic value had long ceased, was to cost thousands of German soldiers their lives.

In Army Group North's sector, reconnaissance aircraft had alerted ground units to the build-up of large Red Army units to the east. Therefore in December 1941 the Germans concentrated their efforts on strengthening and firming up their defence lines. Both II Corps and X Corps were positioned in the area between Lake Ilmen and Lake Seliger, and to the west along the River Lovat. The SS *Totenkopf* Division was part of this deployment, and its men dug themselves into the natural defensive position of the Valdai Hills.

Marshal Zhukov unleashed his divisions against Army Group North during the night of 7/8 January 1942. The *Totenkopf*'s neighbours, the 30th and 290th Infantry Divisions, were hit by the Eleventh Army, Thirty-Fourth Army and First Shock Army. The German lines buckled, and the two divisions were smashed.

As the Red Army sliced into the German units, the Sixteenth Army was in danger of being surrounded. The *Totenkopf* Division was divided up and deployed at various crisis points,

▼ A well-equipped German patrol moves forward to deal with a Soviet incursion in the Demyansk Pocket in February 1942. Though heavily outnumbered, the Germans in the pocket were helped by the fact that the Russians, halted by the deep snow, were often unable to bring forward their heavy weapons to support attacks.

while its reconnaissance battalions were deployed at Staraya Russa, which they were ordered to hold at all costs.

By 12 January 1942, Field Marshal von Leeb believed the best course of action was to withdraw both his corps over the River Lovat to form a new defensive line. If not the Sixteenth Army would be annihilated. Hitler, unsurprisingly, refused permission, ordering his troops to hold fast. Von Leeb offered to resign, a request Hitler readily agreed to. The former commander of the Eighteenth Army, Colonel-General Küchler, replaced von Leeb on 17 January.

At the front the two German corps were forced into a pocket centred around Demyansk On 20 January, the Soviets broke through along the River Lovat. The German units were now separated on the west and east banks of the river. At Staraya Russa, though, the *Totenkopf* Division and the army's 18th Motorized Division held firm against fanatical attacks.

Some 40km (25 miles) west of Demyansk, units of the Soviet Eleventh and First Shock Armies linked up on the Lovat on 8 February – the Soviet ring had closed firmly around II and X Corps, trapping the 12th, 30th, 32nd, 123rd and 290th Infantry Divisions, plus what was left of the *Totenkopf* Division. The enemy deployed 15 fresh infantry divisions, well equipped and supported by an assortment of armoured units and independent ski battalions. Inside the pocket there were 95,000 men and 20,000 horses. With the total collapse of supply lines, Hitler was assured by Göring, head of the Luftwaffe, that the pocket could be supplied by air. For his part Hitler forbade any withdrawals from the Demyansk Pocket. The trapped German divisions were instructed to hold their positions and stand firm until a new front west of the River Lovat was built, and a relief attack launched to rescue them.

▼ German troops in "Fortress Demyansk" in February 1942. During the second half of the month the pocket was attacked every day by the Red Army, and units such as the SS *Totenkopf* Division were split into small, isolated groups by the enemy.

An estimated 200 tonnes (203 tons) of supplies would be required daily for the men in the pocket – weapons, ammunition, food and medical supplies. Initially, Göring's aircraft were more than able to meet the defenders' daily requirements. However, the air drops gradually tailed off, with the Luftwaffe finally struggling to meet even half the estimated requirements. At least the *Totenkopf* Division did not freeze – an ample supply of warm winter clothing had been procured though SS channels for their troops before the supply lines were cut.

▲ A Panzer 38(t) moves up to the front. By early 1942 the T-34 had established a clear superiority over its German opponents. Tank driver Karl Rupp, 5th Panzer Division, recalled the T-34s "were shooting up our tanks like rabbits."

Death at Demyansk

Inside the pocket, Soviet aircraft dropped incendiary bombs on buildings to deny any form of shelter to the SS troops. They were fighting in snow well over waist deep and in temperatures far below freezing. In a number of places the Soviet forces had penetrated the German lines by late February. These penetrations had produced their own little pockets as individual villages were cut off and surrounded. The artillery of the Soviet Red Army had incessantly pounded Eicke's men, with losses mounting dramatically for the *Totenkopf* Division, but it still held on doggedly to its positions. The situation on the ground had become so confused that the Waffen-SS troops were strafed by their own side, as Luftwaffe transport aircraft dropped supplies behind Soviet lines.

The frenzied assault on the German positions was undertaken by even more fresh Soviet divisions. This involved prolonged and bitter fighting, with both sides giving no quarter.

▶ A Panzer 35(t) light tank. The 6th Panzer Division had begun Barbarossa with 155 of these vehicles. Armed with a 37mm gun, nearly all had been knocked out by the end of 1941. There are recorded instances of German light tanks opening fire against T-34s at a range of 36.5m (120ft), only to see their rounds having no effect!

Eicke appealed directly to Heinrich Himmler, head of the SS, for replacements, now fearing for the very survival of his fragmented and mauled division. When Himmler was eventually able to muster several hundred replacements that could be flown directly into the pocket, the Luftwaffe insisted that its supply flights did not have the capacity to carry them.

Soviet attacks became an even greater problem for the Germans as time went on because

▲ Typical appearance of the average German soldier on the Eastern Front in early 1942: quilted jacket and Russian-type fur cap. Many items of winter clothing had been taken from dead Russian soldiers, of which there was an ample supply. In addition, furs and felt boots were also purchased from civilians.

the spring thaw would turn the frozen battleground into a muddy quagmire, which would bog down the German operations, disadvantaging them far more than the Soviet defenders. Every effort therefore had to be made to crush the Demyansk Pocket before this happened.

The dire situation that the *Totenkopf* Division now found itself in was brought to Hitler's notice when Himmler intervened and spoke personally to him. It was agreed that the replacements procured by Himmler would be flown in as soon as possible. The Luftwaffe, due to an improvement in weather conditions, was permitted to make a substantial drop to the beleaguered defenders of essential ammunition, food and medicines. On 7 March the fresh SS troops finally arrived at Demyansk.

In mid-March, as the spring thaws set in, the Soviet attacks began to tail off. In their attempt to annihilate the Demyansk Pocket they had suffered well over 20,000 casualties,. During the same period the *Totenkopf* Division had lost 7000 men.

Outside the pocket, Lieutenant-General Walter von Seydlitz-Kurzbach assembled a relief force. German forces had been built up on the west bank of the River Lovat since the beginning of March 1942: the 5th and 8th Light Divisions, as well as the 122nd, 127th and 329th Infantry Divisions. Their objective was to drive eastwards crossing the River Lovat and heading towards the pocket, while Eicke's battle group would make a corresponding push to the west, when the time was appropriate. The relief operation was codenamed "Fallreep".

Supported by massive air power, the offensive began on 21 March and good progress for the first two days. But then the advance slowed as Soviet resistance began to stiffen, with the enemy frantically battling to prevent a link-up between the German forces. It was not until two weeks after the push eastwards had begun that Seydlitz-Kurzbach felt confident enough to give Eicke his orders to begin his attack westwards. The delay meant the spring thaw would once more turn the ground into boggy marshland, through which Eicke's troops would have to trudge yet again. The Soviets were attacked with a frenzied determination by the *Totenkopf* Division infantry, with vicious hand-to-hand combat often resulting. Due to stiff Soviet resistance and the horrendous conditions, a rate of advance of only around 1.6 km (one mile) per day was achieved by the *Totenkopf* troops.

The east bank of the River Lovat was reached by a company from the *Totenkopf*'s tank-destroyer battalion on 20 April, and on the following day it was joined by the remainder of the German battle group. The bridgehead over the River Lovat was sufficiently secured after 73 days to start moving into what had now become the Demyansk Pocket, and Seydlitz-Kurzbach dispatched the first troops and supplies into it on 22 April.

It was a victory, of sorts, and the Führer was delighted that his Waffen-SS troops had proved that units could stand fast if they had the strength of will. However, what he did not see was the psychologically and physically shattered troops who came out of the pocket. For the *Totenkopf* Division was a ghost formation, and would have to be totally rebuilt.

▼ The fate of tens of thousands of German soldiers on the Eastern Front in the winter of 1941–42. Poorly equipped for the winter, fighting an enemy who was familiar with the terrain, the ordinary German soldier still prevented a total Wehrmacht collapse.

The racial war

Close on the heels of the advancing German armies came the Einsatzgruppen, special SS squads whose task was to "cleanse" the newly conquered lands of Jews, communists and others who had no place in the Thousand Year Reich.

The destruction of the Jews and other "unmentionables" who inhabited the Soviet Union was the avowed intention of Adolf Hitler. Shortly after the invasion of the Soviet Union he had stated: "This Russian desert, we shall populate it ... We'll take away its character of an Asiatic steppe, we'll Europeanize it ... And above all, no remorse on this subject! We're absolutely without obligations as far as these people are concerned. To struggle against the hovels, chase away the fleas, provide German teachers, bring out newspapers – very little of that for us!" He believed his dream of racial purity and the eradication of Bolshevism, which was in his eyes "a social criminality", was at hand. In fact what was really at hand for the peoples of the Soviet Union under German occupation was a period of brutality, exploitation and extermination.

From the early 1920s Hitler was obsessed by the notion of *Lebensraum* (living space) for Germany at the expense of the Soviet Union.

▼ Russian Jews forced to work for an SS Einsatzgruppe (Special Action Group) during the early stages of Operation Barbarossa. Made to wear the Star of David, they would be shot after they had carried out their work duties.

▶ German soldiers hang Russian civilians in late 1941. Both the Einsatzgruppen and Wehrmacht participated in executing "Jewish plunderers" or "Jewish Bolshevists" – largely catch-all phrases.

In *Mein Kampf* Hitler ominously wrote: "If we speak of soil in Europe today, we can primarily have in mind only Russia and her vassal border states ... For centuries Russia drew nourishment from the Germanic nucleus of its upper leading strata. Today it can be regarded as almost totally exterminated and extinguished. It has been replaced by the Jew ... He himself is no element of organization, but a ferment of decomposition. The giant empire in the east is ripe for collapse. And the end of Jewish rule in Russia will also be the end of Russia as a state." Nearly 20 years later the Führer was at last in a position to wage a racial-biological war against the "Jewish-Bolshevik intelligentsia."

The agents of the racial war

But such a special mission required special men. Hitler realized that the extermination of the Jews in the East was no undertaking for regular soldiers. Therefore, Reichsführer-SS Heinrich Himmler was ordered to form special units to follow the German armies into the Soviet Union to undertake "special actions". These units were called Einsatzgruppen (Special Action Groups).

During the invasion of the Soviet Union, Hitler granted Himmler special powers over the occupied territory in the East. On 3 March 1940, Himmler took responsibility for "certain tasks which stem from the necessity finally to settle the conflict between the two opposing political systems." The *Instructions on Special*

▶ These Jews were murdered in the Ukrainian town of Lemberg in 1941. An SS NCO once stated: "What can they be thinking? I believe each still has the hope of not being shot. I don't feel the slightest pity."

▲ **At first the Germans were welcomed as liberators, especially in the Baltic states and the Ukraine. But even as the troops were fraternizing, senior Nazis were putting in motion plans for the enslavement of the indigenous population.**

Matters of 13 March 1941 divided occupied Russia into "ethnographic areas", each of which was to be ruled by a Reichskommissar.

Reinhard Heydrich, head of the SS Reich Main Security Security Office (RSHA) and Himmler's deputy, quickly worked out the areas of responsibility between the army and the Einsatzgruppen during Barbarossa. This task was simplified as far as the SS was concerned when Hitler's Commissar Order placed communist commissars and officials, both military and civilian, beyond any law save one which automatically sentenced them to summary execution. Commissars when captured would be shot out of hand, if not by German frontline troops then by the Einsatzgruppen, to whom they would be handed over: "Political leaders and commissars who are captured will not be sent to the rear."

On the eve of Barbarossa it had been established that "the Einsatzgruppen are authorized, within the framework of their task and on their own responsibility, to take executive measures affecting the civilian population." There were four Einsatzgruppen: Einsatzgruppe A, assigned to operations in Latvia, Lithuania and Estonia, was commanded by SS-Gruppenführer Franz Stahlecker; Einsatzgruppe B, assigned to the Baltic states and the Ukraine, was commanded by SS-Gruppenführer Arthur Nebe; Einsatzgruppe C, assigned to the Ukraine south of Einsatzgruppen B, was led by SS-Oberführer Carl Rasch; and Einsatzgruppe D, which assumed responsibility for the remainder of the Ukraine, was commanded by SS-Gruppenführer Otto Ohlendorf.

Units of the Sicherheitsdienst (SD) – SS Security Service – Waffen-SS and Ordnungspolizei – Order Police, or the regular uniformed police – provided men for the Einsatzgruppen, which were forces that were armed with light automatic weapons. The strength of the various Einsatzgruppen varied. Einsatzgruppe A had 990 men, while Einsatzgruppe D numbered 500.

Categories of victims

The atrocities began as soon as Barbarossa started. At the village of Virbalis, for example, Jews were forced to lie down and were then shot. The children were spared being shot, but were subsequently buried alive. The Einsatzgruppen took to their task with relish. They had been instructed by Heydrich: "Communist functionaries and activists, Jews, gypsies, saboteurs and agents must basically be regarded as persons who, by their very existence, endanger the security of the troops and are therefore to be executed without further ado." In fact the list of those who were to be executed "without further ado" became all encompassing: Russian commissars, communists, looters, saboteurs, Jews with false papers, agents of the NKVD, traitorous Ethnic Germans, "sadistic Jews", "unwanted elements", carriers of epidemics, members of partisan bands, armed insurgents, partisan helpers, rebels, agitators, young vagabonds, and Jews in general.

Soon the Einsatzgruppen had murdered hundreds of thousands of people. Ohlendorf, for example, kept scores of his "achievements". By the winter of 1941–42, his group had liquidated 92,000 Jews alone. The wording of the reports of SS commanders made for chilling reading. On 18 July 1941, for example, SS-Obergruppenführer and General of the Waffen-SS and Polizei, Erich von dem Bach-Zelewski, Ordnungspolizei commander in the Soviet republic of Belorussia, sent the following to his superiors in Berlin: "In yesterday's cleansing action in Slonim, carried out by Police Regiment Centre, 1153 Jewish plunderers were shot." By 7 August, he again reported, this time to SS-Oberstgruppenführer and Generaloberst of the Polizei, Kurt Daluege: "The total number of executions in territory under my jurisdiction has now exceeded 30,000." The murderous drive

▲ German troops in the Ukraine are welcomed by the locals. Hermann Göring, head of the Luftwaffe, stated: "The best thing would be to kill all men in the Ukraine over 15 years of age, and then to send in the SS stallions."

◀ Hitler was particularly concerned that contact with the locals would lead to Slav women seducing young German soldiers and corrupting them away from the ideals of National Socialism.

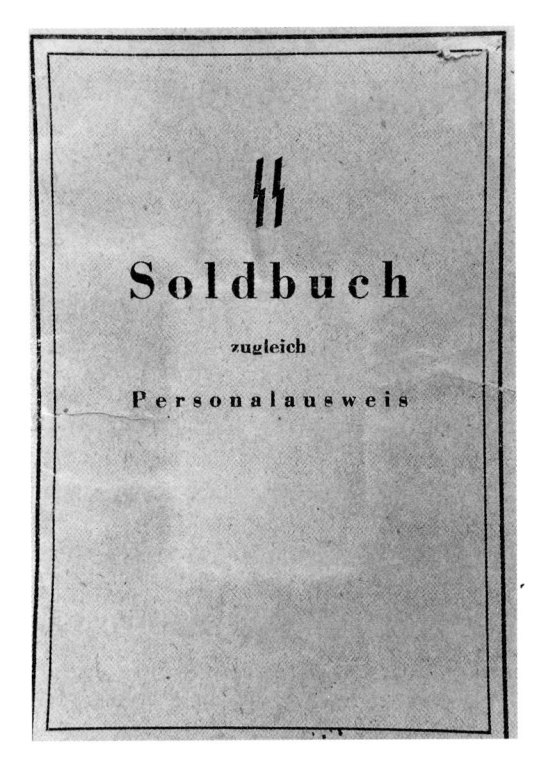
ϟϟ

Soldbuch

zugleich

Personalausweis

◀ **Each SS man carried a "Soldbuch", a record of his personal details and SS activities. During Barbarossa many would record assignments to Einsatzgruppen to undertake "resettlement measures" or "cleansing actions" against Jews, both pseudonyms for mass killings. By mid-October the Einsatzgruppen had killed 300,000 Jews.**

against the Jews was made easier because over 90 percent of Russian Jews were concentrated in Russia's cities. Einsatzgruppen tactics were to follow close behind the advancing German troops, then seal off any town they came across.

Once the German Army had taken control of a town, the Einsatzgruppe commanders would move in and deviously go about their task. Jews were often tricked into surrendering themselves. In Kiev, for example, Einsatzgruppe C proudly reported that, "The Jewish population was invited by poster to present themselves for resettlement. Although initially we had only counted on 5000–6000 Jews reporting, more than 30,000 Jews appeared: by a remarkably efficient piece of organization they were led to believe in the resettlement story until shortly before their execution."

The list of murders was endless: 4200 Jews shot near the town of Kamenets-Podolsk; 1255 Jews killed near the town of Ovruch; 12,361 Ukrainian Jews executed at the end of August 1941; in Lithuania, "about 500 Jews, among other saboteurs, are currently being liquidated every day"; and near Ogilev "a total of 135 people, most of them Jews, were seized. 127 people were shot."

The murderers went about their task with a barbaric glee, smashing babies' heads against doors and stone walls, which one SS man remembered thus: "It went off with a bang like a bursting motorcycle tyre."

However, even hardened fanatics have their limits, for by the winter of 1941–42 the Einsatzgruppen leaders were feeling the effects of the mass murders. Nebe had a nervous breakdown. In hospital he ranted at his doctor:

▶ **The image of its soldiers the SS liked to portray to the world. But the death's head insignia on the cap was a symbol of terror for the local population. Many SS personnel took great delight in sadistic murders as German rule spread. A favourite method was whipping unfortunate victims to death.**

▲ "Sepp" Dietrich, commander of the Waffen-SS *Leibstandarte* Division, originally Hitler's bodyguard. The Führer described him as a man "simultaneously cunning, energetic and brutal". The same could be said of most members of the SS.

"Thank God, I'm through with it. Don't you know what's happening in Russia? The entire Jewish population is being exterminated there." Nebe even pleaded with Himmler to halt the murders, to be told by the Reichsführer: "That is a Führer order. The Jews are the disseminators of Bolshevism ... if you don't keep your nose out of the Jewish business, you'll see what'll happen to you."

Alarmed by outbreaks of conscience among his henchmen, Himmler travelled to Minsk to encourage them. After attending the shooting of 200 Jews, which shocked him greatly, he told Nebe that a more efficient way of killing must be found. Nebe agreed, for the psychological effect on those who had to carry out the executions was very great. He began experimenting with killing people, in one case 80 inhabitants of a lunatic asylum, using exhaust gas from his car. He went about the task with an enthusiasm that he was incapable of keeping to himself. He was a keen amateur film maker, and recorded his crude gas chamber on celluloid.

A like-minded individual was SS-Oberführer Christian Wirth, a former Stuttgart police officer, he was an "expert" in experiments in mass sterilization. Wirth was eventually assigned to Poland, under Odilo Globocnik, head of the SS Jewish extermination programme in Poland. Wirth's mission was to find an efficient method of dispatching one million Polish Jews. He selected an area along the Lublin–Lwow railway for his first experimental camp, and went on to head an organization of a group of four extermination camps.

Wirth focused his efforts on a stationary killing unit which had three "shower rooms", which was built at the centre of the camp. Once inside, the victims were killed by the exhaust gas from diesel engines. He had wide doors on both front and back walls to make the removal of gassed victims easier. In this way the camp was able to murder 1500 Jews daily. As they entered the gas chamber they saw a banner made from a synagogue curtain which stated in Hebrew: "This is the gate of the Lord into which the righteous shall enter".

A fellow SS officer noted in his journal the behaviour of Wirth at the Belzec death camp in the aftermath of the gassing of a group of Jews:

▼ Nazi doctors, and also Reichsführer-SS Heinrich Himmler, were obsessed with racial differences in bone structure and the hereditary transmission of abnormalities. Any "suitable" guinea pigs, such as the dwarf photographed with police personnel, were sent to concentration camps for experimentation.

"Among it all the chief, Wirth, leaps about. He is in his element. Some workers check genitalia and backsides for gold, diamonds and valuables. Wirth calls me over: 'Feel the weight of this tin of gold teeth, that is only from yesterday and the day before!"

Once Barbarossa had finally stalled at the end of 1941, the Einsatzgruppen became static. They took over the existing auxiliary units or formed their own with recruits drawn from the ethnic Germans, pro-Germans in general, and reliable members of the defunct Soviet militia. It is sad to report that they found many willing participants among the indigenous populations within German-occupied territory, and tapped into a rich vein of anti-Semitism. These units were often unreliable, poorly organized, ill-disciplined, badly equipped and trained, but they could still take part in the hunting down and murder of Jews. In the Ukraine, for example, a Ukrainian Security Service in Cherson undertook guarding factories and stores against looters and saboteurs. Its tasks also included "the maintenance of peace", a euphemism for the rounding up of Jews.

▲ Himmler believed that gypsies (such as the women pictured here) were capable of doing racial harm to his Nordic master race. Consequently, during Barbarossa German police units were ordered to round up gypsies. Many were shot along with Jews. Later, gypsies were sent to Auschwitz, to be housed in a separate enclosure before death.

By the end of 1941 the various Einsatzgruppen submitted their figures of Jews killed to Himmler: Einsatzgruppe A – 249,420; Einsatzgruppe B – 45,467; Einsatzgruppe C – 95,000; Einsatzgruppe D – 92, 000. This figure of nearly 500,000 took place during the so-called "wild period" of Einsatzgruppen activities, when they followed hot on the heels of the German armies invading the Soviet Union.

The second period of SS rule in the Soviet Union was more organized though similarly brutal. Alfred Rosenberg was appointed Reich Minister for the Occupied Eastern Territories, being responsible for two Reich Commissariats – Ostland and Ukraine. Ostland consisted of Estonia, Latvia, Lithuania and Belorussia, which

comprised much of the Ukraine. To carry out his orders, Himmler had appointed a number of Senior SS and Police (HSSPF) commanders in the occupied territories: SS-Gruppenführer Hans Prützmann as HSSPF North in Riga; SS-Gruppenführer Erich von dem Bach-Zelewski as HSSPF Centre in Minsk; and SS-Obergruppenführer Freidrich Jeckeln as HSSPF South in Kiev. Later, in 1942, SS-Brigadeführer Gerret Korsemann was appointed HSSPF Caucasus. On Himmler's orders dated 6 November 1941, all auxiliaries were formed into auxiliary police units. These battalions were placed at the disposal of the order police commander and the HSSPF.

Systematically the Germans purged existing police and paramilitary organizations and reformed them to suit their own needs. For

▲ Unusually, these auxiliaries are digging a grave themselves. Normally they would get their victims to make the hole, after which they would be lined up on its edge and shot. This photograph suggests the victims were too weak to dig the frozen soil.

▶ One of the Jews described by Himmler as being "the eternal enemies of the German people, and must be exterminated ... All Jews are to be exterminated."

▶ **Einsatzgruppe commander Otto Ohlendorf stated: "I surrendered my moral conscience to the fact that I was a soldier ... I never permitted the shooting by individuals, but ordered that several men should shoot at the same time to avoid direct personal responsibility."**

example, all anti-Soviet partisans in and around Kovno, Lithuania, were disbanded on 28 June 1941, with five auxiliary companies subsequently formed from "reliable elements". The Jewish concentration camp at Kovno was guarded by one company while another undertook police duties. In Wilna, the Lithuanian political police was disbanded in July 1941, with around 150 of its men being sent to the Einsatzgruppen. In Belorussia an auxiliary police unit was formed from Polish and Belorussian criminal police officials. All these units readily assisted in the round-up and extermination of Jews.

A brutal breed apart

However, it was the Einsatzgruppen that committed the most murders in the Soviet Union. As the historian Heinz Höhne stated: "Wholly dedicated to 'hardness' and camaraderies, they reached a degree of insensibility surpassed only by those soulless automata, the concentration camp guards. Here was to be found the élite of that barbaric type of mankind, intoxicated by its own achievements, which Himmler exalted as the SS ideal; it was indeed an Order of the Death's Head, divorced from the world of ordinary mortals and from their moral standards, ready to undertake any mission ordered by its masters, and prisoner of a community claiming the sole right to decide the SS man's social and ethical standards ... Moreover, the deeds demanded of them took place in the vast expanses of Russia, so far distant from their normal environment that the whole murder business seemed like a dream ... so that what occurred had never really taken place."

As the murders were taking place throughout German-occupied territory, many Wehrmacht commanders turned a blind eye to what was going on, or subsequently claimed that they had no knowledge of the atrocities being committed by the SS. After all, they argued, the delineation between army areas of responsibility and that of the SS was firmly established from the beginning of Barbarossa, and Himmler would brook no infringement on his sphere of influence. In this way, Wehrmacht personnel were able to distance themselves from the horrors being committed against the indigenous population.

However, there is abundant evidence to prove that not only did army commanders know what was going on, but that they actively participated in Nazi ideological policy. The commander of the Sixth Army, Field Marshal Walther von Reichenau, Army Group South, reacted to reports of the "softness" of his troops by instilling them with particularly strong statements about their role in suppressing communism and Soviet Jewry. Von Reichenau was known as one of the most strongly Nazi of the leading German Army commanders. He died of a stroke only a few months after he issued the document below to his troops. Other German commanders in the Soviet Union also used this document to instruct their troops. The order was issued on 10 October 1941, entitled *Conduct of Troops in Eastern Territories.*

"Regarding the conduct of troops towards the bolshevistic system, vague ideas are still prevalent in many cases. The most essential aim of war against the Jewish-bolshevistic system is a complete destruction of their means of power and the elimination of Asiatic influence from the European culture. In this connection the troops are facing tasks which exceed the one-sided routine of soldiering. The soldier in the Eastern territories is not merely a fighter according to the rules of the art of war, but also a bearer of ruthless national ideology and the avenger of bestialities which have been inflicted upon German and racially related nations. Therefore, the soldier must have full understanding for the necessity of a severe but just revenge on subhuman Jewry. The Army has to aim at another purpose, i.e. the annihilation of revolts in the hinterland, which, as experience proves, have always been caused by Jews.

"The combating of the enemy behind the frontline is still not being taken seriously

▼ Treatment towards the peoples of the Baltic states, many of whom were considered by the Nazis to be "Nordic" in racial characteristics, was more lenient than towards "subhumans". Many thousands of Estonians and Latvians joined the ranks of the Waffen-SS during the war.

▲ A police detachment operating in German-occupied territory. Tens of thousands of locals were recruited by the Germans to implement Nazi policy in the conquered territories. Of little use militarily, they were often recruited from the worst elements of society. Murder and savagery came easily to them.

enough. Treacherous, cruel partisans and degenerate women are still being made prisoners-of-war, and guerrilla fighters dressed partly in uniform or plain clothes and vagabonds are still being treated as proper soldiers, and sent to prisoner-of-war camps. In fact, captured Russian officers talk even mockingly about Soviet agents moving openly about the roads, and very often eating at German field kitchens. Such an attitude of the troops can only be explained by complete thoughtlessness, so it is now high time for the commanders to clarify the meaning of the pressing struggle.

"The feeding of the natives and of prisoners-of-war who are not working for the armed forces from army kitchens is an equally misunderstood humanitarian act as is the giving of cigarettes and bread. Things which the people at home can spare under great sacrifices and things which are being brought by the command to the front under great difficulties, should not be given to the enemy by the soldier even if they originate from booty. It is an important part of our supply.

"When retreating, the Soviets have often set buildings on fire. The troops should be interested in the extinguishing of fires only as far as it is necessary to secure sufficient numbers of billets. Otherwise, the disappearance of symbols of the former bolshevistic rule even in the form of buildings is part of the struggle

◀ **Jews are rounded up before being transported to a ghetto. The Jewish ghettos had been established by the Nazis during the winter of 1939–40, all of which quickly became overcrowded. By 1942 the Warsaw ghetto, which housed over 500,000 people, became so destitute that an average of 5000 were dying there every month.**

of destruction. Neither historic nor artistic considerations are of any importance in the Eastern territories. The command issues the necessary directives for the securing of raw material and plants, essential for war economy. The complete disarming of the civilian population in the rear of the fighting troops is imperative considering the long vulnerable lines of communications. Where possible, captured weapons and ammunition should be stored and guarded. Should this be impossible because of the situation of the battle, the weapons and ammunition will be rendered useless.

"If isolated partisans are found using firearms in the rear of the army drastic measures are to be taken. These measures will be extended to that part of the male population who were in a position to hinder or report the attacks. The indifference of numerous apparently anti-Soviet elements which originates from a 'wait and see' attitude, must give way to a clear decision for active collaboration. If not, no one can complain about being judged and treated a member of the Soviet system. The fear of German countermeasures must be stronger than threats of the wandering bolshevistic remnants. Regardless of all future political considerations the soldier has to fulfil two tasks:

"1.) Complete annihilation of the false Bolshevist doctrine of the Soviet State and its armed forces.

"2.) The pitiless extermination of foreign treachery and cruelty and thus the protection of the lives of military personnel in Russia.

"This is the only way to fulfil our historic task to liberate the German people once and for all from the Asiatic-Jewish danger.

"[signed] von Reichenau"

In this way the Wehrmacht became actively involved in Nazi ideology in the East. The Germans had no military guidelines for combating partisan bands, and as the frustration of trying to battle an elusive foe grew, a foe who often committed atrocities against isolated German patrols, reprisals became more widespread and indiscriminate. The partisan war is beyond the

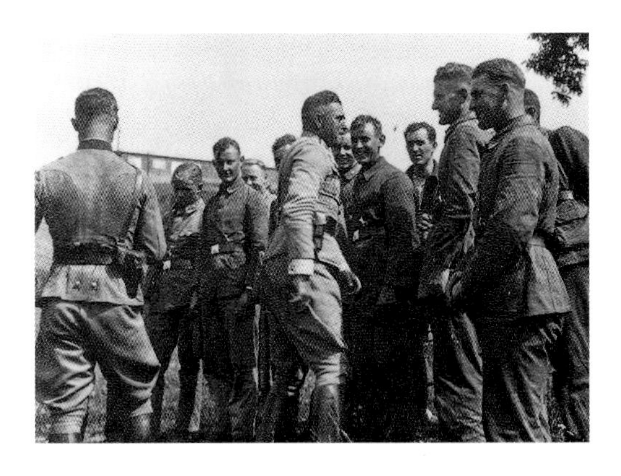

▶ **The murderers take time to relax. It has been estimated that as many as 1,400,000 Jews had been murdered as a result of German Einsatzgruppen activities by the spring of 1942.**

▲ **The man in the foreground is a German policeman, while those around him are members of a Russian auxiliary unit raised to assist the Einsatzgruppen. The members of such units were shot out of hand if captured by the Red Army.**

scope of this chapter, but suffice to say that it did help to reinforce the view of the devious, subhuman Bolshevik Russian peasant, against whom only pitiless action was effective. Hitler himself encouraged "freedom of action against any evilly-disposed civilian enemy encountered during the course of a military operation."

Nazi racial policy had disastrous consequences in the Ukraine, where many towns and villages had welcome the Germans as liberators (it is estimated that up to seven million Ukrainians had died of starvation during Stalin's collectivization policies in the 1930s – the terror of Soviet communism convinced many Ukrainians that they would be better off under a cultured country such as Germany), only to discover the terrible truth as the Wehrmacht conquered their land. For the "subhuman" inhabitants of the Ukraine, Hitler planned that they would "disappear". A few might be left as slave labourers, who would serve the German colonists. In this way the Germans alienated 40 million Ukrainians who might otherwise have aided the anti-Soviet war effort.

The historian George Stein summarizes the German war in the Soviet Union thus: "When the enemy is regarded as a repulsive and evil animal, an *Untermensch*, a subhuman, the result is an unmatched brutalization of warfare, for the soldier is generally set free from feelings of guilt or remorse for his grisly deeds ... the deplorable effects that resulted from the artificial dehumanization are well known – the shooting of prisoners, the murder of civilians, the destruction of peaceful villages." Such were the results of Hitler's racial crusade to save Western civilization against "Asiatic Bolshevism".

Recriminations

Hitler's distrust and dislike of his senior army commanders came to the surface following the failure at Moscow. Incensed by what he saw as defeatism among the army High Command, he purged Germany's top brass.

▲ The plaque at this German cemetery of Barbarossa dead in Russia reads: "Men's worth will be reckoned by what they gave for their fatherland – these gave their lives."

The defeat of the German Army near Moscow in December 1941 brought to a head the resentment and disputes between Hitler and his senior Wehrmacht commanders.

The Führer had earlier established his personal ascendancy over the army beginning in 1938 with the dismissal of Field Marshal Werner von Blomberg, Minister of Defence, following a Nazi-organized scandal, and the trial of the Army Commander-in-Chief, Field Marshal Freiherr Werner von Fritsch, following an SS-organized sex scandal. The vacant posts were filled by Hitler himself, as Minister of War, and his pliant nominee von Brauchitsch as Commander-in Chief. In 1939, the three service ministries were unified into a small executive body, the Armed Forces High Command (OKW), headed by Hitler, who filled senior posts with yes-men: Keitel and Jodl.

An emasculated army?

The Army High Command (OKH) had no direct influence on the higher direction of the war, except through the person of von Brauchitsch, himself a personal nominee of Hitler's. Franz Halder, the Chief of the Army Staff, was little more than a staff officer.

Despite Nazi efforts to emasculate the army, it stood high in reputation up to and including Barbarossa. After all, the Luftwaffe had failed in the Battle of Britain, and the Kriegsmarine had put in a mediocre performance, whereas the army stood undefeated. Indeed, it appeared that Nazi Germany itself relied on the training, discipline and courage of the German Army.

During Barbarossa, German senior commanders began to develop their own views about how best to conduct the war, which did not fit in at all with Hitler's view of the army as a totally obedient arm of the Nazi state. For example, Field Marshal von Leeb had ordered an assault on Leningrad three days after receipt of orders to release the bulk of his armour and air force for operations in Army Group Centre's sector. He had ignored the final paragraph of the Führer directive: "Any saving of time and consequence advance of the timetable will be to the advantage of the whole operation [that is, the attack by Army Group Centre] and its preparation." Heinz Guderian, commander of the Second Panzer Group, had been even more disobedient during Barbarossa.

With the tacit approval of his commander, Field Marshal von Bock, Guderian had kept his tanks in action against the Soviets at Yelnya, despite being ordered to regroup his panzer divisions for the drive south on Kiev. This had led

▲ A German artillery unit displays a sign celebrating one of its guns firing its 10,000th shot on the Eastern Front, February 1942. Yet victory was still a dream.

▼ A familiar sight in early 1942 – German reinforcements being shipped to the Eastern Front for another grand offensive designed to defeat the Soviet Union.

◀ **Von Brauchitsch, Chief of OKH, was made the scapegoat for the failure of Operation Barbarossa and forced to resign.**

to a number of insignificant victories which exhausted the panzer crews, and wasted precious dry campaigning days in early August 1941.

Von Rundstedt, who had always been unenthusiastic about the war in the East, considered in September 1941 that the campaign should be halted, and a "Winter Line" established on the River Dnieper.

Panzers versus the infantry

At lower levels, there was also disagreement between panzer and infantry commanders. The panzer commanders – Guderian, von Manstein, Hoth and Kleist – favoured ambitious encirclements and ever-deeper penetrations. But those who commanded the infantry divisions, which moved at a slower pace, saw things very differently. It was their men who had to reduce the vast pockets formed by the panzers, which often resulted in heavy casualties while the tanks were off "enjoying themselves".

As Barbarossa developed, many senior commanders became increasingly disenchanted with Hitler's leadership. They even talked about the Führer's "replacement" openly (Halder had actually been privy to a scheme to assassinate Hitler in 1938).

Like the Emperor Caligula, Hitler saw intrigue and plots everywhere, especially when Barbarossa started to go wrong and his orders were being disobeyed. Therefore, at the end of 1941, the German Army High Command, in his eyes disloyal in speech and thought, if not in action, at odds with one another on questions of strategy and tactics and ever ready to blatantly ignore OKW, was long overdue for a shake-up.

◀ **Franz Halder, von Brauchitsch's successor, was dismissed by Hitler in 1942 over the conduct of strategy in the East.**

▲ **Von Rundstedt, commander of Army Group South, was dismissed and reinstated by Hitler three times during the war.**

The "disaster" of December of 1941 gave Hitler his chance. At the front near Moscow, the men were exhausted and had no protection against the sub-zero temperatures of the Russian winter. Worse, they were having to face attack from high-quality Russian divisions recently arrived from Siberia.

In such circumstances, senior German commanders reacted according to their training; that is, if a penetration cannot be sealed off, the flanks must be withdrawn in order to prevent them being turned. Unfortunately, on the Eastern Front a combination of dreadful weather and fast-moving Red Army divisions meant the Germans could not retreat as fast as the Russians could advance. Within three days of the start of Zhukov's counteroffensive, for example, Army Group Centre was becoming badly fragmented.

At this point the Army High Command became almost paralyzed: Von Brauchitsch suffered a serious heart attack; von Bock had stomach cramps and could only rise from his bed for three or four hours each day; and Hoepner had

▼ **Heinz Guderian (right), brilliant panzer commander, was dismissed in December 1941 for carrying out a withdrawal in contravention of the "stand fast" order.**

▲ Faced with a long war in Russia, German soldiers adopted measures to cope with the terrain and weather. These men are wearing mosquito nets – essential for warding off malaria in swamp and marsh areas.

dysentery. Hitler decided enough was enough. He began communicating direct with army and corps commanders, bypassing Halder. Von Brauchitsch resigned on 7 December on the grounds of "ill-health". Hitler remarked: "If he had remained at his post only another few weeks, things would have ended in catastrophe." He told Josef Göbbels, Nazi Propaganda Minister, that von Brauchitsch was "a vain, cowardly wretch and a nincompoop". Within the next three weeks, no less than 35 army, corps and divisional generals had joined him in disgrace and exile. These included such distinguished commanders as Guderian, Hoepner and Hans Count von Sponeck, who was sentenced to death for withdrawing, though this was commuted to seven years in prison.

In this way Hitler forced the army leadership into standing firm wherever they found themselves, and thus construct a network of fortified positions behind the front.

Franz Halder was made Commander-in-Chief, though he was under no illusion as to what was expected of him. Hitler told him: "The task of the Commander-in-Chief of the army is to train the army in a National Socialist way. I know of no general who could do that, as I want it done."

Ironically, many officers believed that Hitler's purge of his generals and "stand fast" order saved the German Army. Field Marshal von Kluge's Chief-of-Staff wrote: "Hitler's fanatical order that the troops must hold fast regardless, in every position and in the most impossible circumstances, was undoubtedly correct. Hitler realized instinctively that any retreat across the snow and ice must, within a few days, lead to the dissolution of the front and that if this happened the Wehrmacht would suffer the same fate that had befallen the *Grande Armée*."

▶ The German Army had lost 75,000 motor vehicles during Barbarossa. Replacements could not make up this shortfall, so some units were forced to adopt more exotic means of transporting supplies.

Unfortunately, though the decision may have been right at the end of 1941, Hitler's inflexible determination never to yield ground cost the German Army dearly in the years to come. In addition, the winter of 1941–42 also saw the rise of the Waffen-SS in both prestige and power. Hitler had seen the performance of units such as the *Totenkopf* Division in the Demyansk Pocket (see Chapter 10), which had followed his orders to the letter and had tied down many Red Army divisions. What could he achieve with entire SS corps, or even armies?

The increase in Waffen-SS divisions was stepped up in 1942 so that the new divisions were grouped into corps, and later there were SS armies that had regular units subordinated to them. Waffen-SS officers got faster promotion and were often to be given commands of critical responsibility in preference to regular officers. Yet, as SS standards of training and experience were lower than those of the army, this resulted in heavy casualties.

The Waffen-SS was also allocated large quantities of precious hardware, especially the new Tiger and Panther tanks that began to roll off the production lines in 1943. This denied the army's panzer divisions of tanks, which did nothing to ease the antagonism between the Waffen-SS and the German Army.

The German Army had not only suffered defeat at the hands of the Soviets in December 1941. It had also suffered a political defeat. Henceforth it would be under Hitler's complete political domination, which would only increase as the war progressed and the tide turned against Nazi Germany. Having cowed his generals, Hitler became the supreme warlord. Yet even in this position he remained suspicious of his senior commanders in the Wehrmacht. During World War I he had served in the trenches, and afterwards believed that among others, the General Staff had stabbed the undefeated German Army in the back. He was determined that the same thing would not happen again.

◀ Erich von Manstein became a field marshal in 1942, but was dismissed by Hitler in 1944 for making tactical withdrawals.

Conclusion

The failure of Barbarossa meant that Germany faced a war of attrition on the Eastern Front unless Hitler could achieve victory in mid-1942. But the omens for success were not good, and the Soviet Union was growing in strength.

The failure of Barbarossa did not augur well for the German Army's war on the Eastern Front. Germany simply did not have the manpower or industrial capacity to replace the huge losses suffered in Russia. For example, 75,000 motor vehicles were lost during the campaign, yet between 1 November 1941 and 15 March 1942 only 7500 vehicles arrived at the front as replacements. The panzer arm was in a worse state. Losses in tanks between June 1941 and March 1942, in all theatres, amounted to 3424, yet during the same period only 2843 rolled off the production lines. And the figures became even more dire when the Panzer IIs and 38(t)s were declared officially obsolete.

With regard to manpower, owing to growing responsibilities on other fronts, such as North Africa, the number of German soldiers on the Eastern Front actually declined from over three million in June 1941 to 2,847,000 in June 1942. No less than 1,101,000 troops were deployed elsewhere. To compound the problem, the army was experiencing shortages of fuel oil and ammunition. No wonder Hitler talked of defeating the Soviet Union before it got its "second wind", specifically acquiring the Caucasus oil fields. Of course, he still wanted "to obliterate Moscow and Leningrad".

◀ "Ivan" – the ordinary Russian civilian turned fighter – would be the agent of the Third Reich's destruction. Between 20–25 million Russians died during World War II, but their sacrifice ensured the defeat of one of the most infamous regimes in history.

Objectively, the Germans had to deliver a mortal blow against the Soviet Union in mid-1942, because Stalin's factories were starting to out-produce those of their adversary, notwithstanding the massive industrial dislocation of 1941. Prior to May 1942, Soviet factories in the Urals and Transcaucasus turned out 4500 tanks, 14,000 artillery pieces and over 50,000 mortars. With such hardware, plus the material being supplied by the Western Allies, *Stavka* was able to create new tank corps and even tank armies. The latter averaged a strength of 35,000 men, up to 500 tanks and up to 200 large towed artillery pieces. Four such formations had been formed by July 1942.

Of course war is not just a matter of out-producing an adversary. Material superiority has to be allied to effective leadership, strategies and tactics to produce ultimate victory. And in early 1942 the Red Army was inexperienced in offensive operations at all levels. Thus the badly planned and executed Second Battle of Kharkov in May 1942 cost the Soviets three rifle armies and a tank army, and did not interrupt German plans for their own summer offensive.

The supreme irony was, though, that in a war Hitler characterized as being a trial of national and racial willpower, it was the Soviet people who were coming out on top. A major factor that had contributed to the failure of Barbarossa had been the sacrifice and tenacity of the Soviet population. In the face of losses that are difficult to comprehend, the people had rallied behind Stalin's appeal to defend the Motherland – and they would see it through to the end.

APPENDIX 1: GERMAN ORDER OF BATTLE, 22 JUNE 1941

Note: formations smaller than divisions are not listed. All corps had attached artillery and antiaircraft units.

NORWAY ARMY

XXXVI Corps
169th Infantry Division
6th Finnish Infantry Division

Norway Mountain Corps
2nd Mountain Division
3rd Mountain Division

ARMY GROUP NORTH

Luftflotte I

Eighteenth Army
291st Infantry Division

I Corps
1st Infantry Division
11th Infantry Division
21st Infantry Division

XXVI Corps
61st Infantry Division
217th Infantry Division

XXXVIII Corps
58th Infantry Division

Fourth Panzer Group
SS *Totenkopf* Division (motorized)

XLI Panzer Corps
1st Panzer Division
6th Panzer Division
36th Infantry Division (motorized)
269th Infantry Division

LVI Panzer Corps
8th Panzer Division
3rd Infantry Division (motorized)
290th Infantry Division

Sixteenth Army
253rd Infantry Division

II Corps
12th Infantry Division
32nd Infantry Division
121st Infantry Division

X Corps
30th Infantry Division
126th Infantry Division

XXVIII Corps
122nd Infantry Division
123rd Infantry Division

ARMY GROUP CENTRE

Luftflotte II

LII Corps
293rd Infantry Division

Ninth Army
VIII Corps
8th Infantry Division
28th Infantry Division
161st Infantry Division

XX Corps
162nd Infantry Division
256th Infantry Division

XXXXII Corps
87th Infantry Division
129th Infantry Division
102nd Infantry Division

Third Panzer Group
V Corps
5th Infantry Division
35th Infantry Division

VI Corps
6th Infantry Division
26th Infantry Division

XXXIX Panzer Corps
7th Panzer Division
20th Panzer Division
14th Infantry Division (motorized)
20th Infantry Division (motorized)

LVII Panzer Corps
12th Panzer Division
19th Panzer Division
18th Infantry Division (motorized)

Fourth Army
286th Security Division

VII Corps
7th Infantry Division
23rd Infantry Division
258th Infantry Division
268th Infantry Division
221st Security Division

IX Corps
137th Infantry Division
263rd Infantry Division
292nd Infantry Division

XIII Corps
17th Infantry Division
78th Infantry Division

XXXXIII Corps
131st Infantry Division
134th Infantry Division
252nd Infantry Division

Second Panzer Group
255th Infantry Division

XII Corps
31st Infantry Division
34th Infantry Division
45th Infantry Division

XXIV Panzer Corps
3rd Panzer Division
4th Panzer Division
10th Infantry Division (motorized)
1st Cavalry Division
267th Infantry Division

XXXXVI Panzer Corps
10th Panzer Division
SS Division *Das Reich* (motorized)

XXXXVII Panzer Corps
17th Panzer Division
18th Panzer Division
29th Infantry Division (motorized)
167th Infantry Division

ARMY GROUP SOUTH

Luftflotte IV
99th Light Division

Seventeenth Army
97th Light Division
100th Light Division

IV Corps
24th Infantry Division
71st Infantry Division
262nd Infantry Division

295th Infantry Division
296th Infantry Division

XXXXIX Mountain Corps
68th Infantry Division
257th Infantry Division
1st Mountain Division

LII Corps
101st Light Division
444th Security Division
454th Security Division

Slovakian Corps Group
1st Slovakian Division
2nd Slovakian Division

Sixth Army
168th Infantry Division
213th Security Division

XVII Corps
56th Infantry Division
62nd Infantry Division

XXXXIV Corps
9th Infantry Division
297th Infantry Division

First Panzer Group
9th Panzer Division
16th Panzer Division
SS Division *Wiking* (motorized)
16th Infantry Division (motorized)
25th Infantry Division (motorized)
SS Division *Leibstandarte* (motorized)

XIV Panzer Corps
13th Panzer Division

III Panzer Corps
14th Panzer Division
44th Infantry Division
298th Infantry Division

XXIX Corps
111th Infantry Division
299th Infantry Division

XXXVIII Panzer Corps
11th Panzer Division
57th Infantry Division
75th Infantry Division

Eleventh Army
22nd Infantry Division
72nd Infantry Division

XI Corps
76th Infantry Division
239th Infantry Division
1st Romanian Panzer Division
6th Romanian Cavalry Division

XXX Corps
198th Infantry Division
8th Romanian Infantry Division
13th Romanian Infantry Division
14th Romanian Infantry Division

LIV Corps
50th Infantry Division
170th Infantry Division
5th Romanian Infantry Division

Third Romanian Army

IV Corps
6th Infantry Division
7th Infantry Division

Mountain Corps
(regiments only)

Cavalry Corps
(regiments only)

APPENDIX 2: SOVIET FRONTS, JUNE 1941

NORTHERN FRONT
Formed on 24 June 1941 from HQ of Leningrad Military District

Seventh Army
54th Rifle Division
71st Rifle Division
168th Rifle Division
237th Rifle Division
208st Independent Air Defence Division

Fourteenth Army
XLII Rifle Corps
104th Rifle Division
122nd Rifle Division

14th Rifle Division
52nd Rifle Division
1st Tank Division

Twenty-Third Army
XLII Rifle Corps
115th Rifle Division
142nd Rifle Division

L Rifle Corps
43rd Rifle Division
70th Rifle Division
123rd Rifle Division

X Mechanized Corps
21st Tank Division
24th Tank Division
198th Motorized Division

27th Independent Air Defence Division
241st Independent Air Defence Division
177th Rifle Division
191st Rifle Division

I Mechanized Corps
3rd Tank Division
163rd Motorized Division

II Air Defence Corps

NORTHWESTERN FRONT
Formed on 22 June from HQ of the Baltic Special Military District

Eighth Army
X Rifle Corps
10th Rifle Division
48th Rifle Division
90th Rifle Division

XI Rifle Corps
11th Rifle Division
125th Rifle Division

XII Mechanized Corps
23th Tank Division
28th Tank Division
202nd Motorized Division

Eleventh Army
XVI Rifle Corps
5th Rifle Division
33rd Rifle Division
188th Rifle Division

XXIX Rifle Corps
179th Rifle Division
184th Rifle Division

III Mechanized Corps
2nd Tank Division
5th Tank Division
84th Motorized Division

23rd Rifle Division
126th Rifle Division
128th Rifle Division
19th Independent Air Defence Division
327th Independent Air Defence Division

Twenty-Seventh Army
XXII Rifle Corps
180th Rifle Division
182nd Rifle Division

XXIV Rifle Corps
181st Rifle Division
183rd Rifle Division

16th Rifle Division
67th Rifle Division
103rd Independent Air Defence Division
111th Independent Air Defence Division

V Airborne Corps

WESTERN FRONT
Formed on 22 June 1941 from HQ of the Western Special Military District

Third Army
IV Rifle Corps
27th Rifle Division
56th Rifle Division
85th Rifle Division

XI Mechanized Corps
29th Tank Division
33rd Tank Division
204th Motorized Division
16th Motorcycle Regiment

243rd Independent Air Defence Division

Fourth Army
XXVIII Rifle Corps
6th Rifle Division
42nd Rifle Division
49th Rifle Division
75th Rifle Division

XIV Mechanized Corps
22nd Tank Division
30th Tank Division
205th Motorized Division

12th Independent Air Defence Division

Tenth Army
I Rifle Corps
2nd Rifle Division
8th Rifle Division

V Rifle Corps
13th Rifle Division
86th Rifle Division
113th Rifle Division

VI Cavalry Corps
6th Cavalry Division
36th Cavalry Division

VI Mechanized Corps
4th Tank Division
7th Tank Division
29th Motorized Division

XIII Mechanized Corps
25th Tank Division
31st Tank Division
208th Motorized Division
155th Rifle Division

38th Independent Air Defence Division
71st Independent Air Defence Division

II Rifle Corps
100th Rifle Division
161st Rifle Division

XXI Rifle Corps
17th Rifle Division

24th Rifle Division
37th Rifle Division
XLIV Rifle Corps
64th Rifle Division
108th Rifle Division

XLVII Rifle Corps
55th Rifle Division
121st Rifle Division
143rd Rifle Division

IV Airborne Corps

XVII Mechanized Corps
27th Tank Division
36th Tank Division
209th Motorized Division

XX Mechanized Corps
26th Tank Division
38th Tank Division
210th Motorized Division

50th Rifle Division
32nd Special Artillery Division (Reserve)
86th Independent Air Defence Division

SOUTHWESTERN FRONT
Formed on 22 June from HQ of the Kiev Special Military District

Fifth Army
XV Rifle Corps
45th Rifle Division
62nd Rifle Division

XXVII Rifle Corps
87th Rifle Division
124th Rifle Division
135th Rifle Division

IX Mechanized Corps
20th Tank Division
35th Tank Division

XXII Mechanized Corps
19th Tank Division
41st Tank Division
215th Motorized Division

23rd Independent Air Defence Division
243rd Independent Air Defence Division

Sixth Army
VI Rifle Corps
41st Rifle Division
97th Rifle Division
159th Rifle Division

XXXVII Rifle Corps
80th Rifle Division
139th Rifle Division
141st Rifle Division

V Cavalry Corps
3rd Cavalry Division
14th Cavalry Division

IV Mechanized Corps
8th Tank Division
32nd Tank Division
Motorized Division

XV Mechanized Corps
10th Tank Division
37th Tank Division
212th Motorized Division

17th Independent Air Defence Division
307th Independent Air Defence Division

Twelfth Army
XIII Rifle Corps
44th Mountain-Infantry Division
58th Mountain-Infantry Division
192nd Mountain-Infantry Division

XVII Rifle Corps
60th Mountain-Infantry Division

96th Mountain-Infantry Division
164th Rifle Division

XVI Mechanized Corps
15th Tank Division
39th Tank Division
240th Motorized Division

20th Independent Air Defence Division
30th Independent Air Defence Division

Twenty-Sixth Army
VIII Rifle Corps
99th Rifle Division
173rd Rifle Division
72nd Mountain-Infantry Division

VIII Mechanized Corps
12th Tank Division
34th Tank Division
7th Motorized Division

28th Independent Air Defence Division

XXXI Rifle Corps
193rd Rifle Division
195th Rifle Division
200th Rifle Division

XXXVI Rifle Corps
140th Rifle Division
146th Rifle Division
228th Rifle Division

XLIX Rifle Corps
190th Rifle Division
197th Rifle Division
199th Rifle Division

LV Rifle Corps
130th Rifle Division
169th Rifle Division
189th Rifle Division

I Airborne Corps

XIX Mechanized Corps
40th Tank Division
43rd Tank Division
213th Motorized Division

XXIV Mechanized Corps
45th Tank Division
49th Tank Division
216th Motorized Division

263rd Independent Air Defence Regiment

Ninth Separate Army
Formed in Odessa Military District

XIV Rifle Corps
25th Rifle Divisions
51st Rifle Divisions

XXXV Rifle Corps
95th Rifle Division
176th Rifle Division

XLVIII Rifle Corps
30th Mountain Rifle Division
74th Rifle Division
150th Rifle Division

II Cavalry Corps
5th Cavalry Division
9th Cavalry Division

II Mechanized Corps
11th Tank Division
16th Tank Division
15th Mechanized Division

XVIII Mechanized Corps
44th Tank Division
47th Tank Division
218th Mechanized Division

STAVKA RESERVES

Sixteenth Army
XXXII Rifle Corps
46th Rifle Division
152nd Rifle Division

V Mechanized Corps
13th Tank Division
17th Tank Division
109th Mechanized Division

Nineteenth Army
XXV Rifle Corps
127th Rifle Division
134th Rifle Division
162nd Rifle Division

XXXIV Rifle Corps
129th Rifle Division
158th Rifle Division
171st Rifle Division

XXVI Mechanized Corps
52nd Tank Division
56th Tank Division
103rd Mechanized Division

XXXVIII Rifle Division

Twentieth Army
LXI Rifle Corps
110th Rifle Division
144th Rifle Division
172nd Rifle Division

LXIX Rifle Corps
73rd Rifle Division
229th Rifle Division
233rd Rifle Division

VII Mechanized Corps
14th Tank Division
18th Tank Division
1st Mechanized Division

18th Rifle Division

Twenty-First Army
LXIII Rifle Corps
53rd Rifle Division
148th Rifle Division
167th Rifle Division

LXVI Rifle Corps
61st Rifle Division
117th Rifle Division
154th Rifle Division

XXV Mechanized Corps
50th Tank Division
55th Tank Division
219th Mechanized Division

Twenty-Second Army
LI Rifle Corps
98th Rifle Division
112th Rifle Division
153rd Rifle Division

LXII Rifle Corps
170th Rifle Division
174th Rifle Division
186th Rifle Division

Twenty-Fourth Army
LII Rifle Corps
91st Rifle Division
119th Rifle Division
166th Rifle Division

LIII Rifle Corps
107th Rifle Division
133rd Rifle Division
178th Rifle Division

Note: units smaller than divisions not listed.
All armies had attached artillery regiments.

APPENDIX 3: RED ARMY LOSSES IN 1941

Baltic region, 22 June to 9 July (average daily casualties: 4916)

Unit	Manpower strength	Killed	Wounded	Total
Northwestern Front	440,000	73,924	13,284	87,208

Belorussian region, 22 June to 9 July (average daily casualties: 23,210)

Unit	Manpower strength	Killed	Wounded	Total
Western Front	625,000	341,012	76,717	417,729

Lvov-Chernovitsk area, 22 June to 9 July (average daily casualties: 16,106)

Unit	Manpower strength	Killed	Wounded	Total
Southwestern Front	864,600	165,452	65,755	213,207

Trans-polar and Karelia region, 29 June to 10 October (average daily casualties: 1305)

Unit	Manpower strength	Killed	Wounded	Total
Northern Front	358,390	36,822	35,714	72,536
Karelian Front	n/a	29,856	32,336	62,192

Kiev region, 7 July to 26 September (average daily casualties: 8543)

Unit	Manpower strength	Killed	Wounded	Total
Southern Front	627,000	531,471	54,127	585,598
Twenty-First Army	n/a	31,792	3793	35,585
Sixth & Twelfth Armies	n/a	52,900	26,320	79,220

Leningrad area, 10 July to 30 September (average daily casualties: 4155)

Unit	Manpower strength	Killed	Wounded	Total
Northern Front	153,000	40,491	15,044	55,535
Northwestern Front	272,000	96,953	47,835	144,788
Leningrad Front	n/a	65,629	50,787	116,316
Fifty-Second Army	n/a	1721	2389	4110

Battle of Smolensk, 10 July to 10 September (average daily casualties: 12,063)

Unit	Manpower strength	Killed	Wounded	Total
Western Front	579,400	309,959	159,625	469,584
Central Front	n/a	79,216	28,009	107,225
Reserve Front	n/a	50,972	28,603	79,575

Donbass-Rostov region, 29 September to 16 November (average daily casualties: 3277)

Unit	Manpower strength	Killed	Wounded	Total
Southern Front	491,500	132,014	15,356	147,370
Sixth Army	45,000	11,201	1862	13,063

Moscow region, 30 September to 5 December (average daily casualties: 9825)

Unit	Manpower strength	Killed	Wounded	Total
Western Front	558,000	254,726	55,514	310,240
Reserve Front	448,000	127,566	61,195	188,761
Bryansk Front	244,000	103,378	6537	109,915
Kalinin Front	n/a	28,668	20,695	49,363

Index

Page numbers in *italics* refer to picture captions

picture credits

All pictures Christopher Ailsby Historical Archives except the following:

Robert Hunt Library: 7, 8 (both), 9, 14, 15, 16 (bottom), 17, 19 (left), 20, 21, 22, 23, 24, 25 (both), 53 (right), 57, 63, 81 (bottom), 102, 116 (top), 117 (top), 120, 121 (both), 122, 123, 125, 126, 127, 128, 129 (bottom left), 130, 131 (both), 132, 138 (bottom), 140, 160, 161 (bottom), 166, 167 (both), 170, 174, 175, 176, 177, 193 (both), 207 (top), 212

Robert Hunt Library/Bundesarchiv: 6, 12 (top), 26 (bottom left), 27, 30, 34 (bottom right), 35 (both), 51, 54 (top), 60 (top), 81 (top), 98, 101, 103 (top), 143, 154 (bottom), 192, 208 (both), 209 (both).
Robert Hunt Library/Camera Press: 12 (bottom).
Robert Hunt Library/IWM: 19 (right), 161 (top), 191.
Robert Hunt Library/Novosti: 18, 171.